Aristotle in China

Language, Categories and Translation

In his latest book, Robert Wardy, a philosopher and classicist, turns his attention to the relation between language and thought. He explores this huge topic in an analysis of linguistic relativism, with specific reference to a reading of the *ming li t'an* (*The Investigation of the Theory of Names*), a seventeenth-century Chinese translation of Aristotle's *Categories*. Throughout his investigation, Wardy addresses important questions. Do the basic structures of language shape the major thought-patterns of its native speakers? Could philosophy be guided and constrained by the language in which it is done? What factors, from grammar and logic to cultural and religious expectations, influence translation? And does Aristotle survive rendition into Chinese intact? His answers will fascinate philosophers, Sinologists, classicists, linguists and anthropologists, and promise to make a major contribution to the existing literature.

Robert Wardy is Lecturer in Classics at the University of Cambridge, and Director of Studies in Philosophy and Classics, St Catharine's College. His publications include *The Birth of Rhetoric: Gorgias, Plato and their Successors* (1996) and *The Chain of Change: A Study of Aristotle's Physics VII* (1990).

The Needham Research Institute Studies series publishes important and original new work on East Asian culture and science which develops or links in with the publication of the *Science and Civilisation in China* series. The series will be under the editorial control of the Publications Board of the Needham Research Institute.

1 Christopher Cullen, *Astronomy and Mathematics in Ancient China: The 'Zhou Bi Suan Jing'*.
ISBN 0 521 55089 0

Aristotle in China

Language, Categories and Translation

Robert Wardy

University of Cambridge

CAMBRIDGE
UNIVERSITY PRESS

CAMBRIDGE UNIVERSITY PRESS
Cambridge, New York, Melbourne, Madrid, Cape Town, Singapore, São Paulo

Cambridge University Press
The Edinburgh Building, Cambridge CB2 2RU, UK

Published in the United States of America by Cambridge University Press, New York

www.cambridge.org
Information on this title: www.cambridge.org/9780521771184

First published 2000
This digitally printed first paperback version 2006

A catalogue record for this publication is available from the British Library

ISBN-13 978-0-521-77118-4 hardback
ISBN-10 0-521-77118-8 hardback

ISBN-13 978-0-521-02847-9 paperback
ISBN-10 0-521-02847-7 paperback

Contents

Preface   *page* ix

**1 The China syndrome: language, logical form,
   translation**   1

  1 Introduction   1
  2 Guidance and constraint   3
  3 On the very idea of translation   11
3.1 Whorf's hypothesis   11
3.2 Deflationary philosophical anthropology   16
3.3 Von Humboldt's legacy   19
  4 Case-study 1: conditionals   25
  5 Case-study 2: Chinese is a list   30
  6 Logical form   35
6.1 Against 'logical' translation   35
6.2 Why form might matter   39
6.3 Procrustean logic   44
  7 Case-study 3: being   51
  8 Case-study 4: truth   55
  9 Case-study 5: nouns and ontology   59
10 Conclusion   62

2 Aristotelian whispers   69

  1 Introduction   69
  2 What's in a name?   87
  3 Disputation, discrimination, inference   98
  4 The need for logic   107

5 Finite and infinite   112
6 The simple and the complex   116
7 All the things there are   120
8 How many questions?   131
9 Relatively speaking   134
10 Particular and general   137
11 Translating the untranslatable   146

Epilogue   150

Glossary of technical terms   153

References   161

Index   166

Preface

Aristotle in China is about the relation between language and thought. That is, of course, a topic of absurdly ambitious scope: it is only slightly less absurd to say that it concerns the particular question of the relation between language and philosophical thought, or even the relation between the Chinese language and Chinese logic. Perhaps readers will concede at the outset that my decision to explore these huge issues through reading Aristotle's *Categories* in Chinese is mere wilful circuitousness, rather than outright absurdity; and I trust that, if they persevere, they will discover that indirection has its compensations.

Chapter 1 introduces, defines and dissects varieties of linguistic relativism, with specific reference to the China question. Chapter 2 is entirely devoted to a reading of the 名理探 (*ming li t'an*), 'The Investigation of the Theory of Names', a seventeenth-century translation of Aristotle's *Categories* into Chinese; indeed, one of my goals is to reanimate an ancient tradition, both Chinese and Western, by producing a sort of meta-commentary. In principle, philosophers could read chapter 1 and dispense with chapter 2; and Sinologists could study chapter 2 and avoid philosophy: but of course my intention is to address philosophers, classicists, Sinologists, linguists, anthropologists and devotees of missionary studies throughout. The inevitable consequence of this inter-disciplinary brief is that I am bound to be guilty of howlers philosophical, linguistic, historical and anthropological; I can only humbly confess my limitations and beg the indulgence of those willing to look further than their immediate academic horizons. I have taken measures to make it possible, I trust in more than principle, for scholars from diverse backgrounds to take advantage of my research. All Greek, Latin and Chinese is translated (although readers will have to cope with citations from the secondary literature in modern European languages; and both Japanese and modern Chinese are beyond me). In chapter 2 I err on the side of generous citation because copies of both the Latin original and its Chinese translation are extremely rare, even in major libraries. Since I quote extensively from the Chinese, I do not always transliterate; but I Romanise (using the Wade–Giles system) whenever a graph or set of graphs is discussed.

In chapter 1 I express fairly complete disagreement with the arguments of Angus Graham. Puzzled dissatisfaction with the Whorfian case presented in his *magnum opus*, *Disputers of the Tao*, planted the original seed of this study. I hope that the tribute the author of so splendidly disputative a book would best have appreciated is critical response. He was kind enough to accept my invitation to speak in Cambridge on this very question, and I suppose that this might have been his last public academic appearance. The argument initiated then must sadly proceed without his irreplaceable contributions, but I have tried to compose the right sort of disrespectful *hommage*. In attempting to articulate my dissatisfaction I have benefited substantially from the assistance of Myles Burnyeat, Roger Crisp, Christoph Harbsmeier, Geoffrey Horrocks, Cathérine Jami, Paul Sanford and – above all – from the detailed and astute comments of Richard Davies, Nicholas Denyer and Stephen Makin. When I presented an embryonic version of this material at the Needham Research Institute my audience's reaction did much to reassure me that the topic was not without interest; and it would certainly have been impossible for me to complete so taxing a project without the luxury of a British Academy/Leverhulme Trust Senior Research Fellowship. I received additional friendly encouragement in Berlin from the participants in the conference Europe in China III, and profited especially from the advice of Nicholas Standaert. The Needham Institute's librarian, John Moffett, was a model of amicable efficiency in tracking down rare research materials. The recommendations of Michael Lackner and David Sedley, readers for the monograph series, were most helpful in the revision stages. Catherine Atherton's sustained and profound criticism has proved invaluable. David McMullen showed me what the true gentleman, the 君子, is by selflessly devoting too many hours to the correction of my gauche efforts at translation. Finally, I dedicate this book to Geoffrey Lloyd. Although he has no great interest in China after the era of the Han, I doubt that, without the example he set, I should ever have strayed so far from what I have come to regard as my native tongues.

Ad 2.

tem, & poteftatem literarum, ignorata earum natura, ita Logici cognofcunt vim prædicationum, fuppofito earum fundamento quod Metaphyfici exponunt. Ad tertiam refpondetur opus effe Dialectico, omnia rerum genera, quoad rationem prædicandi, & fubijciendi, cognofcere, non vt earum rerum notitiam per fe comparet, fed vt medijs abundet, ad quancunque de re propofita quæftionem pertractandam. Argumentum fecundæ refolutum iam eft.

Ad varias intellectus operationes variæ quoqꝫ Logicæ trationes ordinantur.

Hactenùs de ordine huius tractationis ad cæteras difciplinas, nunc de illo, quem ad alias Logicæ Ariftotelis partes obtinet; is verò eft idem, qui in operationibus mentis confpicitur. Nam primæ operationi, qua fimplicia apprehenduntur, refpondet hæc prædicamentorum doctrina, vbi fimplicia nomina in claffes rediguntur. Secundæ, qua componimus, & diuidimus, aptantur libri

de interpretatione, in quibus de enuntiatione difputatur. Tertiæ, qua ratiocinamur, congruunt Analytica, & Topica, vbi confequentiæ, argumentationes, fyllogifmíque fabricantur.

Huius doctrinæ commoditas, & vtilitas eft quam maxima ad omnem vfum dialecticum, nam ad diuifiones, definitionefque conficiendas expeditam præbet materiam, Genera, Species, Differentiafque diftinguendo. Ad argumentationem verò de quacunque re inftituendam, omnè fubijcit naturã, omnè proprietatè. Diftributio operis eft in tres partes, in ante Prædicamenta, in Prædicamenta, & poft Prædicamenta. Prima quatuor capitib. continetur. Secunda, quæ præcipua eft, quinque fequentibus. Tertia, vt ordine, ita vtilitate, & dignitate vltima, totidem extremis.

Hæc doctrina ad omnè vfum dialecticum eft maximè neceffaria. Tractatio Prædicamentorum in tres partes diuiditur.

EXPLANATIO CAPITIS PRIMI,

DE AEQVIVOCIS, VNIVO-
cis, & Denominatiuis.

SVMMA CAPITIS.

Definitio Aequiuoc.

Definitio Vniuoc.

Definitio Denominatiui.

Hoc caput tres continet definitiones, & totidem in partes diuidi poteft. Prima eft Aequiuocorum in hunc modum; Aequiuoca funt ea, quorum nomen commune eft, ratio verò fubftantiæ nomini accommodata, diuerfa; hoc eft, quæ nomine conueniunt, conceptibus autem, vel effentia difcrepant. Secunda eft Vniuocorum, & fic habet; Vniuoca funt, quorum & nomen commune eft, & ratio fubftantiæ nomini accommodata, eadem, feu quæ & nomine, & effentia conueniunt. Tertia, defcribuntur Denominatiua hac ratione. Denominatiua funt, quæ ab aliquo nominis habent appellationem folo differentia cafu; hoc eft, quæ tribuunt fubiecto appellationem alicuius formæ, quæ afficitur vocabulo initio eodem, fine tamen diuerfo.

CAPVT I.

COMMENTARIVS.

a *Æquiuoca dicuntur*] Quoniam huius primæ partis doctrina eo tendit, vt nonnulla explicentur ad prædicamentorum intelligentiam neceffaria, quæ fi pofteà traderentur, inchoatam difputationis feriem interrüperent, idcircò primis quatuor capitibus, quædam; omnibus, vel pluribus Categorijs, partim repugnantia, partim conuenientia, ediferit. Huius confilij ratio, vt in hoc primo capite eluceat, aduertit Albertus Magnus tractatu primo, capite 2. Aegydius hic, & alij trifariam conferri poffe Prædicamenta, cuius membra funt. Secundo, fingula cum fuis inferioribus. Tertiò, quædam ad alia, verbi caufa, Prædicamenta accidentium ad fubftantiam. Si comparatio fiat primo modo, omnia funt Aequiuoca, feu analoga; qua de caufa, differit hoc loco de Aequiuocis, adde etiam, vt oftendat ea excludenda effe à Prædicamentis. Si fecundo modo omnia conueniunt vniuocè, vt planum eft. Si denique tertio, fingula nonë Categoriarum accidentia dicuntur de fubftantia, non æquiuocè; quia prædicari poffunt eadem ratione, vt in Prædicabilibus vifum eft; non vniuocè, quia non

Trifariam conferri poffunt prædicamenta.

A a *Equiuoca dicuntur ea,* **b** § *Quorum nomen folum commune eft:* **c** § *ratio verò fubftãtia* **d** § *Nomini accõmodata, diuerfa: vt animal dicitur, & ipfe homo, & id, quod eft pictũ.* Horũ enim nomẽ cõmune tantũmodo eft, ratio verò fubftãtia nomini accõmodata diuerfa. Si quifpiã enim, quænã fit vtriufqꝫ ratio animalis voluerit affignare ratione vtrifqꝫ profecto propriã affignabit. **e** § *Vniuoca ea dicũtur, quorũ & nomẽ commu-*

Alb. Mag.
Ægyd.

affir-

古 物倫首辯同名岐義活人塑人皆謂之人厭名
雖同體義則異

解 此論分別十倫從幾端物理推較而定所較有
三。舉卝倫與總存而較二。舉各倫與其屬之下
性而較三。舉各倫自立者之倫與他諸倫而較也。舉總
有之較則十倫之諸性皆同名岐義者。同為有者。故同名。各
自一理。故岐義。西云額計勿加者是也。舉下性之較則十
倫之諸性皆同名同義者。西云悟尼勿加者是也。

Sample page of the *ming li t'an*

1

The China syndrome: language, logical form, translation

The only generalisation to make about language and science is to make no generalisation.

Yuen Ren Chao

Die Sprache verkleidet den Gedanken. Und zwar so, daß man nach der äußeren Form des Kleides, nicht auf die Form des bekleideten Gedankens schließen kann; weil die äußere Form des Kleides nach ganz anderen Zwecken gebildet ist, als danach, die Form des Körpers erkennen zu lassen.[1]

Wittgenstein, *Tractatus Logico-Philosophicus* 4.002

1 Introduction

My intention in this first chapter is to address a methodological presumption which, for better or worse, influences a great portion of the work done on Chinese philosophy, both in the West and in the East. I refer to the presumption that there is something distinctively Chinese about Chinese philosophy taken more or less in its entirety; that this feature (or these features) set(s) the path of its development; and that it (or they) must be invoked to account for whatever large and deep contrasts are perceived between it and that other strange monolith, Western philosophy.

The suggestion that we should pay attention to what is Chinese (in some very broad sense) in Chinese thought will sound rather bizarre to anyone not wedded to a radically abstract conception of argument – and will do so precisely because it is so resoundingly truistic. But of course what is characteristic of Chinese philosophical studies, not to mention the whole scientific project inspired by Joseph Needham, is not merely a proper sensitivity to some set of more or less diverse cultural factors impinging on Chinese intellectual evolution in one or another, more or less decisive fashion: what dominates is the perceived contrast with the West. Sometimes this takes the form of a trial, the

---

[1] 'Language disguises thought. So much so, that from the outward form of the clothing it is impossible to infer the form of the thought beneath it, because the outward form of the clothing is not designed to reveal the form of the body, but for entirely different purposes.'

Chinese being seen to have diverged from – almost inevitably to have fallen grievously short of – some Western achievement, and the question is then, why so? But such studies, whether they plead for the defence or for the prosecution, always impose investigative patterns which Chinese material is made to fit, usually by distortion, at best by omission.

Geoffrey Lloyd has recently subjected one large family of comparativist methodologies to blistering attack in his *Demystifying Mentalities*.[2] I shall make my beginning with a cognate group of theories, those which cast their principles in linguistic terms, and which are of particular interest both because they prevail in philosophical studies and because their evaluation presents a special, and especially philosophical, difficulty. The mentalities approach seeks to explain a host of anthropological issues by associating a distinctive set of intellectual capacities (and limitations) with a given culture. A running theme of Lloyd's book is that it is swiftly brought to grief by the insuperable difficulties which beset any attempt to specify a well-defined social unit to which a dominant mentality might be attributed without begging all the interesting questions. Lloyd's moral is that in this sphere, at least, totalising tendencies are well nigh indefensible. But the hypotheses I shall scrutinise can boast at least one especially challenging feature. For, in comparison with most mentality approaches, their basic presumption that linguistic communities are relatively homogeneous is not patently outrageous.[3]

There is a twist, however. Their presumption will fail to be truly outrageous only if, paradoxically, it motivates interpretative strategies of a vauntingly ambitious character. We begin far beyond the range of dialectal differences, diachronic linguistics, the relation between spoken and written language, or the proprietary modes of expression of given cultural groupings. We begin with the structure of the language itself, as it were with *langue* rather than *parole*; structure must be understood as so fundamental as not to be subject to any of the enormous variations I have enumerated, on pain of losing that putative unitary theoretical entity, *the* language. So here is the first shift of comparativist linguistic hypotheses outside the narrow circle of the mentalities debate: their favoured terms of comparison are less vulnerable to the accusation of being mere figments of the theoretical imagination. Second, champions of linguistic comparativism do not always regard thought as intrinsically linguistic. But they *do* happily claim both

[2] Lloyd 1990.
[3] Jean-Paul Reding's 'Greek and Chinese Categories: A Reexamination of the Problem of Linguistic Relativism' develops a judicious critique of what he considers over-hasty recognition of the relativistic influence exercised by particular languages on disparate philosophical traditions: 'if categories can be discovered through a language, this does not mean that they are relative to that language; it only means that the categories mirror themselves – though imperfectly – in language. It would also be wrong to say that language channels our thinking: it rather floods it, and it is the philosopher's duty to find the fordable places' (Reding 1986, pp. 355–6).

that linguistic structure is to some significant extent isomorphic with major thought-patterns and that it is necessarily language which imposes those patterns on thought, not the other way around. Third, this isomorphism is supposed to be apparent in the articulation of reason called philosophy, and philosophical development is judged to be positively guided and negatively constrained by the language in which it is done.

The hypothesis that basic linguistic structure at once encourages and constrains the development of philosophical tendencies and doctrines, whether fruitful or disastrous, has enjoyed a curiously persistent vogue amongst students of Chinese philosophy. For ease of reference I designate it 'the guidance and constraint hypothesis', and shall investigate its continuing popularity by considering the genesis of the trend both inside and outside the boundaries of Sinology proper. Quite apart from the obvious attraction it holds of affording insight into why a significant group of scholars should be wedded to a given procedure,[4] my approach has the added advantage of helping to explain an otherwise surprising feature of comparativist methodology: its ostensible conflict with dominant philosophical anthropology. Once its pedigree has been established, the various fortunes of proponents of the hypothesis will be assessed in a series of case-studies covering topics of the greatest potential interest and importance. Dubbing the Sinological vogue for the hypothesis a 'syndrome' is obviously pejorative. Yet my evaluations, even if largely negative, will not only help diagnose what I shall argue is a remarkable affliction besetting comparativist philosophy of language. They will also suggest alternative ways of understanding the all-imporant but protean concepts of linguistic and logical form.

2 Guidance and constraint

'Guidance and constraint' is easy enough to enunciate; it is far less easy to make the hypothesis usefully determinate or to work out what types of linguistic phenomena should count as evidence *pro* or *contra*. 'Guidance' takes two forms. In its first form, where the relativist perceives success, a feature of linguistic structure will be invoked which either strongly encourages or, more commonly, at least enables the discovery of philosophical truth. In its second form, where philosophy goes 'wrong', we have 'misguidance'; for example the reification of linguistic detail deemed not to correspond with reality. 'Constraint' can overlap with 'misguidance', but is usually invoked to

---

[4] Some, if not all, of the scholars to be discussed critically in the sequel might very well object that I have grossly misrepresented them at the outset: since they differ so sharply over basic issues in the interpretation of Chinese philosophy and language, they can hardly constitute a real 'group'. What I shall seek to demonstrate is that adherence to 'the guidance and constraint hypothesis' constitutes a problematic methodological unity more fundamental than the level on which they part company.

explain the absence from one language, and thus from one philosophical tradition, of whole departments of enquiry energetically pursued in another.

At this juncture a cardinal principle must be introduced, one flouted regularly in the literature, just as the basic requirement of thorough knowledge of the languages in question is only partially satisfied at best. Again and again participants in these discussions adduce supposedly striking and decisive instances of what might be labelled linguistic 'dissonance' or 'shock', that is, alleged examples of baulked translation whose intractability is to be ascribed (the story goes) to structural divergence. But the fact is that much of this evidence constitutes, if anything, a set of counter-examples to 'the guidance and constraint hypothesis'. That some philosophical thesis can be formulated in ancient Chinese or ancient Greek or modern English or French only by creating or adapting terminology, by novel definition or redefinition, or even by speaking in what might be felt as an alien idiom, establishes that the philosophy *is* expressible – albeit at the expense of considerable ingenuity, prolixity or both. Sinologists impressed by the trickiness of getting certain European philosophical texts into Chinese should take note of how elaborately hedged about is, and must always be, the study of ancient Greek texts in English translation. When the complex of Chinese language and thought is set against the Western model, the linguistic explanation of their differences is supposed to be fundamental, and where, as is customary, the contrast is with ancient Greek, the foundation is taken to be whatever differentiates Indo-European from all other language groups. As a result, registering examples of 'shock' and 'dissonance' will hit home if and only if they demonstrate a real inability, in principle and as a consequence of basic structure, to get something from or into Chinese: mere occasions for ingenuity will not suffice.

In several works[5] Angus Graham took up 'the guidance and constraint hypothesis' and adapted it to the large-scale evaluation of Chinese philosophy.[6] His *Disputers of the Tao* is a text to which I shall return again and again. Since Graham's unparalleled linguistic expertise was explicitly set to philosophical work of great force and scope, both the particular form of 'guidance and constraint' he advocated and his objections to rival versions will amply repay study.

Graham's exploitation of 'dissonance' appears to hover unstably between exaggeration of its significance and willingness to moderate his own linguistic determination strategy. Citing what he sees as Plato's and Anselm's 'confusion between existence and

---

[5] Most notably appendix 2 to *Disputers of the Tao: Philosophical Argument in Ancient China* (Graham 1989).
[6] Although various earlier, interesting formulations of Graham's position are easy enough to find scattered throughout his voluminous writings, which do not simply repeat themselves on this score, the fact remains that in all essentials appendix 2 is the definitive, final enunciation of his thesis.

essence', he asserts without qualification that 'such a fallacy cannot be reproduced in Chinese'.[7] So translation is impossible. But not quite, provided we are prepared to pay the cost of destructive syntactical innovation: 'one sees that philosophical translation from another language, which seems to enrich terminology, can involve a deterioration of syntax'.[8] We are reassured, however, that untranslatability does not threaten 'the extreme sort of linguistic relativism', perhaps to be glossed by Graham's phrase 'invalidity is independent of particular language structures'.[9]

Now, in this particular case, as Graham is confident that treating existence as a predicate is a philosophical error (indeed *the* error of 2,000 years of Western philosophy), and I certainly am not, then – if we must talk of East/West competition – I will certainly not want to judge this round in it as he does. But the comparative exercise in any case depends on his assumption that a Chinese word or turn of phrase whose sole function is to translate Western philosophical arguments is not a real word or phrase, that is, does not represent a legitimate translation; and I fail to see that that is any better than arbitrary stipulation. Graham's defence would presumably be that when attempts to translate foreign philosophy into Chinese cause syntactical 'deterioration', the suspicion that authentic translation has not actually been achieved is well grounded: no question has been begged. Such a response persuades only if we have access to a neutral criterion for distinguishing a species of 'deterioration' favouring 'the guidance and constraint hypothesis' from (philosophically, at least) benign linguistic innovation, whether lexical or syntactical; and such a criterion should be objective in the obvious sense that the rationale for detection of 'deterioration' must not merely be falling foul of the researcher's *philosophical* convictions. Unfortunately, as Graham fails to meet this condition, mere feelings of linguistic oddity, even on the part of the *doyen* of modern Sinologists, do not carry conviction.

Perhaps the condition *is* unsatisfiable, but for an interesting reason. It is simply impossible, even for native speakers, to draw a firm line between 'odd' sentences and ones they find truly unintelligible.[10] For him to avoid question-begging, Graham's

---

[7] Graham 1989, p. 412.   [8] *Ibid.*, p. 413.

[9] *Ibid.*, p. 414. Reding neatly reverses Graham's procedure, detecting logical distortions *by* rather than *of* Chinese: 'the only road which can lead us to the Chinese categories is a study of how logical distinctions can be distorted by Chinese syntax . . . "Distortion", here, is not meant to be an abstract concept: it manifests itself as a kind of uneasiness or frustration felt by the philosopher, who, while using the language, stumbles against its limits and reacts against its imperfections by pointing them out or by propounding new forms of expression' (Reding 1986, pp. 361–2). The ultimate ancestry of something like Reding's linguistically hobbled philosophy is explored in section 6.2.

[10] Much as the line between sentences and non-sentences, or grammatical and ungrammatical sentences, is not there to be drawn – except, say, by someone dogmatically committed to a meta-theory of grammar which dictates that all grammars must be sets of rules generating all and only the sentences of a language.

philosophical convictions should not influence his linguistic judgements. But they do –
and in fact it may be that *no-one* can make purely linguistic judgements in any case
(except grammarians, and then only about their *ad hoc*, maximally decontextualised
sentences).

A related point concerns what we mean by 'a language'. I have already emphasised
that evaluation of 'the guidance and constraint hypothesis' is bedevilled by its proponents' failure to apply and test it at a structural level so fundamental that the tremendous
linguistic variation which threatens to dissolve the terms of cultural comparison has
not yet emerged. But even when that condition is respected, it remains unclear just
how much is to be abstracted away. That not blindly begging questions here is vitally
important finds vivid exemplification in the prevalence of the assumption that Chinese
morphology – or rather the *absence* of Chinese morphology – is quite distinctive. If
anything is going to count as a significant fundamental linguistic feature, then lack of
morphology in Chinese will.

This, of course, is what everyone who knows anything about Chinese knows, and it is
intimately bound up with the general presumption that Chinese is fantastically ambiguous[11] – a presumption which goes all the way back to primary contacts, as this quotation
from Matteo Ricci confirms:

> I have recently given myself to the study of the Chinese language and I can
> promise you that it's something quite different from either Greek or German. In
> speaking it, there is so much ambiguity that there are many words that can signify
> more than a thousand things, and at many times the only difference between one
> word and another is the way you pitch them high or low in four different tones.
> Thus when [the Chinese] are speaking to each other they write out the words they
> wish to say so that they can be sure to understand – for all the written letters are
> different from each other. As for these written letters you would not be able to
> believe them had you not both seen and used them, as I have done. They have as
> many letters as there are words and things, so that there are more than 70,000 of
> them, every one quite different and complex.[12]

---

[11] E.g. 'the average lexical item found in the literature (especially the basic 2500+[i.e. graphs]) is so rich
in semantic content that meaning differentiation is very difficult, with the consequence that virtually
every passage is ambiguous, being subject to a multiplicity of readings until and unless a specific
interpretation is given to it' (Rosemont 1974, p. 83; this supposed near-universal ambiguity is cited in
support of Rosemont's astounding contention that written ancient Chinese, in sharp distinction from
spoken, is not a natural language).

[12] Letter to Martino de Fornari (1583), quoted from Spence 1985, pp. 136–7. Ricci takes words to be
(primarily) spoken objects, and apparently fails fully to absorb the fact that written signs are signs
for words, and are not letters, i.e. signs for units of speech. But it is his so regarding graphs which guarantees his also regarding both them and what they stand for ((spoken) words) as invariant.

In contrast, John Webb imagined that absence of morphology must constitute a sort of grand linguistic liberation, or rather the state of original freedom from which all but the Chinese have since fallen:

> the Chinese are never put to that irksome vexation of searching out a radix for the derivation of any of their words, as generally all other nations are, but the radix is the word and the word is the radix . . . Besides they are not troubled with variety of Declensions, Conjugations, Numbers, Genders, Moods, Tenses and the like grammatical niceties, but are absolutely free from all such perplexing accidents, having no other Rules in use than what the light of nature has dictated unto them; whereby their language is plain, easie and simple as NATURAL speech ought to be.[13]

But is Chinese so boundlessly ambiguous? And, if so, is this ambiguity integral to 'the guidance and constraint hypothesis'? There is and can be no single acceptable answer to the question of ancient Chinese's alleged hyper-ambiguity, for the simple reason that languages are not in themselves ambiguous. 'Ambiguity', in any precisely definable sense, and with any precisely delimitable extension, is a technical term which derives its meaning from this or that linguistic theory; given the range of theories on offer, there is not even agreement over the boundaries of the set of communicative phenomena dubbed 'ambiguous', let alone over what makes them ambiguous.[14] To put this another way, the nature and degree of ambiguity one is inclined to detect in a language will depend in large part on where one favours placing the line between semantics and pragmatics, and on whether one will concede that pragmatic determination should count as resolution of meaning within the language proper. Thus, Rosemont hardly assumes that the ambiguity he insists is rife in written ancient Chinese[15] is irresoluble, although his refusal to acknowledge the contribution of syntax is incomprehensible: 'context provides the basic setting for the interpretation of passages, aided not by syntax or phonetics but by semantic information'.[16] He does not pause to consider the possibility that, if context regularly determines or even dictates a single reading – or at least a manageable range of readings comparable to the flexibility evinced by most, perhaps all, languages – then the flat assertion that 'virtually every passage is ambiguous' is at best highly misleading. What Rosemont calls 'interpretations' are not items

---

[13] Webb 1669, p. 192; cf. Webb 1678.

[14] The point is a general one: homophony, homography, equivocity, etc. are likewise dependent on difficult decisions about both the bearers and the nature of meaning. For example, the statement that 'homophones sound alike, but have different meanings' is an unacceptably lax definition: but clarifying what is meant both by 'sounding alike' and by 'different meanings' will carry us into the deepest theoretical waters.

[15] See n. 11 above. [16] Rosemont 1974, p. 82.

extrinsic to ancient Chinese helpfully imposed on it by the reader; rather, they are there
to be discovered *in* the language, so long as one is prepared to recognise that the extent
and complexity of the textual surroundings required to grasp the meaning of selected
passages might differ radically between linguistic cultures.

Again, neither ancient nor modern Chinese verbs are marked for tense or the sub-
junctive mood. In their different ways, neither ancient nor modern Chinese marks or
specifies conditional relationships to quite the extent that they are explicitly indicated
in modern English, let alone in ancient Greek. But if we widen our view to take in
signals beyond what morphology and syntax alone clarify, then we must resist any
initial inclination to discern limits to Chinese thought imposed by Chinese language. It
is convenient, perhaps inevitable, for those most familiar with Western languages and
the study thereof to conceive of such extra-morphological and -syntactical signals as
occurring in something called 'the context'. Of course there is nothing objectionable as
such in that designation, so long as all that is implied is that neglecting such signals will
impair, perhaps even destroy, one's ability to retrieve whatever is being said. Yet it is
both difficult, and essential, to withstand the insidious temptation further to assume that
since 'context' complements 'text', and 'text' is – obviously – semantically primary,
languages which rely on contextual disambiguation for the effective communication
of meaning must indeed be ambiguous at the core. The rejoinder is to insist that fixing
on a given type of linguistic unit as a candidate for semantic evaluation is certainly not a
theoretically innocent manœuvre, at least from the perspective of the semanticist. If
fixing semantic units for Chinese which are roughly comparable to what theorists have
typically attributed to Western languages results in 'discovering' disproportionate
ambiguity in Chinese, then the suitability of the theoretical imposition, not the communicative efficacy of the language, ought to be questioned. To take a single example,
Christoph Harbsmeier displays admirable sensitivity to the importance of contextual-
isation in ancient Chinese (which he abbreviates to 'AC'), but draws some surprising
and unwarranted conclusions:

> Aus der Kontext-Gebundenheit von AC-Sätzen ergeben sich Konsequenzen für
> die allgemeine pragmatische Charakterisierung dieser Sätze. Ein Satz, dessen
> Bedeutung sich erst aus dem Zusammenhang ergibt, ist im allgemeinen nicht
> primär als Abbild oder objektive Darstellung des Sachverhaltes gemeint, sondern
> primär als Mitteilung. Man ist versucht zu sagen, daß nur wer mitteilen will, ohne
> notwendigerweise auch abbilden oder objektiv darstellen zu wollen, so elliptisch
> reden und schreiben würde, wie das die alten Chinesen anscheinend zu tun
> pflegten.[17]

---

[17] Harbsmeier 1979, p. 115.

I should add that I am not at all sure that I grasp what 'communication' might be which can omit 'objective representation' while ostensibly not of necessity precluding it (Harbsmeier does not elaborate on these technicalities). This reasoning betrays the theoretical bias just highlighted: if the *Satz* bereft of context is strikingly elliptical, etc., then impressive consequences for the pragmatics of ancient Chinese can be seen to flow only on the supposition that the *isolated Satz* is unquestionably the primary semantic unit to which we rightly attribute such qualities as elleipsis.[18]

When there is a job of communication to be done, which segments of what I think I have every right to call 'the language' get it done can vary considerably between languages, without affecting how well the job gets done.[19] The moral for application of 'the guidance and constraint hypothesis' to ancient Chinese philosophy is fairly obvious. Lack of morphology is a star candidate for recognition as a fundamental linguistic influence on thought, probably under the 'constraint' half of the rubric. It ought to manifest itself in the guise of indeterminacy and/or ambiguity. But we must at the same time have due regard for the resources of contextual disambiguation, which of course in the case of philosophical texts emphatically do not coincide with the types of indicator governing spoken language, ancient or modern. It then emerges that the 'ambiguity' of ancient Chinese philosophy might indeed exist, and might be a function of language (if we are flexible enough about what we mean by a 'function' of language). But it cannot be viewed as an unproblematic consequence of language on

---

[18] Harbsmeier himself later provides an extremely useful characterisation of ancient Chinese grammaticality which effectively undermines the basis for his earlier inferences: 'Grammatikalität ist für ihn [meinen chinesischen Meister] nicht eine Eigenschaft von Sätzen als solchen, sondern eine Relation zwischen Satz, Interpretation und Kontext. Eine Theorie der Grammatikalität im Altchinesischen ist also in ganz elementarer Weise zugleich eine Theorie der Kommunikations-Kontexte. Dem Versuch, Grammatikalität rekursiv und pragmatisch kontextfrei im Hinblick auf das AC zu klären, geht jede Plausibilität ab' (*ibid.*, p. 266). Further, his formulation of what he calls 'das Entbehrlichkeitsprinzip' might help us to shake off the blinkers imposed by too parochial a grammatical background: 'Abgesehen von idiomatischen Wendungen sind im AC alle informationstheoretisch (pragmatisch) redundanten Wörter grundsätzlich grammatisch fakultative' (*ibid.*, p. 119).

[19] Roy Harris, with his customary pungency, expresses a similar attitude to 'the metalinguistic terminology a language provides or does not provide, its resources or lack of resources for talk about language [which] reflect differences – sometimes subtle and sometimes quite obvious – between the ways in which different cultures treat language-using as a form of behaviour' (Harris 1980, p. 21). He goes on to argue that 'someone who agrees that this is so may none the less feel that it is going too far to say that different cultures have different concepts of what a language is. He may not realise that this view may itself be seen as reflecting a particular cultural background. For the European is the inheritor of an intellectual tradition which is strongly biased in favour of regarding languages as superficially different but fundamentally equivalent systems of expression. This assumption reveals itself in a variety of ways, including a willingness to draw a sharp distinction between "the language" and "the culture" which the language happens to serve' (*ibid.*).

the level at which the champions of 'guidance and constraint' must operate – that is, on the only level at which they do not run the risk of all the fearsome problems of interpretation not generated and circumscribed by the Chinese 'language' (as the hypothesis must understand it).

It would be as well to remember at this juncture that generalisation over the entire range of ancient Chinese philosophy is an extremely rash undertaking. Graham claims that the later Mohist concern with both linguistic and logical accuracy impelled them to produce a form of Chinese unique in its independence from context:

> in most kinds of Chinese writing one expects a word to have a variety of meanings, distinguishable in theory by looking up a dictionary, distinguishable in practice only when we have become familiar with the sort of context to which each is confined. But the key words of Mohist dialectic are shorn of all but their basic meanings; and this semantic restriction, together with the precision of the syntax, frees them from their ordinary contextual limitations.[20]

Among many other impressive examples of both lexical and syntactic innovation undertaken for the sake of clarity, he cites the following arresting, if speculative, instance: 'the Mohist dialecticians deliberately reserved the pre-verbal 有 (*yu*)/ 無 (*wu*) ("there are"/"there are not") for quantification, and avoided the confusion which might result from their use in other constructions by choosing other graphs and particles'.[21] Certainly, the Mohist logicians were atypical in both their ruling concerns and the techniques they developed to address them; but one cannot afford to dismiss the intriguing linguistic implications of their unusual writings on that score.

We have now learnt why 'dissonance' should not impress us, and discerned some of the difficulties for 'the guidance and constraint hypothesis' thrown up by the ambiguity of 'ambiguity' and the obscure polyvalence of the theoretical term 'language'; our next step is to invoke the name of Benjamin Whorf, and investigate why its resonance has proved unusually persistent in Sinological circles. As a preliminary, I shall note that Graham began his study 'The Relation of Chinese Thought to the Chinese Language' with these words: 'Chinese thought before the introduction of Buddhism from India is the unique instance of a philosophical tradition which, as far as our information goes, is wholly independent of traditions developed in Indo-European languages . . . It therefore provides the ideal test case for Whorf's hypothesis that the thought of a culture is guided and constrained by the structure of its language.'[22]

---

[20] Graham 1978, p. 162.   [21] *Ibid.*, p. 134.   [22] Graham 1989, p. 389.

3 On the very idea of translation

3.1 *Whorf's hypothesis*

Whorf's *Language, Thought and Reality* of 1956, which, on the basis of a study of the Hopi language, propounds something quite close to what I have called 'the guidance and constraint hypothesis', has proved enormously, if indirectly, influential both on philosophy, through Quine, and on anthropology, in the relativism and rationality debate, where it interacts with the complementary sources highlighted by Geoffrey Lloyd in his *Demystifying Mentalities*. Whorf was himself deeply interested in the work of Lévy-Bruhl, and in fact believed that the viability of the mentalities scheme 'is only one of the great psychological world-questions that fall into the domain of linguistics and await the impersonal and positive type of answer that linguistic research can give'.[23]

What is infuriating about reading Whorf – and this, paradoxically, may be in no small measure responsible for the breadth of his influence – is the constant difficulty of gauging the exact import of his principle of linguistic relativity. Clearly, Whorf is wedded to the idea that linguistic structure influences thought and action; but just what he intends by 'structure', the manner and extent of its influence on human perception of and reaction to reality, and the nature and strength of the evidence for relativity, all remain far from clear, for Whorf never produced a definitive statement of his position. Indeed, there are grounds for a suspicion that at least the implications of some of his assertions might not be compatible. Thus, although he most frequently cites purported lexical data in support of his claims, he accords vocabulary less weight than 'structure and grammar', whose nature he apparently assumes to be self-evident. He claims, for example, that 'these abstractions [i.e. for which *our* language lacks adequate terms] are definitely given either explicitly in words – psychological or metaphysical terms – in the Hopi language, or, even more, are implicit in the very structure and grammar of that language, as well as being observable in Hopi culture and behavior'.[24] Whorf explicitly denies that all thinking is linguistic,[25] and once, disconcertingly, rejects even the relatively modest thesis that there is any determinate correlation between language and culture, let alone a causal one.[26] But, on the other hand, he often permits himself (quasi-) metaphorical expressions which imply strong determination of thought by

---

[23] Whorf 1967, p. 80; from 'A Linguistic Consideration of Thinking in Primitive Communities' (*c.* 1936).

[24] *Ibid.*, pp. 58–9; from 'An American Indian Model of the Universe' (*c.* 1936).

[25] *Ibid.*, p. 66; from 'A Linguistic Consideration of Thinking in Primitive Communities'.

[26] *Ibid.*, pp. 138–9; from *Language, Culture, and Personality: Essays in Memory of Edward Sapir* (1941).

language;[27] claims that 'this study [of language] shows that the forms of a person's thoughts are controlled by inexorable laws of pattern of which he is unconscious';[28] and goes so far as to attribute a partial linguistic genesis to Newtonian concepts: 'Newtonian space, time, and matter are no intuitions. They are recepts from culture and language. That is where Newton got them.'[29] If this oscillation in Whorf's commitments never ceases, it was the memorable turns of phrase tilting towards fairly hard 'guidance and constraint' which nevertheless lodged themselves in the public mind and established his fame,[30] such as his most celebrated pronouncement, in which he embraces pure 'guidance and constraint' without the slightest inhibition: 'thinking also follows a network of tracks laid down in the given language, an organisation which may concentrate systematically upon certain phases of reality, certain aspects of intelligence, and may systematically discard others featured by other languages. The individual is utterly unaware of this organisation and is constrained completely within its unbreakable bonds.'[31]

---

[27] E.g. 'the three-tense system of . . . [European] verbs colors all our thinking about time' (1967, p. 143; from *Language, Culture, and Personality: Essays in Memory of Edward Sapir*); or 'English and similar tongues lead us to think of the universe as a collection of rather distinct objects and events corresponding to words' (1967, p. 240; from 'Language and Logic' (1941)).

[28] 1967, p. 252; from 'Language, Mind, and Reality' (1942).

[29] 1967, p. 153; from *Language, Culture, and Personality: Essays in Memory of Edward Sapir*. Lest it be imagined that it is unfair to suppose that this is a radical manifestation of 'guidance and constraint', since the passage couples 'culture' with 'language' as causal factors, one should recognise that Whorf explains that by a 'thought world' he intends 'all the give-and-take between language and the culture as a whole, wherein is a vast amount that is not linguistic but yet shows the shaping influence of language' (1967, p. 147): evocative but imprecise expressions like 'the shaping influence of language' shield Whorf from the uncomfortable obligation to articulate and defend his hypothesis.

[30] 'Which was first: the language patterns or the cultural norms? In main they have grown up together, constantly influencing each other. But in this partnership the nature of the language is the factor that limits free plasticity and rigidifies channels of development in the more autocratic way. This is so because a language is a system, not just as assemblage of norms . . . Language thus represents the mass mind; it is affected by inventions and innovations, but affected little and slowly, whereas TO inventors and innovators it legislates with the decree immediate' (1967, p. 156; from *Language, Culture, and Personality: Essays in Memory of Edward Sapir*). Note also the relatively unguarded expression of what one might label 'hard-core guidance and constraint': 'when anyone, as a natural logician ['natural logic' = 'deeply rooted ideas about talking and its relation to thinking'], is talking about reason, logic, and the laws of correct thinking, he is apt to be simply marching in step with purely grammatical facts that have somewhat of a background character in his own language or family of languages but are by no means universal in all languages and in no sense a common substratum of reason' (1967, p. 211; from 'Science and Linguistics' (1940); cf. 'We dissect nature along lines laid down by our native languages', p. 213).

[31] 1967, p. 256; from 'Language, Mind, and Reality'. To set the record straight, while Whorf himself *usually* argues that linguistic structure strongly encourages rather than absolutely determines the thought it expresses (creates?), many of his followers did indeed go over the top, advocating wildly extremist versions of 'guidance and constraint' (a small selection: Hall 1959; Girdansky 1963; Müller (*Anthropos* 57)).

As so often happens in cases of interdisciplinary cross-fertilisation, Whorf is no longer a name to conjure with in linguistics proper. One reason for his eclipse was the new ascendancy of transformational grammar, whose leading exponents assumed (perhaps too quickly) that their revivified universalism exploded the pretensions of Whorfian linguistic relativity. Thus, Jerrold Katz has claimed that the 'well-known doctrine of linguistic relativity, which states that cultural differences produce incommensurate conceptual frameworks, derives neither from the discovery of exceptional facts about exotic languages by linguists like Whorf nor from important breakthroughs in the study of methodology by philosophers like Quine. Rather, the doctrine derives from the empiricism common to these linguists and philosophers.'[32] Katz supposes that linguistic relativity jeopardises the universal intertranslatability he assumes to be immediately entailed by rationalist transformationalism; but aspects of this pioneering defence of universal grammar against the threat of the then popular relativism suggest that he is perhaps mistaken:

> it is commonly held that modern linguistic and anthropological investigations have conclusively refuted the doctrines of classical universal grammar, but this claim seems to me very much exaggerated. Modern work has, indeed, shown a great diversity in the surface structures of languages. However, since the study of deep structure has not been its concern, it has not attempted to show a corresponding diversity of underlying structures, and, in fact, the evidence that has been accumulated in modern study of language does not appear to suggest anything of this sort.[33]

Evidently there is nothing to preclude the peaceful co-existence of transformational grammar and some version of Whorfian relativity, so long as 'guidance and constraint' is confined to surface rather than deep structure.[34] It all depends on just how incommensurate 'incommensurate conceptual frameworks' must be.

But it is the second reason for Whorf's fall from prominence which is immediately pertinent to our present concerns. What was most startling about Whorfian relativity was that it was held to be true of particular human communities in the real world. A confusing characteristic of the chief philosophical discussions of radical translation, the inscrutability of reference, and the very idea of a conceptual scheme is that they are cast

---

[32] Katz 1978, p. 220.   [33] Chomsky 1967, p. 118.

[34] I have been at pains to stress that the plausibility of 'guidance and constraint' is conditional on the location and exploitation of *fundamental* linguistic structure, but since 'depth' is a relative notion, there is nothing to preclude a structure deep enough to satisfy the needs of an advocate of 'guidance and constraint' from being shallow relative to transformationalist deep structure. Cf. 'one could say that in Whorf's time the structures of the structuralists and of Whorf's linguistic writings were surface structures' (Robins 1976, p. 103).

as thought-experiments insulated in principle from empirical verification and objection, a factor routinely ignored in anthropological borrowings from and disagreements with the philosophers. Whatever success the philosophers might or might not achieve,[35] Whorf bluntly urged as a matter of fact that Hopi language does manifest basic features entailing that Hopi thought, for example in its treatment of time, diverges markedly from the language and thus thought employed by his own audience:

> after long and careful study and analysis, the Hopi language is seen to contain no words, grammatical forms, constructions or expressions that refer directly to what we call 'time', or to past, present, or future, or to enduring or lasting . . . or that even refer to space in such a way as to exclude that element of extension or existence that we call 'time', and so by implication leave a residue that could be referred to as 'time'. Hence, the Hopi language contains no reference to 'time', either explicit or implicit.[36]

The problem is that the best current work on Amerindian languages seriously undermines Whorf's results: both his data and their interpretation are, let us say, highly questionable. Most devastating, perhaps, is Ekkehart Malotki's eloquent juxtaposition (without further comment) of part of the passage from Whorf just quoted with this Hopi quotation from Malotki's own field notes of 1980: 'then indeed, the following day, quite early in the morning at the hour when people pray to the sun, around that time then he woke up the girl again'.[37] Malotki's *magnum opus* (the very length of a book entitled *Hopi Time* (677 pages) speaks volumes) exposes Whorf's alternative 'thought world' as a complete fantasy: 'while many other contributing factors instrumental in disambiguating present and past time interpretations of Hopi nonfactive verbs cannot be detailed here, suffice it to say that Hopi speakers never consider themselves at a loss in determining whether a particular utterance refers to past, present, or future time'.[38]

---

[35] I directly confront such thought-experiments, and the morals which have been drawn from them, in the next section.

[36] Whorf 1967, pp. 57–8; from 'An American Indian Model of the Universe'; and a typically unqualified assertion: 'Hopi may be called a timeless language' (1967, p. 216; from 'Science and Linguistics'). In marked contrast to the pervasive ambiguity we have detected in his various formulations of and references to the relativity hypothesis itself, Whorf never wavers in his commitment to the full-blooded reality of Hopi timelessness, at once linguistic and conceptual.

[37] Epigraph to Malotki 1983.

[38] *Ibid.*, p. 625. Malotki refrains from formulating the harsh judgement his illustrious predecessor palpably deserves: 'while I do not want to contend that all of my observations are flawless, one wonders, however, why Whorf erred so drastically in many of the Hopi time issues' (p. 631); a combination of quite basic linguistic incompetence and wishful thinking springs to mind as the obvious answer. However, Malotki's project is by no means unremittingly negative: with great anthropological sophistication he develops an impressive case for the thesis that Hopi deployment of their elaborate temporal concepts diverges sharply from the Western European paradigm – if hardly for the imaginary Whorfian reasons.

Thus much of the force of a supposedly 'hard' case dissipates: if anyone is inhabiting a distinct world, it isn't the Hopi, at least not for the reasons Whorf pretended he had unearthed. If the Hopi are profoundly alienated from main-stream American society, this may have a little more to do with economic and political oppression than with their delightful tense-system.

We have seen that Whorf himself was not at all averse to taking what he called 'culture', as opposed to 'language', into consideration in his study of the Hopi. In general terms, such catholicity is, of course, all to the good; but no *consistent* advocate of 'guidance and constraint' can afford to pay 'culture' the attention it would otherwise demand, if any progress is to be made towards charting the connections between language, thought and society. As a matter of historical fact, scholars reacting to the hypothesis of linguistic relativity were acutely aware of a set of problems closely resembling this dilemma. In the immediate aftermath of Whorf's celebrity, numerous linguists and anthropologists were rightly much exercised by the puzzle of *defining* language.[39] This was because so many of them were uneasy with that Whorfian construct, the 'thought world'. For his ideas to acquire substantive content, they believed, those ideas should in principle support inferences from 'language' to 'culture' (or, say, from linguistic results to pertinent ethnographic questions); so then 'language' had better not be coterminous with 'culture', but rather be at once theoretically and empirically extricable from it. No consensus emerged, however, on how best to specify the conditions Whorfian relativity should meet to achieve legitimacy in this way; on what the chances for success were; or, finally, on what salutary lessons for directing future research might be learnt from the Whorfian problematic.

In contrast, my version of 'the guidance and constraint hypothesis' was deliberately phrased to afford some protection from the dilemma, at least initially: the intention was that investigating the relation between fundamental syntactic and semantic features of a language and the philosophy done in that language should remain *within* 'language' as such, as distinct from 'culture'. Furthermore, if Chinese philosophy is to constitute a unity 'shaped' or 'coloured' by Chinese language, the latter must form a linguistic foundation which can be perceived to vary neither synchronically nor diachronically. Unlike the field anthropologist, therefore, who works on communities inhabiting real stretches of space and time, the philosophical neo-Whorfian will be forced to dive deep below the surface phenomena and stay there, if the thesis of an integrated type of distinctively Chinese thought is to be maintained.

---

[39] One can get a particularly vivid sense of the intellectual climate from Hoijer 1954, which is largely devoted to discussions of the Whorfian thesis that languages contain 'a hidden metaphysics' (pp. viii–ix).

3.2 Deflationary philosophical anthropology

In the last section we noted a significant contrast between Whorf's timeless Hopi 'thought
world' and a particularly influential trend in contemporary philosophical anthropology
occupied with the topics of radical translation and the inscrutability of reference. While
the Hopi were supposed to constitute an actual alternative to the way we talk and think,
the 'aliens' inhabiting philosophical thought-experiments are, of course, not real. One
might, however, object that, so far as our understanding of language is concerned, this
is a distinction without a difference. Surely such thought-experiments are designed to
open our minds to the possibility that there might be alternative (even incompatible)
conceptual schemes; to the extent that this is a *serious* possibility (and, in philosophy,
possibility 'in principle' is serious enough), its occurring, say, on 'Mars' rather than
in New Mexico makes no difference. According to Quine's famous scenario, a field
linguist is plunged into the midst of an exotic tribe with whose language he is entirely
unfamiliar.[40] Working exclusively on the basis of observed behaviour – the only basis
available to him[41] – the linguist begins the task of ascribing meanings to samples of
the native language on the charitable presumption that their beliefs resemble our own:
when not true, their falsehood should at least make sense in terms of the canons of rationality which we all share (although Quine is clear that the principle of charity does not
automatically outweigh other, obvious, methodological considerations).[42] The linguist's
task is done when he has completed a manual of translation for 'Jungle'. But – so Quine
avers – proceeding along the obligatory behaviourist lines will not necessarily produce
a *unique* best manual: native behaviour, the only criterion for selection between rival
manuals, might very well be equally compatible with incompatible translations. (Quine
is at pains to guard against the misguided supposition that this renders translation
impossible; quite the reverse: 'translation remains, and is indispensable. Indeterminacy
means not that there is no acceptable translation, but that there are many.'[43]) Finally,
since these translation options, being under-determined by all possible evidence, can

---

[40] Radical translation receives its most celebrated formulation in Quine 1960; but from many points of
view, as Quine himself acknowledges, the exposition in 'Speaking of Objects' (in Quine 1969, but
actually written before *Word and Object*) is more helpful.

[41] 'In psychology one may or may not be a behaviourist, but in linguistics one has no choice' (Quine
1987, p. 5).

[42] 'He [the translator] will favour translations that ascribe beliefs to the native that stand to reason or are
consonant with the native's observed way of life. But he will not cultivate these values at the cost of
unduly complicating the structure to be imputed to the native's grammar and semantics, for this again
would be bad psychology; the language must have been simple enough for acquisition by the natives,
whose minds, failing evidence to the contrary, are presumed to be pretty much like our own' (*ibid.*, p. 7).

[43] *Ibid.*, p. 9.

involve determining which characteristic, or sort of thing, is referred to by a 'Jungle' term, and since these possible references may be incompatible, as in Quine's own example of 'gavagai', the indeterminacy of translation apparently yields a full-blown relativistic metaphysics, mutually exclusive ontologies being relative to the alternative manuals.[44] But if that is so, surely Quinean methodology, by generating incommensurate conceptual schemes, fully matches the shattering implications of Whorf's 'thought worlds'?[45]

That this impression is profoundly mistaken is demonstrated most emphatically by Quine's constant correlation of 'Jungle' speakers with *English* learners: we are all, in real life, radical interpreters when we acquire our mother tongue in infancy.[46] But does this not just entail an even more destabilising relativity? We need not travel to New Mexico to encounter aliens: for all we know, our closest fellows subscribe to conceptual schemes different from or even incompatible with our own; when on a country walk I point out a rabbit to my wife, what 'rabbit' signifies to her is, unbeknownst (and unknowably) to me, what I would describe as 'undetached rabbit part'. The inference is fallacious because it ignores the dominant pragmatism of Quine's methodology: his thought-experiment is anti-semantic not out of despair at selecting amongst the burgeoning multiplicity of rival meanings, but rather because there is, by his principles, *no* meaning to postulate beyond what observation indicates, so that the residual indeterminacy of translation or interpretation is ineliminable: 'it makes no real difference that the linguist will turn bilingual and come to think as the natives do – whatever that means. For the arbitrariness of reading our objectifications into the heathen speech reflects not so much the inscrutability of the heathen mind, as that there is nothing to scrute.'[47] To make the semantic aspect of the issue more prominent, I have added a disjunct, 'interpretation', borrowed from Davidson: 'the term "radical interpretation" is meant to suggest strong kinship with Quine's "radical translation". Kinship is not identity,

---

[44] Of course incommensurability does not *entail* incompatibility. A rainbow has colour but no weight, and there is no way to 'translate' colour vocabulary into weight vocabulary; but having a weight does not exclude having a colour, nor is the ability to notice and describe colours incompatible with the ability to notice and describe weights. However, all that is required for the argument which I have developed is that the renderings of a 'Jungle' term in alternative, level-pegging translation manuals *might* have incompatible references.

[45] Jerrold Katz evidently presumes as much when he links Quine with Whorf as advocates of linguistic relativity (see p. 13 above). Presumably he intends to refer to the behaviouristic premiss employed in the construction of the thought-experiment when he attributes the doctrine to 'empiricism', although in that case what 'important breakthroughs in the study of methodology' remain to Quine's credit is rather obscure.

[46] 'Each of us learns his language by observing other people's verbal behaviour and having his own faltering verbal behaviour observed and reinforced or corrected by others' (Quine 1987, p. 5).

[47] Quine 1969, p. 5.

however, and "interpretation" in place of "translation" marks one of the differences: a greater emphasis on the explicitly semantical in the former.'[48] Davidson is very much in deflationary accord with Quine, on my reading: 'indeterminacy of meaning or translation does not represent a failure to capture significant distinctions; it marks the fact that certain apparent distinctions are not significant'.[49] But if 'there is nothing to scrute', the moral must surely be that deciding between rival translation manuals is no *real* choice. Portraying Quine as sharing Whorf's company in championing the reality of incompatible conceptual schemes must, in consequence, be a dismal error.[50]

A second objection to a deflationary construal of philosophical anthropology would attempt to pit Davidson against Quine by focusing on the subset of strictly incompatible (not merely different) conceptual schemes or languages. Davidson not only dismisses Whorfian relativity;[51] he also accuses Quine of surreptitiously cleaving to a 'third dogma of empiricism', an untenable dualism of scheme and content.[52] In essence, the Davidsonian argument runs as follows. Breakdown of translation can speak in favour of the existence of divergent conceptual schemes only if we suppose that there is something independent of the incommensurable languages – 'experience' – for the languages' associated schemes to be schemes *of*. But, since such concept-neutral 'experience' would have, by definition, to lie beyond all schemes (since otherwise it *could* be expressed (variously) in the various languages, which would then be intertranslatable), it remains permanently inconceivable – which is an absurdity. Davidson draws a moral which

[48] 'Radical Interpretation', in Davidson 1984, p. 126, n. 1.
[49] 'Belief and the Basis of Meaning', in Davidson 1984, p. 154.
[50] Elsewhere Katz demonstrates a better understanding of the status of Quine's thought-experiment: 'he presents radical translation as the limiting case of actual translation, i.e. as the case where historical differences between the languages and cultural differences between its speakers are maximal. It is presented as the most philosophically perspicacious case of actual translation in virtue of being the one where the issue about meaning is least likely to be confused by historical and cultural similarities' (Katz 1988, p. 232). Katz contends that Quine's strictures on meaning are illegitimate because they rely on outmoded Bloomfieldian substitution criteria for semantic definitions which have been replaced by axiomatic/recursive definitional techniques in generative grammars (pp. 240–2); but his question 'is Quine to be construed as claiming that English speaking linguists and their English speaking informants do not share a language in which they can communicate?' (p. 249) bespeaks considerable persisting confusion. I have not attempted to adjudicate between Quine and the defenders of *Sinn* because a decision on the viability of intensional semantics is not necessary for comprehending what in Quine is germane to our project, namely, what is *not* implied by the indeterminacy thesis.
[51] In effect Davidson charges Whorf with having been taken in by what I have labelled linguistic 'dissonance': 'Whorf, wanting to demonstrate that Hopi incorporates a metaphysics so alien to ours that Hopi and English cannot, as he puts it, "be calibrated", uses English to convey the contents of sample Hopi sentences' (Davidson 1984, p. 184, from 'On the Very Idea of a Conceptual Scheme'; the reference is to Whorf 1967, p. 55, from 'The Punctual and Segmentative Aspects of Verbs in Hopi').
[52] Davidson 1984, p. 189.

advances an extended principle of charity as the cure for the third dogma: 'we improve the clarity and bite of declarations of difference, whether of scheme or opinion, by enlarging the basis of shared (translatable) language or of shared opinion'.[53]

A decisive response to this second objection is not hard to discover. First, Quine flatly protests that Davidson's accusation is unjust:

> a triad – conceptual scheme, language, and world – is not what I envisage. I think rather, like Davidson, in terms of language and the world. I scant the *tertium quid* as a myth of a museum of labeled ideas. Where I have spoken of a conceptual scheme I could have spoken of a language. Where I have spoken of a very alien conceptual scheme I would have been content, Davidson will be glad to know, to speak of a language awkward or baffling to translate.[54]

The response seems perfectly adequate – so far as it goes. A genuine difference of opinion might nevertheless separate Quine's and Davidson's positions: perhaps Quine would be willing to contemplate translation situations 'awkward or baffling' to a degree Davidson is inclined to disallow *a priori*. But even were we to accept the validity of Davidson's critique, it would simply reinforce the general message we are most closely concerned to extract from this brief foray into one important field of contemporary semantics: that any notion that there might be languages differing to the extent of bringing incompatible conceptual schemes in their wake is to be rejected – as we have seen, only confused exaggeration of the import of linguistic 'dissonance', or allegiance to an incoherent notion of content somehow transcending linguistic/conceptual 'schemes', could tempt one into error. Thus, if we are truly to come to grips with the China syndrome, we must grapple with the conundrum of how it is that the Sinologists we are seeking to understand have fallen so strikingly out of step with the dominant movement in philosophical anthropology. We shall make some progress by exploring the distinctive genealogy of linguistic Sinology in the next section.

3.3 Von Humboldt's legacy

While in Europe the heritage of Lévy-Bruhl, positing a prelogical primitive mentality, was dominant for a long period, and to some extent remains so today,[55] American anthropology (*in primis* Whorf himself) tended pugnaciously to exalt 'the primitive' as a repository of potentially valuable alternatives to the deadening legacy of mainstream Western culture. But it would be a grotesque distortion to posit complete disparity

---

[53] *Ibid.*, p. 197.   [54] 'On the Very Idea of a Third Dogma', in Quine 1981, p. 41.
[55] See Lloyd 1990.

between the anthropological traditions of the two continents: Alexander von Humboldt continues to exercise a profound and lasting European influence that hybridises much more easily with the American school. Since Sapir studied under Boas, who conveyed to America knowledge of the ideas of Wilhelm von Humboldt, Alexander's brother, and since Whorf finally studied under Sapir, there is even a real pedagogical link joining W. von Humboldt's linguistic theories to Whorf's.[56] This family tree is for us very suggestive because Humboldt made a seminal contribution to European thinking about the special character of the Chinese language. Our working hypothesis will be, therefore, that the unusual cast of much Sinology is at least partially explicable in these genetic terms. Because 'the primitive' is all too easily assimilated to 'the oriental', whether with disreputable or with benign intent, and because Eastern 'advanced' languages have historically been bracketed with 'barbaric' but equally 'exotic' Amerindian languages, the confluence of European and American streams, flowing from W. von Humboldt and from Whorf, has produced the unique methodology of 'guidance and constraint' Chinese scholarship – a scholarship in tension with the prevalent methodology in semantics detailed in the previous section. To refine and test this thesis, I shall concentrate on Humboldt's brilliant monograph, *Lettre à M. Abel-Rémusat sur la nature des formes grammaticales en général, et sur le génie de la langue chinoise en particulier.*[57]

A preliminary point: the genetic story I suggest is not proffered in a reductive spirit, nor is it intended as a sufficient explanation of the China syndrome; it is not even meant to be the only plausible genetic account. For example, as in so much else, Nietzsche fully anticipates the most provocative work of this century in his challenging evocation of the purest 'guidance and constraint':

> Die wunderliche Familien-Ähnlichkeit alles indischen, griechischen, deutschen Philosophierens erklärt sich einfach genug. Gerade, wo Sprach-Verwandtschaft vorliegt, ist es gar nicht zu vermeiden, daß, dank der gemeinsamen Philosophie der Grammatik – ich meine dank der unbewußten Herrschaft und Führung durch gleiche grammatische Funktionen – von vornherein alles für eine gleichartige Entwicklung und Reihenfolge der philosophischen Systeme vorbereitet liegt:

---

[56] Were one to believe Chomsky, it would be impossible to make this association. Chomsky appeals to the Humboldtian idea that language cannot be taught (Chomsky 1969, pp. 17ff.) as a precursor of his own theory that there is an innate learning module which constructs a generative grammar of any given *langue* on the basis of fragmentary *parole*: 'to perform this task, it utilises its given *faculté de langage* [Humboldtian jargon], its innate specification of certain heuristic procedures and certain built-in constraints on the character of the task to be performed' (p. 26). But he only manages to enrol Humboldt in the universalist camp opposed to proponents of linguistic relativity by ignoring the strong evidence to the contrary contained in such documents as the *Lettre à M. Abel-Rémusat*.

[57] von Humboldt 1827.

ebenso wie zu gewissen anderen Möglichkeiten der Welt-Ausdeutung der Weg wie abgesperrt erscheint.[58]

I am not at all concerned to deny that Nietzsche's 'unconscious domination and directing' of philosophy by grammar might also have contributed significantly, if indirectly, to the creation of an intellectual inclination to detect a peculiar relationship between Chinese language and Chinese thought: I only insist that the Humboldt pedigree has won special prestige on account of the celebrity which the *Lettre* justifiably enjoys.

According to Abel-Rémusat, the question 'of the nature and actual importance of grammatical forms' has been given a new lease of life by advances in the study of two Asian languages which stand in almost polar opposition to each other: 'remarquables, l'une [Sanskrit] par la perfection de son système, l'autre [Chinese] par la pauvreté apparente qui la caractérise'.[59] It is because both Sanskrit and Chinese are oriental 'exotica' that Abel-Rémusat is able to bring them together in this spurious but highly charged contrariety. What must never be forgotten when one is assessing this material is that the linguistic theorising of the period not only subscribed to a now-vanished normativity – at least, the uninhibited normative extremism so evident in the nineteenth century has vanished – but also, as a consequence of the not yet extinct classical inheritance, felt free to evaluate entire languages against the standard of grammaticality deriving from traditional study of Greek and Latin. Thus the 'perfection' of Sanskrit's 'system' will be readily applauded, because the intimidating ramifications of its morphology and syntax easily impress someone with a classical education as linguistically elaborate on a familiar scale of grammatical complexity. By the same token, Chinese – when judged according to what is now accepted as an utterly inappropriate grammatical conception, stemming from the Western classical languages – will emerge as 'impoverished'. This strictly biased normativity must never be lost sight of as we review Humboldt's description of 'le *génie* de la langue chinoise'.

The first cardinal point to note about Humboldt's conception of Chinese is that, although he is perfectly well aware that it lacks word-classes and grammatical categories as traditionally conceived, this unusually does not suggest to him that it thereby also lacks proper linguistic structure: 'elle fixe *d'une autre manière* les rapports des éléments du langage dans l'enchaînement de la pensée'.[60] In fact, such is Humboldt's

---

[58] Nietzsche 1987, p. 24: 'the singular family resemblance between all Indian, Greek and German philosophising is easy enough to explain. Where there exists a language affinity it is quite impossible, thanks to the common philosophy of grammar – I mean thanks to unconscious domination and directing by similar grammatical functions – to avoid everything being prepared in advance for a similar evolution and succession of philosophical systems: just as the road seems to be barred to certain other possibilities of world interpretation.'

[59] p.v of his 'avertissement' to the *Lettre*. [60] von Humboldt 1827, p. 2 (my italics).

grammatical perspicacity that he pays attention to Rosemont's benighted ancestors[61] and neatly dissects their capital mistake: 'je pense que les savants qui se sont presque laissés entraîner à oublier que le chinois est une langue parlée, ont tellement exagéré l'influence de l'écriture chinoise, qu'ils ont, pour ainsi dire, mis l'écriture à la place de la langue'.[62] He insists that, even in languages which neglect to mark categories, words combined into phrases must nevertheless possess 'une valeur grammaticale', although this grammatical force will not be apparent in the word taken in isolation. From where does this force come? Humboldt conceives of grammatical categories as deriving from, and perhaps representing, categories in the real world (whether these ontological categories owe more to Aristotelian or to Kantian philosophy is not clear); the derivation is effected by 'la pensée', which somehow intervenes between the world and language. So he suggests a variety of sources for a word's force: most directly, if it refers to an object which must belong to a single ontological category, then the verbal signifier has the force associated with the grammatical category analogous to the referent's ontological category; or a word of multiple signification can be restricted to a single category by convention; finally, and most interestingly, grammatical force can arise simply from either a given phrase's syntax or its larger context.[63] This rather baroque metaphysical semantics has the signal advantage of permitting Humboldt to attribute grammatical *function* to the Chinese language, even in the absence of morphological *form*: 'la langue chinoise ne connaît donc, à parler grammaticalement, point de verbe fléchi; elle n'a pas proprement de verbes, mais seulement *des expressions d'idées verbales*, et ces dernières paraissent sous la forme d'infinitifs, c'est-à-dire, sous la plus vague de celles que nous connaissons'.[64]

Not that Humboldt does not subscribe to a version of 'the guidance and constraint hypothesis', at least to the 'constraint' component: 'si un rapport grammatical ne trouve pas d'expression dans une langue, il ne frappe pas vivement la nation qui la parle, et n'en est pas senti avec clarté et précision'.[65] Humboldt's postulation of a noetic intermediary between reality and language keeps him from thorough-going 'guidance and constraint', since the thought which captures ontological categories and transmits them to language cannot be entirely in thrall to linguistic determination; if anything, there would seem to be interdependence between thought and language, on Humboldt's scheme. He nevertheless concludes that Chinese is markedly inferior to its linguistic 'opposites' 'comme organe de la pensée'.[66] His judgement is quite particular: it is precisely the demand which Chinese places on its readers to *infer* so very much that constrains the easy, effortless movement of thought along lengthy deductive chains,

[61] See n. 11 above.   [62] von Humboldt 1827, p. 80.   [63] *Ibid.*, pp. 8–9.
[64] *Ibid.*, p. 16; my italics.   [65] *Ibid.*, p. 27.   [66] *Ibid.*, p. 65.

since only explicit grammatical forms can guide reasoning on so complicated a journey.[67] Humboldt does not, however, castigate Chinese accordingly as linguistically 'primitive': on the contrary, and despite appearances, Chinese is not to be confused with the 'imperfect' languages of nations which have never attained any significant intellectual development.[68] Not only is Chinese an 'advanced' language; it also, and somewhat paradoxically, achieves parity with Greek and Latin by virtue of the absolute regularity with which its exiguous grammaticality is maintained (indeed here is its 'characteristic genius'),[69] although this parity does not extend to the use of Chinese for reasoning. Chinese is no good 'comme organe de la pensée' because its syntax, which articulates no more than the basic distinction between subject and attribute, cannot represent the more sophisticated logical relationships required to depict the various 'logical' categories.[70] If 'le génie de la langue chinoise' makes a remarkable impression, its logical imperfection is so pronounced that Humboldt goes so far as to assert that language *should* aim in the opposite direction;[71] in the last analysis, the perfection of Chinese remains constricted within limits which the ratiocinative capacities of Western classical languages break.[72]

Humboldt's legacy to Sinology is momentous, if fraught with ambiguity. On the one hand, he gives lasting shape to the impression, prevalent since the very first Western contacts with China, that its language is remarkable, perhaps unique, by conveying this impression in philosophically evocative terms, those of a metaphysically loaded theoretical semantics and grammar. But, on the other, the style of his defence of Chinese linguistic 'genius', which vindicates the language by sacrificing its claims to efficacy as an instrument of reason, is partially responsible for one key Sinological attitude: if not 'primitive' in the sense favoured by Lévy-Bruhl, the Chinese mind is nevertheless not comparable to the Western intellect, nor, consequently, should one

---

[67] *Ibid.*, pp. 66–7.   [68] *Ibid.*, p. 47.

[69] 'C'est, au contraire, par la netteté et la pureté qu'elle met dans l'application de son système grammatical, que la langue chinoise se place absolument à l'égal et au rang des langues classiques, c'est-à-dire, des plus parfaites parmi celles que nous connaissons, mais avec un système non pas seulement différent, mais opposé, autant que la nature générale des langues le permet' (*ibid.*, p. 48). Humboldt's own genius does not lie in his being an exception to the ruling normative paradigm of his time (although he does at one point insist that so many different qualitative criteria for evaluating languages are available that such judgements cannot be certain (*ibid.*, p. 50)); it is, rather, to be discovered in the brilliant originality with which he both radically expands and transforms the normative canons otherwise merely taken for granted.

[70] *Ibid.*, p. 68.

[71] '. . . les langues d'un système grammatical opposé nous étonnent par une perfection que nous reconnaissons comme étant celle à laquelle le langage doit réellement viser' (*ibid.*, p. 67).

[72] '. . . l'art de sa grammaire consiste à lui en fournir les moyens sans sortir de son système, mais l'étendue et la tournure qu'elle donne aux périodes est toujours renfermée dans la mesure de ses moyens' (*ibid.*, p. 69).

expect it to be informed by a standard of rationality that can be rightly demanded only of thinking undertaken in Greek, Latin or their descendants. In other words, part of Humboldt's heritage is a conception of thinking which is at loggerheads with the implications of the principle of charity applied by the deflationary philosophical anthropology canvassed in the previous section. Furthermore, Humboldt's employment of 'thought' as a vital theoretical term separate from 'language' also feeds into a distinctively mentalistic strain in later Sinological discussion of the Chinese language in relation to Chinese culture.

All components of this inheritance are especially apparent in the French tradition of Chinese studies; unfortunately, however, Humboldt's all-important insight that there can be grammatical function in the absence of familiar morphology and word-classes tends not to be preserved. For example, Granet metamorphoses the thesis that Chinese linguistic rationality is defective into the much more extreme hypothesis that it is *conceptually* impoverished, favouring symbolically loaded imprecision: 'la langue chinoise ne paraît point organisée pour exprimer des *concepts*. Aux signes abstraits qui peuvent aider à spécifier les idées, elle préfère des symboles riches de suggestions pratiques; au lieu d'une acception définie, ils possèdent une efficacité indéterminée.'[73] Amazingly, he suggests that rhythm substitutes for syntax in Chinese ('il [le chinois] a su réserver au rhythme seul le soin d'organiser l'expression de la pensée');[74] and he concludes that the language deliberately abstains from analytical discussion so as to specialise in emotional communication and rhetorical persuasion (one suspects that Granet conceived of 'la langue chinoise' as a woman): 'la langue chinoise n'apparaît point organisée pour noter des concepts, analyser des idées, exposer discursivement des doctrines. Elle est tout entière façonnée pour communiquer des attitudes sentimentales, pour suggérer des conduites, pour convaincre, pour convertir.'[75]

Gernet, an enthusiastic exponent of a crudely enunciated 'guidance and constraint',[76] quite clearly sees the Humboldtian *aperçu* that Chinese lacks morphologically discriminated word-classes; but he travesties it by assuming that Chinese words can be made to appear functionally distinct only by the *arbitrary* importation of alien grammatical categories:

> of all the languages in the world, Chinese has the peculiar, distinctive feature of possessing no grammatical categories systematically differentiated by morphology: there appears to be nothing to distinguish a verb from an adjective, an adverb from a complement, a subject from an attribute. The fact is that, in Chinese, these

---

[73] Granet 1934, p. 8. Cf. 'Il [le mot en Chinois] évoque, en faisant d'abord apparaître la plus active d'entre elles, un complexe indéfini d'images particulières' (p. 37).

[74] *Ibid.*, pp. 79, 82.   [75] *Ibid.*, p. 82.   [76] Gernet 1985, p. 240.

categories only exist by implicit and arbitrary reference to other languages which do possess them.[77]

He insists that in Chinese syntactical articulation is at a bare minimum, and derives from this supposition the quite incredible notion that 'every Chinese text has in general an impersonal tone'.[78] In the end he chooses – whether consciously or not – to account for cultural clash by replicating Humboldt perfectly, removing the Chinese mind and the Chinese language together from the exclusively Western preserve of rational argument: 'in the manipulation of the Chinese language, the mental mechanisms and aptitudes that are at work are different from those which have been favoured in the West. Comparisons and combinations are preferred to logical articulations.'[79] We have now seen how Humboldt's legacy might very well have rendered certain Sinological schools uniquely receptive to the stimulus of Whorfian relativity and more or less unaffected by the antidote to 'guidance and constraint' provided by Quinean and Davidsonian principles of charity. In the next section I broach my first case-study, which will reveal how the syndrome forges a more specific link between the undeniable (from a Western perspective) peculiarities of Chinese grammar and alleged peculiarities of Chinese engagement in abstract and scientific thought.

4 Case-study 1: conditionals

As it happens there is a notorious case in the study of modern Chinese of the influence of such theoretical commitments. Alfred Bloom's *The Linguistic Shaping of Thought: A Study in the Impact of Language on Thinking in China and the West*[80] is an extreme Whorfian manifesto.[81] Bloom contends that Chinese conditionals are indeterminate in that they do not distinguish between simple, hypothetical and counterfactual conditions, distinctions unavoidable in English if standard (received) morphological and syntactical rules are obeyed.[82] Therefore, he concludes, abstract thought which springs from hypothetical exercises does not come easily to Chinese people, a result which Bloom argues he has verified with four pieces of evidence: the claim that Hong Kong subjects

---

[77] *Ibid.*, p. 241. The text continues: 'furthermore, there was no word to denote existence in Chinese, nothing to convey the concept of being or essence, which in Greek is so conveniently expressed by the noun οὐσία or the neuter τὸ ὄν' (p. 241). I directly address the issue of Western versus Chinese 'being' in sections 7 and 9, and in chapter 2.

[78] '. . . the subject is no more than whatever an assertion is being made about. There is no necessary link, made manifest through morphology, to connect subject, verb and complement' (*ibid.*, p. 246).

[79] *Ibid.*, p. 242.   [80] Bloom 1981.   [81] The allegiance is made explicit at Bloom 1981, p. 11.

[82] '. . . the Chinese language has no distinct lexical, grammatical, or intonational device to signal entry into the counterfactual realm, to indicate explicitly that the events referred to have definitely not occurred and are being discussed for the purpose only of exploring the might-have-been or the might-be' (*ibid.*, p. 16).

are noticeably loath to indulge in counterfactual hypothesising, and that invitations to do so are met with such responses as 'it's unnatural', 'it's unChinese';[83] the claim that monolingual Chinese subjects fail to perceive conditionals as ambiguous between indicative and counterfactual construals, which they supposedly would do, were their thought-patterns uninfluenced by 'guidance and constraint';[84] the claim that Chinese students supposedly encounter particular difficulty in mastering the English counterfactual;[85] and the data yielded by a battery of psychological tests administered to sample Chinese and American groups. Although he readily concedes that Chinese people do use the recognisable classes of conditional, with presupposition determining whether a given sentence expresses a straight implication or a counterfactual, he hankers after nothing less than explicit marking, and decides, in a diluted Whorfian spirit, that its absence 'does not encourage' the Chinese to evolve a 'cognitive schema' which would correspond to the absent marked category (rather than actively discouraging them from such development).[86]

These claims have been replicated for ancient Chinese philosophy by David Hall and Roger Ames in their book *Thinking Through Confucius*, where we learn that 'scientific and ethical reflections and deliberations' would have been 'unappealing' to the ancient Chinese as a direct consequence of indeterminate conditional structure.[87] They are evidently unaware that Harbsmeier presents extensive and irrefutable evidence for firm recognition in ancient China of the distinction between plain and counterfactual conditionals;[88] he demonstrates that 使 (*shih*), as opposed to 若 (*jo*) or 如 (*ju*), introduces a counterfactual construction.[89]

Bloom lays particular emphasis on his experimental findings. He administered questionnaires containing stories of the form 'X was not the case; but if X was, then W, then Y, then Z, etc. . . .', and appended questions asking in one way or another whether the consequents refer to actual happenings. The results were as follows: 25 of 28 American college students were successful (89 per cent); 37 of 54 Chinese college students[90] were (69 per cent); 6 of 36 Chinese hotel workers were (17 per cent). Bloom is convinced that these figures constitute hard scientific evidence for 'the guidance and constraint hypothesis'.[91]

---

[83] *Ibid.*, p. 13.   [84] *Ibid.*, p. 17.   [85] *Ibid.*   [86] *Ibid.*, p. 20.   [87] Hall and Ames 1987, p. 265.
[88] In the section 'Counterfactual *shih* 使' of his magisterial *Aspects of Classical Chinese Syntax* (Harbsmeier 1981, pp. 272–87).
[89] Hall and Ames's linguistic theorising comes under direct scrutiny in the next section.
[90] '. . . all of whom had some exposure to English and some of whom had very considerable exposure to English' (Bloom 1981, p. 24).
[91] 'The results . . . speak not only to the absence of a scheme corresponding to the English and Indo-European counterfactual among the majority of Chinese speakers, but also to the specific relevance of linguistic variables to that fact . . . many of the Chinese subjects who responded correctly wrote the words "would have" in English in the margin of the stories they were reading, even though the questionnaire was written in Chinese and distributed by a Chinese research assistant' (*ibid.*).

But his experimental procedure is very seriously flawed. First, Bloom takes no account of the fact that his study includes no sample of working-class Americans. Presumably he used two sets of Chinese subjects precisely because he wanted to test for the influence of exposure to English or some other Western language. And even were one to grant that the variation in scores is significant, despite the tiny numbers involved, the difference cannot establish anything to do with Indo-European influence, because Bloom has surprisingly neglected the educational disparity between his Chinese groups. As a result the dramatic working-class Chinese figures should be excluded; the remaining numbers for comparison are, therefore, 89 per cent (American college students) as against 69 per cent (Chinese college students).

Second, are even these groups truly comparable? The Chinese were from Taiwan National University,[92] while the Americans came from Swarthmore. But no more information is provided concerning social and cultural backgrounds. Two questions are crucial: were the Chinese primarily engineering students, for example? Given Swarthmore's humanistic ethos, even were all the Americans (say) psychology majors, they would have possessed considerable experience in the parsing of complex written tests. Was this true of the Chinese? We have no way of knowing. And, perhaps even more important, all the Americans would have been veterans at sitting aptitude tests which focus on the rapid logical analysis of short texts – often, indeed, on counterfactuals. What about the Chinese? Unless they had a similar educational history, Bloom was, as so often in experimental psychology, testing for nothing but skill at taking a certain type of test.

Third, even were it the case that these questions about the background of Bloom's Chinese sample were settled in his favour, what follows? Surely not his conclusion that abstract 'cognitive schemata' are 'not encouraged' by Chinese linguistic structure. Bloom presents scattered anecdotal evidence to the effect that counterfactual constructions are (relatively) rare in Chinese. Ignoring the general fallibility of the anecdotal method, let us suppose that this is true, so that a real contrast exists between Chinese and English; that is, between two groups of language-users; that is, finally and precisely, between two linguistic *cultures*. Bloom is eager to correlate this supposed fact with the presence or absence of counterfactual markers. But that move just seems to beg the question, when it is baldly assumed that such correlation betrays a causal influence of (lack of) linguistic structure on cognitive processes. So, were the contrast between Chinese and English a (problematic) fact, we could simply say: there is *something* about Chinese (linguistic) culture which does not encourage counterfactual exercises. Why suppose that lack of markers is at the root of the matter?

---

[92] '. . . the college of highest prestige in Taiwan' (*ibid.*, p. 23).

On this scenario, the bilingual Chinese students attached the *English* gloss 'would have' to their correct counterfactual responses not 'as if those words insured the continued activation of a schema, drawn from their English repertory, which would, in this case, be helpful in processing Chinese',[93] but rather because their familiarity with such trains of thought derived from exposure to English cultural products. Bloom thinks he is testing for counterfactual reasoning 'outside of concrete situational contexts': but nothing could be more sensitive to a multiplicity of interacting educational and social factors than such reasoning. To be fair to Bloom, his further experiments[94] are not similarly flawed, since they involved only college-educated groups. Furthermore, they are considerably more subtle, since the questionnaires included two types of story, one open to a coherent non-counterfactual interpretation, the other making sense only if construed counterfactually, so that minimum (story 1) versus maximum (story 2) willingness to interpret counterfactually would emerge differentially. The result claimed is 29 per cent Chinese counterfactual responses as against 97 per cent American.[95] These tests are not fatally skewed by the inclusion of a relatively uneducated Chinese sample; but even if taken at face-value, they persist in ignoring the central issue of relative cultural familiarity with extended counterfactual texts (especially in tests), and so still flagrantly beg the question of whether the results are the effect of fundamental linguistic structure. Bloom himself seems disconcertingly to admit as much,[96] but then protests: 'the present argument is not that cultural proclivities do not make important contributions to the shaping of thought, but rather that linguistic structures also make their contributions and that *as one moves into increasingly abstract cognitive realms, such as that of the counterfactual, the formative contributions of linguistic structures to both thought and culture become increasingly pronounced*'.[97]

As a companion piece to his Whorfian analysis of conditionals, Bloom also argues that English and Chinese thinking diverge significantly in the ease with which they employ generic concepts. A Chinese test group was confronted with a Chinese sentence which, in order to preserve indeterminacy, could be represented in English as '(the) kangaroo(s) is/are eat turnip(s)', and asked whether the sentence might refer, not just to all kangaroos, but rather to a 'conceptual kangaroo', 'something other than an actual or all actual kangaroos'.[98] The initial, eminently reasonable response was: 'what do you mean by "conceptual" kangaroo? Either you are talking about a single kangaroo or about all kangaroos. What else is there?' Would English speakers (who were not tested on their supposed facility with generic concepts) have reacted any differently? Bloom takes it for granted that an 'extracted theoretical entity' is either a universal, or at least a

---

[93] *Ibid.*, p. 25.   [94] *Ibid.*, pp. 25–30.   [95] *Ibid.*, p. 28.   [96] *Ibid.*, p. 32.
[97] *Ibid.*, p. 33, my italics; cf. p. 70.   [98] *Ibid.*, p. 36.

psychological construct to be used in imaginary or hypothetical contexts. But the statement of his assumption by itself suffices to show that there is no reason to anticipate that competent speakers of any language, merely on the basis of their competence, need share his conception of concepts, generic or otherwise.

Quite apart from his highly questionable testing procedure,[99] Bloom's linguistico-racist findings rely on the conviction that contextual disambiguation, no matter how subtle and effective, simply will not count as a device of the language shaping the thought. If disambiguation is pragmatic, then it serves merely to shore up a ruinously handicapped language, itself riddled with primitive, all-pervasive ambiguity.[100] I am not, of course, pretending that pragmatic principles *are* rules of grammar; rather, we should conceive of grammatical rules as constantly subject to pragmatic constraint. The argument is that since every utterance has a context, whether what requires determination receives it by recourse to grammatical rules or to pragmatic principles (or, of course, to their combination) cannot make a whit of difference; all that matters is that appropriate determination occurs. Since real language just is utterances in contexts, real grammar and pragmatics fuse inextricably.[101]

Allow me to stress that I personally (like many others) do not find the translation of *ancient* Chinese conditionals easy,[102] nor do I deny that hard thinking is necessary about

---

[99] Further extremely serious defects are uncovered by Wu Kuang-ming's review of Bloom's book, 'Counterfactuals, Universals, and Chinese thinking' (Wu 1987), which contends that 'Bloom's test results, then, are due more to an imposition of English formulation (put in Chinese) on Chinese people than to Chinese ignorance of counterfactual thinking' (p. 85), and most interestingly points out that 'the whole of satirical Taoism thrives on skillful manipulation of counterfactuals into stories and arguments' (p. 88); and also by Fang Wan-chuan's 'Chinese Language and Theoretical Thinking: A Review Article' (Fang 1984), which similarly charges that the wording of the Chinese questionnaires, in comparison with the English, is obscure and confusing.

[100] There is a partial phonological analogy. To argue that the high incidence of homophony (that is, to untrained English ears) in isolating languages is a source of disabling ambiguity which pitch variation, by introducing further semantic distinctions, merely helps to alleviate is not much more objectionable than is Bloom's reasoning about conditionals.

[101] Discussion with Geoffrey Horrocks has helped me to clarify my position considerably. He offers a parallel to Bloom's data: the mechanisms of pronominal anaphora are highly grammaticalised in most European languages, and almost entirely ungrammaticalised in many oriental languages; but just as Bloom's counterfactual argument did not survive inspection, so there is no reason to believe that these languages are plagued by special problems in establishing correct pronominal reference.

[102] Not that one should unthinkingly assume that conditionals indubitably of one type rather than another are difficult to come by. Take, for example, *Analects* III.9, 文獻不足也 (*wen hsien pu tsu yeh*), where Confucius insists that the records and wise men of Ch'i and Sung are insufficient to substantiate his description of pristine Hsia and Yin Dynasty ceremonial (he is here deploring the decay of ancient ritual). Out of context, the immediate sequel, 足，則吾能徵之矣 (*tsu, tse wu neng cheng chih i*), could be construed as 'since they suffice, I am able to adduce them'; but in context it must, of course, be rendered '*were* they to suffice, I *should* be able to adduce them'.

how conditionals are deployed in Chinese philosophy, science and medicine. What is worrying is that such investigations can take off from the constraints of basic linguistic structure. Here is a caricatured but, I think, genuinely analogous argument aimed at Western philosophers of science: 'for years now you have been puzzling over how attributions of disposition figure or ought to figure in nomic conditionals. But you have attacked the problem in the wrong way, because you have failed to recognise that it arises from, and can only be comprehended in terms of, the availability of English subjunctives like '*x* is soluble in water because if placed in H_2O, it would have dissolved'. Nobody would think much of this linguistic analysis, and equally nobody should be impressed by the 'guidance and constraint' argument levelled against Chinese facility with conditionals.

5 Case-study 2: Chinese is a list

Hall and Ames cultivate a version of 'the guidance and constraint hypothesis' which is of special interest because it tries to draw conclusions from the Chinese language not just for Chinese thought in general, but for ancient Chinese philosophy in particular, and, most particularly, for Chinese philosophy about language. Since Hall and Ames seem to accept unreservedly Rosemont's untenable theory that written ancient Chinese, an 'artificial language', is more or less completely unrelated to spoken ancient Chinese, a 'natural language',[103] they suppose that what is explicitly identified as 'the Sapir–Whorf hypothesis' 'cannot easily be applied to classical Chinese, since, presumably, the oral form of communication provides the readiest reference to the structure of thinking in early China and it is precisely the oral form that, for the most part, eludes us'.[104]

But this does not keep Hall and Ames from extravagant, if vague, speculation associating linguistic and philosophical character; for example, they link Confucius' ritualistic characterisation of human beings to 'the functional character of Chinese language *per se*',[105] and gnomically declare that 'a wholly immanent vision can only be expressed in a language of concreteness'.[106] Either Hall and Ames believe, then, that ancient Chinese writing does afford at least limited access to a specialised mode of thought – philosophy; or they are actually proposing a modified form of 'guidance and constraint' which somehow replaces 'thought' with 'philosophy', where 'philosophy' is, in a manner left unexplained, to be distinguished from 'thought' no matter how qualified. In any case, Hall and Ames certainly present symptoms characteristic of the China

---

[103] See n. 11 above.   [104] Hall and Ames 1987, pp. 253–4.
[105] *Ibid.*, p. 239: one might ask, in that case, why Confucianism ever had any rivals.   [106] *Ibid.*, p. 263.

syndrome.[107] They introduce a novel interpretation of Confucius' doctrine of 正名 (*cheng ming*), 'the rectification of names': 'naming for Confucius cannot simply be a process of attaching appropriately corresponding labels to an already existing reality. The performative force of language entails the consequence that to interpret the world through language is to impel it towards a certain realisation, to make it known in a certain way.'[108] This argument is supposed to buttress the claim that, on the Confucian conception, language does not neutrally signify, that is, merely represent – accurately or not – an independent realm of objective reference.[109]

The argument fails. Hall and Ames may claim only that a 'reality' must be brought into existence which corresponds rightly to the 名 (*ming*, names); but where is the case for the 名 themselves not constituting *objective* criteria – *true* ones, in a full-blooded sense? There are two possible responses. First, since Hall and Ames favour a 'process' ontology,[110] they might argue that 義 (*i*, which they render 'signification') is inherently fluid, and so never a fixture allowing objective assessment.[111] But unless 'signification' is so fluid as to reach an untenable Heraclitean extreme of constant, exceptionless semantic change, then even on this scheme of things objective answers to questions about the relation of name and object would always be available *pro tem*. Second, Hall and Ames might look for a defence in their 'performative' model of discourse. But the phrase 'language *impels* the world', if taken seriously, is rank nonsense, a sort of phenomenology at once vulgar and untrue to the astute and practical bent in Confucianism

[107] They are nonetheless not prone to cite 'guidance and constraint' at every opportunity (e.g. they propose that the putative deficiency in ancient Chinese of abstract nouns and counterfactuals is 'a consequence of the absence of notions of transcendence in the classical Chinese tradition' (p. 267), rather than seeking a linguistic explanation).

[108] *Ibid.*, pp. 268–9.

[109] 'Language is self-referencing. The meaning of a word is a function of its use within a particular community' (*ibid.*, p. 264); 'the name/thing correlation does not seem to concern Confucius' (*ibid.*); and '(at least for Confucius) language does not serve primarily to refer to a world of objects' (pp. 263–4). Yet Hall and Ames seem to contradict themselves by also appearing to endorse a less iconoclastic semantics, if only in a dismissive aside: 'the meaningfulness of a proposition (its "locutionary" character, its sense and reference) abstracted from its active and responsive (illocutionary and perlocutionary) force is broadly irrelevant' (p. 264). I would guess that if 'language is self-referencing', then the reference here conceded to propositions must be self-reference; but *universal* self-reference is ridiculous. Confidence is not bolstered by the passage's serious miscomprehension of speech-act theory, and is eroded yet further when one reads 'ontological particulars cannot be referenced; they must be alluded to, hinted at, suggested' (p. 275), as if *coy* reference were not reference at all.

[110] '. . . Confucius tempers his respect for antiquity with the practical consideration that inherited wisdom and institutions must be constantly revamped to accommodate *the shifting circumstances of an always unique world*' (*ibid.*, p. 272; my italics).

[111] '. . . naming and the attunement of names is [*sic*] a dynamic enterprise in which the existing structure and definition is [*sic*] qualified by the understanding that names and their achieved harmonies are always fluid within the parameters of a context, and are in continual need of attunement' (*ibid.*, p. 274).

which Hall and Ames, like most people, so appreciate as typical of this strand in the Chinese philosophical tradition.

Their major foray into the philosophy of language is so provocative as to deserve quotation *in extenso*:

> Classical Chinese is not, as are most Western languages, grounded in the propositional utterance. The dominance of the noun function precludes limiting meaningful statements to those possessing the sentential, subject–predicate form. The tendency of classical Chinese philosophers to be concerned with the ordering of names is a consequence of the dominance of the noun function.[112] The striking claim that classical Chinese doesn't depend upon sentences and propositions for the expression of semantic content entails the consequence that all Chinese words are names, and that compound terms, phrases, and sentences are strings of names. This consequence, in turn, requires that one appreciate the lack of interest on the part of the early Chinese in questions of 'truth' and 'falsity'. Words, as names, may be judged appropriate or inappropriate; only propositions may, in the strict sense, be true or false.[113]

Hall and Ames's version of 'the guidance and constraint hypothesis' thus topples into utter absurdity. It asserts not that ancient Chinese is a different language, inhibiting philosophical tendencies familiar in the West and encouraging the discovery of exotic philosophical insights, but rather that it simply is not a language at all – although they are evidently unaware of the unwelcome implication that Chinese is a vast catalogue of lists. Perhaps the ultimate roots of this spectacular error are to be found in the long-standing dispute as to whether Chinese words fall into lexical classes (the claimed 'dominance of the noun function', fictitious as it is, may hint at such an origin). The truth is that words in ancient Chinese, if not confined within the well-defined lexical classes present in Indo-European, nevertheless do not function randomly.[114] I must

---

[112] Graham objects that, if anything, it is *Indo-European* languages which deserve to be described as 'noun-centred' (Graham 1989, p. 394).

[113] Hall and Ames 1987, pp. 298–9. Section 8 will be occupied in part with Graham's views on Chinese 'truth', which he enunciates in response to Hall and Ames's thesis.

[114] Harbsmeier wittily illustrates his theory of 'flexible functional preference' with a metaphor which compares ancient Greek lexical items to chessmen, Chinese ones to football players: 'Sie [Wörter] könnten ein kategoriales Kontinuum bilden, in dem Wörter eine größere oder geringere Tendenz oder Präferenz an den Tag legen, gewisse grammatische Funktionen auszuüben' (Harbsmeier 1979, pp. 156–7). This should be compared to the ideas of the 'category squish' and of 'fuzzy grammar' introduced respectively by other opponents of hard-and-fast lexical classes (e.g. Ross 1972) and by those sceptical about the existence of all-or-nothing grammatical rules (e.g. Lakoff 1973). What remains unclear, however, is whether Harbsmeier is actually a partisan of so-called 'non-discrete' grammar, as distinct from merely being critical of any grammatical theory (such as some types of old-fashioned transformationalism) entailing a degree of functional rigidity at manifest odds with his compelling Chinese data.

confess that I cannot really understand Hall and Ames's position, possibly because it is incoherent: when, as they say, ancient Chinese philosophers judge whether a name is 'appropriate' (rather than 'true'), do they actually think that this judgement lacks propositional content, or that their poor Chinese philosophers so believe?

Graham reads Hall and Ames as imagining that possession of subject–predicate form is a necessary condition for a phrase to have a truth-value, which he calls an (incorrect) 'Aristotelian principle'.[115]

> On this Aristotelian principle one would have to agree that no truths were ever spoken in China, for even a verbal sentence with a subject is not conveniently analysed in subject–predicate form. But surely for modern logic propositions require this form only when quantified . . . Ridding oneself of the subject–predicate presupposition may itself be claimed as one advantage of an education in Chinese which Hall and Ames seem to have missed.[116]

I cannot endorse this critique, because Graham's enunciation of the so-called 'Aristotelian principle', which he rejects, is dangerously vague. It would seem that in the first instance he construes it as a *grammatical* principle, and is certainly correct that not all Chinese sentences (or, for that matter, English or Greek ones) have (grammatical) subject–predicate form. But without perceiving the shift he immediately goes on to speak as if *logical* form were in question, and asserts that only quantified propositions require (logical) subject–predicate form.[117] Not so. Because Graham confuses grammatical and logical subjects and predicates and therefore does not explain precisely what he intends by 'subject–predicate form' in logic, I do not know where he thinks it occurs in formal systems. Presumably he mistakenly sees this form only in a formula which contains a variable bound by a quantifier, where the variable is taken for subject and the function-letter for predicate. But if that is the idea, then he has simply overlooked

---

[115] Graham 1989, p. 394.

[116] *Ibid.* Arguably many ergative languages also lack sentences displaying the subject–predicate cut. Harbsmeier maintains that ancient Chinese theorists did not anatomise the proposition into subject and predicate (Harbsmeier 1979, p. 159), but is willing to compare their division of words into 'full' and 'empty' (lexical and grammatical words respectively) to the Aristotelian distinction between *categoremata* and *syncategoremata* (p. 160). Not that he positively excludes subject–predicate form from grammatical analysis of ancient Chinese: 'im AC scheinen die Subjekt/Prädikat-Sätze ein Grenzfall der Thema/Rhema-Sätze zu sein, in denen Thema und logisches Subjekt zusammenfallen' (p. 235).

[117] Yuen Ren Chao is admirably unconfused on the issue of types of form: 'the grammatical meaning of subject–predicate in a Chinese sentence is not that of actor–action, as in most Indo-European languages, but topic–comment, which includes actor–action as a special case. The logical import of this generality of the subject–predicate relation is that it is much nearer the form used in the symbolism ϕa, where a need not represent the actor of some action ϕ but so long as ϕ is so of a, then one can say ϕa' (Chao 1955, pp. 38–9).

the presence in the predicate calculus of individual names, the proper combination of which with function-letters also yields formulae of subject–predicate form without quantification; so it would not be true that only quantified propositions 'require' it.

Even if Graham were correct about where the form exclusively occurs, most logicians would be taken aback by his 'only', as if devices for handling quantification were some minor appendage to their systems. And that is the way to put it: what logic requires emerges from propositional features such as quantification which grammatical features of language might – or might not – convey. I suspect that Graham has blundered because, ironically, he remains in thrall to Aristotle. In time-honoured fashion he regards traditional syllogistic as central to logical studies. Although at various junctures in the development of his argument he cites modern formal logic as both an antidote to pernicious Aristotelianism and a valuable source for the illumination of ancient Chinese's linguistic structure, he pays attention to only one aspect of the predicate calculus, when he ought to widen his scope to encompass consideration of how predication might be represented in whatever formal system(s) he favours. This confusion of grammar with logic brings us to a position from which to confront the cardinal issue of how best to understand the relation that obtains – or fails to obtain – between linguistic structure and logical form.

Before turning to that problem, we should observe that Chad Hansen has advanced a thesis comparable to Hall and Ames's (and one similarly untenable), but looks precisely to subject–predicate form for 'guidance and constraint': 'Chinese theorists implicitly and explicitly focused attention on the word, not on the sentence nor on sentence counterparts such as beliefs, opinions, judgements. The sentence did not draw theoretical attention because . . . no essential "minimal" form of a complete sentence dominated theoretical attention the way the subject–predicate form did in Western philosophy.'[118] Hansen also duplicates Hall and Ames's *non sequitur* of inferring from ancient Chinese philosophers' preoccupation with ethical matters that they must have subscribed to an embarrassingly primitive semantic theory: 'the Chinese 子 (*tzu*, 'masters') viewed language as playing essentially a guiding rôle, not a descriptive one. (They were interested in ethics, not metaphysics.) Their interest in language centred on the word, not the sentence.'[119] Elsewhere he explains that 'we use traditional Western grammar to analyse Chinese word order. This presumes the sentence is the pivotal structural unit'[120] – as if recognition of sentences (as opposed, say, to the imposition of rigid lexical classes, which we have discussed) were some quaint remnant of outmoded grammatical theory.

---

[118] Hansen 1987, p. 319.   [119] 'Should the Ancient Masters Value Reason?', in Rosemont 1991, p. 193.
[120] 'Language in the Heart-mind', in Allinson 1989, p. 82.

6 Logical form

6.1 Against 'logical' translation

I should now move quickly to protect my flank. A certain wing of analytical philosophy is committed to the thesis that *bona fide* sentences in natural languages conceal as often as they reveal their *true* structure, their logical form. Much philosophy (on this view) is a large, appalling mistake, because it consists of silly metaphysics generated by a confusion of grammatical with logical form; good analytical philosophy clears away the mess, often by perspicuously displaying logical form in an artificial language whose rigour and clarity elevate it far above misleading 'natural' languages. Were one to subscribe to such a programme,[121] the 'guidance and constraint' hypothesis could perhaps be given very short shrift, since at least a core of identical logical forms would inevitably be found to underlie the sentences of 'natural' languages, no matter how disparate these sentences might be at the grammatical level. Of course, part of this programme is the idea that people can certainly be misguided by their language; but its adherents, unlike the partisans of 'guidance and constraint', would insist that at the deepest level – the level of logical form – languages are not distinct. Since, with sufficient analytical acumen, that logical bedrock can always be reached, philosophical thought *need* not suffer at the hands of language, no matter what the language in which the philosophy happens. I do not pretend that analytical enthusiasts achieve lucidity on this matter – but, in principle, this is what their stance *ought* to be. My disagreement with Graham should be understood as a protest against his abuse of the 'Aristotelian principle', not as an insistence that he should have battened onto some particular formal system enshrining uniquely correct representations.

But crucially, I do not regard any such formal representations as *translations* of 'natural' sentences. Why would one think in the first place that depicting 'all animals are mortal' as '$(\forall x)(Ax \supset Mx)$' is on all fours with translating it as 'omnia animalia sunt mortalia'? Samuel Guttenplan's confidence in the rightness of this assumption is evident in the very title of his introductory textbook, *The Languages of Logic*,[122] and at numerous points he explicitly endorses the translation model which I reject; for example, 'we are about to discuss the details of translation from English into Sentential. Sentential is a very different language from, say, French. It is a language of structure. Nonetheless, the move from English to Sentential does involve many of the problems of translation.'[123] One might suppose that Guttenplan intends his conceit of translation

---

[121] The relevance to the China syndrome of this programme's rise and fall is examined in the next section.
[122] Guttenplan 1986.   [123] *Ibid.*, p. 106; cf. pp. 39–40, 166, 220.

into logical languages as no more than a pedagogical device, albeit one to be deprecated, but not so: 'the development of methods of logic will give us insights into the nature of language, and through this, into the nature of thought';[124] since the methods he teaches are consistently presented as (*ersatz?*) translation rules, he must assume that they throw light on language and thought precisely because logical 'translation' is not meant as a (mere) metaphor.

One might reason for the assumption made by Guttenplan and others as follows: logical systems had better be languages (of a sort), because logic is, above all, meant to provide the means to isolate valid argument schemata from invalid ones. Now an inference is valid if and only if it is impossible for its premises to be true but its conclusion false. Thus logic, to be logic, must exploit semantic concepts; and surely a formal system possessing a semantics as well as a rigorous syntax has every right to the title 'language'. Of course, 'A' and 'M', unlike the logical constants, do not have any standard interpretation in the predicate calculus, and in working out its semantics one is utterly indifferent between all the various extensions which might be assigned to these, or any other, predicate letters. But there is nothing wrong with fixing our minds on an interpretation which assigns to 'A' the set of all 1-membered sequences whose members are in the domain and are animals, and to 'M' the set of all 1-membered sequences whose members are in the domain and are mortal. If that is so, and '$(\forall x)(Ax \supset Mx)$' *is* 'all animals are mortal' in the predicate calculus, surely it is a humble example of English *translated* into the predicate calculus?

The reason I urge resistance to this seemingly innocuous conclusion begins to emerge if we reflect on the controversy which surrounds even our banal example: many people react with healthy scepticism on being informed that such quantified sentences of 'natural' language either 'really' are, or perhaps 'conceal', conditional propositions. The problem is that whereas we have unimpeachable evidence for the existence of some (roughly) synonymous sentences in different 'natural' languages (for example our getting more or less what we want when using a foreign phrasebook) even after paying due regard to the mysteries of connotation and metaphor, the only plausible argument for the correctness of the logical 'translation' is that its behaviour in inferences meets (some of) our expectations about how its 'natural' equivalent behaves, or ought to behave, in argument. But the lack of agreement amongst logicians over how to represent various 'natural' forms seriously restricts the availability of even these inferential equivalents. Thus, as Christopher Kirwan warns, 'one might be tempted to think of the whole process of formalising as a kind of translation from words into symbols; but because the steps in it do not have to preserve sameness of meaning they are translations

---

[124] *Ibid.*, p. 36; cf. pp. 221–2.

of a special kind, and in particular schematising is far from coming under the ordinary idea of translating'.[125]

The paramount danger posed by the notion of 'logical' translation only becomes apparent, however, when we realise that if the thesis that formal calculi are 'artificial' languages intertranslatable with 'natural' ones is accepted, then, for example, '$(\forall x) (Ax \supset Mx)$' can serve as a standard for assessing the *relative logicality* of different 'natural' languages. Were we to encounter a language whose translation of '$(\forall x) (Ax \supset Mx)$' retained the conditional structure, we should be obliged to conclude that its speakers had the logical advantage over us. Such logicist normativity is every bit as repellent as – and no better founded than – the tyranny once exerted by Greek and Latin over the linguistics of the past: where is the evidence that structural explicitness ensures fewer mistakes in reasoning?

Nor is this a needless warning against some idle fantasy. Graham pleads that classical Chinese is 'perhaps nearer to symbolic logic than any other language'.[126] Harbsmeier, in contrast, draws our attention to a rather more subtle question:

> Classical Chinese is most certainly not like symbolic logic. No natural language is. But . . . we can indeed inquire whether it is not part of what Wilhelm von Humboldt called *le génie de la langue chinoise*, that being an isolating language it is in some quite fundamental ways more logically transparent [we might ask: 'transparent' to whom?] than the Indo-European languages we are familiar with. There is no reason why some languages might not be logically more transparent than others. Neither is there any reason why all languages should be equally powerful with regard to the representation of logical complexity.[127]

Thus Harbsmeier seems to substitute the notion of 'logical transparency' for that of direct similitude. How might this work in practice? He devotes an entire section to negation, where the thesis is developed that, in ancient Chinese, there is no *illogical* cumulative negation, a feature he explicitly contrasts with the situation in ancient Greek.[128] But such cataloguing delivers, and can deliver, no meaningful comparison of different languages' relative 'logical transparency'. To illustrate, Harbsmeier himself contends that ancient Chinese is plagued by aggravated problems with quantifier scope:[129] how does one measure Chinese's bonus points for negation against its quantifier penalty points? The delusive conception of 'translation' into a formal system lies at the heart of the matter. Harbsmeier makes a most revealing claim:

---

[125] Kirwan 1978, p. 196.   [126] Graham 1989, p. 403.

[127] Harbsmeier 1998, p. 8; he also casually refers to logical 'translation' into a formal language in Harbsmeier 1979, p. 239.

[128] Harbsmeier 1998, pp. 112–13.   [129] *Ibid.*, pp. 154–6.

it seems profoundly significant that, when in logic classes one learns to translate sentences from natural languages into logical notation, one performs tasks that much of the time remind one strongly of the kinds of tasks one would perform if one had to translate that same sentence into Classical Chinese: one performs a process of logical 'factorisation' and reduction to the simplest possible form.[130]

He does not attempt to explain the nature of this 'profound significance': to me his statement is an expression of profoundly mistaken, mystical logicism, founded on the misapprehension that he learnt how to translate into a splendid new language when he attended logic classes.

In various places in *Disputers of the Tao*[131] Graham ridicules the prejudice that a language's conceptual resources are proportional to its degree of inflection.[132] The criticism is of course more than amply justified. But while we have disposed of the view that Chinese lacks counterfactuals, what of the idea that only the capacity of a highly inflected language, say, Greek, to combine specifications of tense, aspect and mood could permit (note: not encourage, let alone entail) the development of a highly sophisticated modal logic, such as we find in the Hellenistic period?

Participants in the Chinese logic argument can all too often be seen to move too swiftly from dubious comparisons between Chinese and, for example, English (usually to the purported disadvantage of Chinese) to equally dubious comparisons between all natural languages and various symbolic scripts (usually as a defensive manœuvre, and executed by Sinophiles, such as Graham). One might do better with what I trust is the relatively harmless hypothesis that certain highly inflected languages just might have the edge in expressing distinctions otherwise impossible to capture prior to the creation of symbolic notation. That is, there might, for example, be no alternative to simply pointing, as it were, to the differing import of imperfect and pluperfect subjunctives to indicate a philosophically crucial difference between modalities. I tentatively suggest that, unlike Graham's bugbears Plato, Anselm and Kant, Diodorus Cronus in his Master Argument concocted a piece of important philosophy well nigh inexpressible in ancient Chinese. How best to represent Diodorus' reasoning remains a hotly contested question for students of Hellenistic philosophy, but any plausible candidate reconstruction will convey how formidably difficult its modal and tense-expressions would be to render into Chinese. Consider Sedley's version:

---

[130] *Ibid.*, p. 172.   [131] E.g. pp. 403–4.

[132] Chinese is not the only victim; within Classics, and not so long ago, certain ridiculous Hellenists were wont to sneer at 'simple' Latin.

What neither is nor will be true is impossible. For if (p) it were or were going to be true, then (q) it would already in the past have been the case that it would be true. But not-q – and necessarily not-q, since every proposition true about the past is necessary. Therefore it is impossible that-q. Therefore it is impossible that-p, since an impossible proposition does not follow from a possible one. Therefore nothing is possible which neither is nor will be true.[133]

Not that (a massive counterfactual), had ancient Chinese philosophers developed an interest in the determinism debate fuelled in Hellenistic times by Diodorus' dialectical challenge, they would have proved incapable of linguistic innovation – Graham might have called it 'syntactical deterioration' – by introducing the needed modal devices into their language.[134] But the impetus would not have been linguistic, at least not in the sense pertinent to 'guidance and constraint'.[135]

An alternative example of what one might label 'pragmatic' or 'processing' constraints on logical expression is supplied by Harbsmeier. In his monograph he discusses the expression of disjunction in ancient Chinese by means of negation and implication[136] before 或 (*huo*) took on the additional meaning of 'or'. This, while hardly indicative of logical impoverishment, does swiftly render multiply disjunctive sentences impenetrable, and might profitably be compared with Floyd Lounsbury's speculations about the linguistic handicapping of Bororo mathematics. The Bororo have only two number words, but can certainly (in principle, at least) express higher numbers (in base 2) – the problem is 'grammatical manipulability'.[137]

6.2 *Why form might matter*

In the very act of conceding that formal calculi do indeed deserve to be called artificial 'languages' (at least in a restricted sense of the word), I have already alluded to the most glaringly obvious reason why form might matter: its intimate connection with validity. After all, 'formal logic' is just that, a logic which abstracts from the content of

---

[133] Sedley 1977, p. 97. Interested readers should compare and contrast Denyer's reconstruction (Denyer 1981).

[134] Various modal locutions – albeit nothing like those required for representing the Master Argument – are to be found in chapter 2's selections from the 名理探 (*ming li t'an*).

[135] Gustave von Grunebaum claims that the reason why Marius Victorinus' attempt to render Plotinus into invented Latin philosophical terminology failed to gain currency, while Bonaventure and Aquinas succeeded brilliantly in privileging technical Latin, is to be discovered in a changing, *extra-linguistic* 'collective drive' (in Hoijer 1954, pp. 228–9).

[136] Harbsmeier 1998, pp. 156–9; cf. Chao 1955, pp. 33–4.

[137] In Hoijer 1954, pp. 129, 139. Givón 1978 provides an extremely interesting and useful compendium of comparative interlingual expressibility and determinacy.

propositions in the effort to discern the inferential patterns into which they fall.[138] Thus if formal logic uses the concept 'same form' as part of its check on validity,[139] it had better be able to explain and defend the concept 'form'. The connection with the China syndrome is made by reformulating the logicism baffled by our argument against the inter-translatability of 'natural' and 'artificial' languages in the previous section: granted that logical formulae are not, strictly speaking, translations of sentences in 'natural' languages, does it not remain possible to identify and assess the relative logicality of these different languages? The problem with 'natural' languages is that they are plagued by lexical ambiguity (as well as vagueness, etc.) and by syntactic inconsistency and misleading-ness. 'Inconsistency' arises from the grammatical obligation to give differential expression to propositions sharing the same logical form at the behest of irrational idiom. 'Misleadingness' means that grammatical form distorts what is independently verified (by logical study) as the logical form of the proposition deformed by its linguistic cara-pace. These are faults common to all 'natural' languages; but to assume *a priori* that they are equally distributed over the languages would be the purest dogmatism. (That this is 'the guidance and constraint hypothesis' is self-evident. But note that it cannot happily be combined with Whorf's relativistic hypothesis, which actively spurns

---

[138] E.g. 'Our overall aim is to define validity in such a way that having a valid form ensures deductive cor-rectness' (Kirwan 1978, p. 41); evidently it would be possible to multiply such citations indefinitely. But Mark Sainsbury offers an apparently rather different definition of validity: 'a formally valid argu-ment is one valid just in virtue of the meanings of the logical constants it contains and the pattern of occurrence of the other expressions' (Sainsbury 1991, p. 312). In its defence he presents an argument inspired by Gareth Evans: 'the notion of a structurally valid argument corresponds to the idea that there are some arguments which are valid, not in virtue of the specific meanings of their expressions, but rather in virtue of the way in which the sentences are constructed. Though formal validity is some-times thought to answer to this intuitive idea, it does not, for formal validity is validity partly in virtue of the specific meanings of certain favoured expressions, the logical constants, and if this idea is to have importance there has to be a deep reason for selecting some expressions rather than others as the logical constants' (p. 311). So it might be thought that I have exaggerated the formality of 'formal' logic. But Sainsbury himself admits that no alternative to the 'topic neutral' criterion for logical constancy under current discussion in the literature is clearly superior to it, while some are inferior (pp. 323–4). Now since that criterion states that 'an expression is a logical constant if either *it intro-duces no specific subject matter*, or there are no objects one needs to learn about in coming to under-stand the expression' (p. 314; my italics), it largely preserves the traditional insistence on logic's occupation with form, not content. (There is little indeed to argue about if one heeds Mark Wilson's warning: 'we frequently do not know enough about our language to rest our inferential practices, including those which seem "purely logical", definitively in either syntax or semantics. Depending upon circumstances, we may cite our semantic theory to correct our syntactic practice or vice versa' (Wilson 1994, pp. 542–3).) In any case, adopting Sainsbury's definition of validity would simply mean taking 'pattern of occurrence' as one of the two necessary conditions for validity, rather than the sole sufficient one, so that my case for why form matters could still proceed.

[139] '. . . an argument can only be counted valid if no argument of the same form will ever lead us from true premises to a false conclusion' (Prior 1955, p. 1).

derogatory labelling of alien 'thought worlds' as 'primitive' – such 'worlds' rather generate canons of right thinking alternative to Western rationality. In contrast, attempts to gauge the relative logicality of ancient Chinese take it for granted that a single set of objective logical standards prevails for all 'natural' languages. Not all sufferers from the China syndrome seem to be altogether aware that relativism and normative logicism mix as well as do oil and water.) So, the objector concludes, one has every reason to persist in posing the question, 'to what extent were ancient Chinese philosophers abetted or betrayed by the language in which they thought in their efforts to construct arguments which were at the very least valid – or to reflect consciously on the criteria for validity – in comparison with, for example, ancient Greek philosophers?'.[140]

In fact, reflection on what the 'formal' in 'formal logic' means prompts yet a further revamping of 'the guidance and constraint hypothesis', as follows. 'Granted, in Chinese a great deal of the work carried out by syntax in Western languages gets done by pragmatic features instead. Hence Western languages give rise to the hope of characterising logical consequence in *syntactic* terms – i.e. the project of *formal* logic. Not that such "guidance" dictates the precise path that the logical project will then take. One project might optimistically predict that syntactic characterisations of logical notions will apply more or less immediately to natural language, or, at worst, to an only slightly modified version thereof. Another might invent special languages just so as to have something for which a syntactic definition of logical consequence will work smoothly. There are no analogies to any such project in Chinese thought. Why? Because it lacks the syntactical spur to logical ambition.' But yet again, everything depends on how ambitious, and thus commensurately on both how interesting and how implausible, this version of the hypothesis is supposed to be. Can (some) speakers of Western languages simply not help engaging in self-conscious reflection on what makes for validity, all at the imperious behest of syntax? Or is the claim very much more moderate, involving a necessary, not a sufficient, condition: that non-Indo-European speakers, disadvantaged syntactically, will not discover formal logic (although in principle they could), while privileged Westerners are at least in a position to do so? My provisional intuition is that this version of the hypothesis attains an acceptable degree of plausibility only when watered down to something very close to the harmless suggestion about the expressive edge of highly inflected languages I made in the previous section when discussing Diodorus Cronus.

---

[140] My project concentrates on comparisons between ancient Chinese on the one hand, and ancient Greek and Latin on the other; but one might note *en passant* that many other languages have claimed linguistic hegemony, if perhaps with not quite the amusing impudence shown by the devotees of French: '. . . quel que soit l'ordre des termes dans une langue ancienne ou moderne, l'esprit de l'écrivain a suivi l'ordre didactique de la syntaxe française' (Diderot 1875, vol. I, p. 390).

We can sharpen this renewed challenge by reviewing the potent historical anteced-
ents of its analytical programme. In a phrasing which (not altogether coincidentally)
finds echoes in my various formulations of logicist 'guidance and constraint', the early
Wittgenstein sang the praises of a symbolic language liberated from the disadvantages,
from the scientific and philosophical point of view, encumbering spoken languages:
'um diesen Irrtümern zu entgehen, müssen wir eine Zeichensprache verwenden, welche
sie ausschließt, indem sie nicht das gleiche Zeichen in verschiedenen Symbolen, und
Zeichen, welche auf verschiedene Art bezeichnen, nicht äußerlich auf die gleiche Art
verwendet. Eine Zeichensprache also, die der logischen Grammatik – der logischen
Syntax – gehorcht.'[141] ('These errors' refers back to 3.323, where the employment of
'is' for copula, identity-sign and the expression of existence is cited in illustration of the
confusions to be avoided by an ideal, symbolic language.[142]) His evocation of 'logical
grammar' and 'logical syntax',[143] were it accepted, would seem to favour an inclination
to indulge in assessment of the relative 'logical transparency' of different 'natural'
languages. But this quotation from the *Tractatus* should not be taken as expressive of
dissatisfaction with the syntax and semantics of 'natural' languages, for consider: 'alle
Sätze unserer Umgangssprache sind tatsächlich, so wie sie sind, logisch vollkommen
geordnet' (5.5563).[144] Any sentence of ordinary language must be logically in order,
that is, must conform to the Tractarian specification; for sentences of ordinary language
are meaningful, and what the *Tractatus* specifies is how a sentence must be, to be meaningful. That conviction is still compatible with maintaining that some sentences are
more liable than others to mislead us; one can – Wittgenstein does – assert this and go in
for constructing artificial languages as the best means of illustrating the point, without
at all wanting such artificial languages to replace the ones we already have.

Thus the *Tractatus* does not denigrate the logical credentials of 'natural' language,
nor does it advocate the construction of a logically ideal symbolic language which

---

[141] *Tractatus* 3.325 (Wittgenstein 1981, p. 54: 'in order to avoid such errors we must make use of a sign-
language that excludes them by not using the same sign for different symbols and by not using in a
superficially similar way signs that have different modes of signification: that is to say, a sign-
language that is governed by *logical* grammar – by logical syntax' (Wittgenstein 1978, p. 16)).

[142] Section 7 will examine Graham's employment of just this example in urging the logical superiority of
ancient Chinese over Indo-European languages in general and ancient Greek in particular.

[143] Elizabeth Anscombe provides an explanation of the *Tractatus*'s concept of logical form, and its
distinctive repercussions for metaphysics and epistemology: 'we call the possibility of the kind of
connection that sets up a proposition "logical form" . . . And since logical form is that through which
a structure can have T and F poles, and for something to be true or false is the very same thing as for
reality to be thus or otherwise, Wittgenstein calls "logical form" also "the form of reality"'' (Anscombe
1959, p. 75).

[144] Wittgenstein 1981, p. 148: 'in fact, all the propositions of our everyday language, just as they stand,
are in perfect logical order' (Wittgenstein 1978, p. 56).

would *replace* our daily speech. This all too common misinterpretation goes all the way back to Russell's introduction to the first edition of the the *Tractatus*, and feeds, of course, into the philosophical movement contributing to logicist 'guidance and constraint'. In fact, Wittgenstein is responsible for one of the most eloquent *denials* of the theoretical basis for the China syndrome: 'daß die Logik *a priori* ist, besteht darin, daß nicht unlogisch gedacht werden kann' (5.4731).[145] So why construct formal languages? Because, even if 'natural' languages express what they express without strictly logical blemish – otherwise they would not *be* languages at all – they are nevertheless faulty as communicative media; and this is because of their ambiguity and fearsome structural complexity. To get at the logic that is already *in* 'natural' language, we construct a formalism which represents logical forms unambiguously and simply.[146]

This will hardly do as exegesis of so challenging a work as the *Tractatus*, but it will suffice for our limited purposes. We wish only to locate the origins of the misguided Russellian reading which contributes to the China syndrome, and to provide at least a tentative illustration of one exceptionally stimulating explication – Wittgenstein's – of the idea of logical form. We draw the immediate moral that in general, as indeed in this particular instance, validation of the belief that heterogeneous expressions share logical form is very hard to come by.[147] It is not as if the very idea of logical form entails

[145] Wittgenstein 1981, p. 128 ('what makes logic *a priori* is the *impossibility* of illogical thought' (Wittgenstein 1978, p. 47)).

[146] I assume this all rests on one condition: 'alles was überhaupt gedacht werden kann, kann klar gedacht werden. Alles was sich aussprechen läßt, läßt sich klar aussprechen' (4.116, Wittgenstein 1981, pp. 76–8: 'everything that can be thought at all can be thought clearly. Everything that can be put into words can be put clearly' (Wittgenstein 1978, p. 26)); that is why 'die Philosophie soll die Gedanken, die sonst, gleichsam, trübe und verschwommen sind, klar machen und scharf abgrenzen' (4.112, Wittgenstein 1981, p. 76: 'without philosophy thoughts are, as it were, cloudy and indistinct: its task is to make them clear and to give them sharp boundaries' (Wittgenstein 1978, p. 25)). Why does Wittgenstein add the *caveat* 'gleichsam', 'as it were'? Is this an admission of an otherwise suppressed uncertainty? Perhaps, because while there is no *necessary* conflict with either 4.116 or 5.5563, surely 4.112 does betray a flutter of doubt as to whether there is a constant, self-same logical content to be thought more or less clearly. This doubt can really be laid to rest only if logical form on the conception of the *Tractatus* exists, and that condition can be satisfied only on the further condition that both reality and *all* its possible representations are so structured that objective vagueness and subjective imprecision are, and can be shown to be, eliminable: hence – in part – the death of the *Tractatus*'s rigorously utopian dreams.

[147] In contrast, Ryle's historically influential analytical programme was more concerned with detection of logical dissimilarity concealed within grammatical uniformity: 'there are many expressions which occur in non-philosophical discourse which, though they are perfectly clearly understood by those who use them and those who hear or read them, are nevertheless couched in grammatical or syntactical forms which are in a demonstrable way *improper* to the states of affairs which they record (or the alleged states of affairs which they profess to record)' (Ryle 1968, pp. 13–14). The rot can set in when people engage in abstract thought about potentially dangerous language: 'pre-philosophical abstract

a commitment to logical atomism. But it remains to be seen whether today's substitutes for the categories and concepts of early twentieth-century analytical philosophy will be any less controversial as rationales for a conception of logical form which permits evaluation of relative linguistic logicality. Accordingly my next step will be to rehearse some features of the movement which Russell's creative misprision of the *Tractatus* helped to generate.

The first thing to register about Russell's delineation of the philosophy of logical atomism is that it includes an unmistakable commitment to philosophical 'guidance and constraint': 'the influence of language on philosophy has, I believe, been profound and almost unrecognised. If we are not to be misled by this influence, it is necessary to become conscious of it, and to ask ourselves deliberately how far it is legitimate.'[148] Not only that, but he fully anticipates the China syndrome itself: 'the subject–predicate logic, with the subject–attribute metaphysic, are a case in point. It is doubtful whether either would have been invented by people speaking a non-Aryan language; certainly they do not seem to have arisen in China, except in connection with Buddhism, which brought Indian philosophy with it.'[149] Russell actively promotes construction of 'an ideal logical language': not, he explains, to supplant 'natural' language outside philosophy, but rather with the negative purpose of safeguarding philosophy from fallacious inference, inference from features of language to features of the world, fallacious because of 'the logical defects of language'; and with the positive purpose of affording true insight into the structure of reality by making valid inferences from a contradiction-free 'artificial' language.[150] The next section will uncover some of the consequences of adherence to a (modified) Russellian programme.

6.3 Procrustean logic

I begin with two cautionary tales demonstrating how ill founded is the confidence that philosophers have access to stable, recognisable forms capable of serving as agreed criteria for the adjudication of disputes over relative 'logical transparency'. The assertion that, even if not omnipresent, such a thing as logical subject–predicate form does exist

---

thinking is always misled by systematically misleading expressions, and even philosophical abstract thinking, the proper function of which is to cure this disease, is actually one of its worst victims' (*ibid.*, p. 35). Thus a Rylean proponent of 'guidance and constraint' might conceivably contend that Chinese's relative paucity of explicit structure makes it an exceptionally large repository of expressions whose grammar fails to discriminate between disparate logical forms.

[148] 'Logical Atomism' (1924), in Russell 1956, p. 330.

[149] *Ibid.* Thus we see that in lambasting the so-called 'Aristotelian principle' (see section 6.1), Graham is following in Russell's tracks exactly (and Russell in Nietzsche's, if not quite exactly: see pp. 20–1 above).

[150] *Ibid.*, p. 338.

might be thought to command universal assent; but no less formidable a philosopher than Frank Ramsey fiercely challenged it, maintaining that subject–predicate form is merely grammatical, and a prime instance of harmful 'guidance and constraint' at that:

> it is a point which has often been made by Mr. Russell that philosophers are very liable to be misled by the subject–predicate construction of our language . . . I shall argue that nearly all philosophers, including Mr. Russell himself, have been misled by language in a far more far-reaching way than that; that the whole theory of particulars and universals is due to mistaking for a fundamental characteristic of reality what is merely a characteristic of language.[151]

Ramsey's idea is that since, in an atomic proposition,[152] subject and predicate are similarly incomplete, there are no grounds for the traditional type-distinction between particular and universal:

> now it seems to me as clear as anything can be in philosophy that the two sentences 'Socrates is wise', 'Wisdom is a characteristic of Socrates' assert the same fact and express the same proposition . . . Now of one of these sentences 'Socrates' is the subject, of the other 'wisdom'; and so which of the two is subject, which predicate, depends upon what particular sentence we use to express our proposition, and has nothing to do with the logical nature of Socrates or wisdom, but is a matter entirely for grammarians.[153]

He concludes that the logical, as distinct from the grammatical, relation between subject and predicate is symmetrical, so that the idea of subject–predicate *logical* form is a delusion brought on by language, itself bringing on some unwanted metaphysical baggage: the notion that universals are peculiarly *incomplete* objects.

It is no part of my brief to maintain that Ramsey's argument commands assent. If, as he says, the words 'individual' and 'quality' are 'devoid of connotation', then how is it that he successfully recognises 'two different types of objects' as designated by them?[154] If symmetrically related in logic, how can they be type-distinct, yet equally (in)complete? And, if they are not distinct, where are the materials for building structure into propositions? Once we look to relations, the difference seems clear-cut: while there is no (logical) upper limit to the number of proper names in an atomic proposition, there can be only one verb. Quantified logic with only individual variables quantified is complete, no matter how many individual variables are permitted in an atomic sentence, while a logic which also quantifies with predicate variables is incomplete. But

---

[151] 'Universals' (1925), in Ramsey 1990, p. 13; and '. . . we must look for senses of subject and predicate which are not purely grammatical, but have a genuine logical significance' (p. 13).

[152] He means 'atomic' in the sense of logical atomism, so that, for example, Socrates is not a 'real' object, and we are in fact unacquainted with any authentic atomic propositions.

[153] 'Universals', p. 12.   [154] *Ibid.*, p. 28.

second-order logic would not be so different from first-order, were there not a difference in type between individuals and relations.

Perhaps, then, Ramsey's commitment to logical atomism fatally influences his reasoning; his statement that '. . . we know and can know nothing whatever about the forms of atomic propositions'[155] prohibits us most effectively from facing the issue of how any proposition acquires structure. This suspicion hardens into certainty when we read Ramsey's 'note on the preceding paper' (1926),[156] where he confesses that his confidence in the inaccessibility of atomic propositions by analysis of familiar ones is shaky; and that, if they can be reached by analysis, then a principled distinction between universal and particular could indeed be drawn (since such analyses would yield atomic subjects incapable of being recast as predicates). All Ramsey can continue to insist on is that it is impossible to be certain that the type-distinction obtains *a priori*. But he by no means capitulates entirely, since he still supposes that the symmetry between (apparent) substantival and adjectival terms could be restored by construing material objects as modifications of events, *à la* Whitehead.

The reason the success (or otherwise) of Ramsey's case is not an issue for us springs from his final manœuvre. The argument comes down to this: it seems to us that there is an important logical difference between 'Socrates' and 'wise'. We lend this intuition some substance by suggesting that what is responsible for the felt asymmetry is that, while 'wise' collects *both* a wider set of propositions (in which 'wise' simply occurs) and a narrower set (one determined by the schema '*x* is wise'), 'Socrates' collects *only* a wider set. Ramsey protests that this is an illusion '. . . because it can be shown to be theoretically possible to make a similar narrower range for Socrates, though we have never needed to do this'.[157] The theoretical possibility mentioned is to proceed *à la* Whitehead, by claiming that events in which he has been involved are 'Socratised'. But one can now protest – if hardly uncontentiously – that this is no possibility, 'theoretical' or otherwise, for it would entail our relinquishing the metaphysics of substance and attribute unavoidable in human thought, and deftly captured in the Fregean distinction between object and concept to which Ramsey was blind.

Again, I am not concerned to persuade the reader that Ramsey is wrong; rather, what is vital is that one perceive that the territory on which I am fighting him lies far beyond the confines of either linguistic or logical form. Ramsey both teaches us that no purported unique or natural logical form is unassailable and helps to confirm my contention that doctrines of form, when defended, inevitably rely on resources drawn from other departments of philosophy. But if that is so, then 'the guidance and constraint hypothesis' cannot appeal to how different languages reveal or conceal logical form for

---

[155] *Ibid.*, p. 29.   [156] *Ibid.*, pp. 31–3.   [157] *Ibid.*, p. 32.

evidence of the influence of language on, say, metaphysics without begging the question: because the case for detecting the logical forms in the languages itself may very well depend on the very metaphysical commitments in question.

My second cautionary tale is about time. In text after text, Quine assures the aspiring logician that analysis is 'facilitated' by treating verbs as tenseless, so that statements do not change their truth-value.[158] So far the recommendation seems nothing but an anodyne representational convenience;[159] yet elsewhere he offers a strikingly different motivation for the removal of tense: 'a drastic departure from English is required in the matter of tense. The view to adopt is the Minkowskian one, which sees time as a fourth dimension on a par with the three dimensions of space. Quantifiers must be read as timeless. The values of "*x*" may themselves be thing-events, four-dimensional denizens of space-time . . .'[160] The student *should* feel disconcerted: what masqueraded as a purely logical *desideratum* has turned out to be a tailoring of logic to meet the requirements of a radical reformation in metaphysics. Quine pretends that his proposal dissolves 'puzzles both conceptual and verbal'; but the gloss that '. . . *much as* Boston and Birmingham are 3000 miles apart, Caesar and Napoleon are 1800 years apart . . .'[161] verges on the disingenuous. Quine's four-dimensional metaphysics has been subject to frequent attack, but perhaps never more energetically than by Geach, who advances against the Minkowskian scheme a number of celebrated arguments concluding that it cannot make sense of change.[162] But, again, we need not adjudicate; what we should take away from the conflict is yet further confirmation that logical form is never innocently 'discovered', innocent, that is, of metaphysical commitments (perhaps unimpeachable in their own right) which close the vicious circle of the effort to compare the logical resources of different languages.

---

[158] E.g. Quine 1980, p. 6.

[159] Cf. 'think *how awkward* it is, without some such view [i.e. that tense should be eliminated from logic], to make sense of applying a predicate to something that no longer exists; or to make sense of quantifying over objects that never coexisted at any one time, and assembling such objects into sets' (Quine 1986, p. 31; my italics); as if Quine were unaware that tense logic 'makes sense' of these things by formalising tense, rather than rejecting it.

[160] Quine 1974, pp. 165–6.   [161] *Ibid.*, p. 166; my italics.

[162] 'Some Problems about Time', in Geach 1981. Geach's own hands are not clean. He argues that '. . . the *natural* expression for simultaneity is not a relative term like "simultaneous with", but a conjunction like "while" joining clauses; it is an accident of English idiom that "at the same time" seems to refer to a certain *time* that has to be *the same*, and the words for "at the same time" in other languages – Latin *simul*, Greek ἅμα, Polish *razem* – have no such suggestion' (p. 312). One can be fairly confident that when a philosophical logician invokes the 'natural' character of a preferred mode of expression, he is concealing a (for the moment) unargued metaphysical doctrine – or even prejudice – beneath the camouflage of the 'natural' formal representation. One should also remark on how happily Geach exploits 'guidance and constraint' against Quine: at least on this issue, there is nothing to choose between them.

Other such cautionary tales are ready to hand. For example, some philosophers (*in primis* Davidson[163]) argue that it is not only licit, but logically mandatory, to rewrite 'Socrates died because he drank hemlock' as 'the drinking of hemlock caused Socrates' death', in part on the grounds that the noun phrases referring to events are crucial, because causal relations actually obtain between events, not substances. Of course, for other philosophers, the noun phrases are, in Kotarbinski's phrase, mere 'onomatoids' (name-like fakes), on the grounds that they misleadingly feign to indicate what isn't there, and isn't required to explain causation. But as in our two main examples, the controversy is not to be settled by appeal to a neutral logical form both parties to the dispute recognise in causal sentences; there is no such form to be found.

The time has come to drive the final nail into the coffin of interlinguistic logicist comparisons. First, the question of the degree of logicality manifested by a given natural language only arises when we have an *argument*,[164] and could only be settled by combining calculations of the degree of logicality attributed to some reasonable proportion of the arguments actually formulated in – or formulable in, if this makes any sense – the language under consideration. The practical challenge of the undertaking, and perhaps even its theoretical feasibility, if formulisability is conceded, are already immense. As the assessments of relative logicality in the literature so often derive, not from actual, formulated reasoning, but rather from the purported implications of one or another morphological feature, lexical item or syntactic arrangement, there are grounds for immediate, and pronounced, scepticism.

Second, to reuse an oft-repeated type of illustration, 'all animals are mortal; Socrates is an animal; therefore Socrates is mortal' goes into the sentential calculus as 'P; Q; therefore R' – which is as choice an example of an invalid *non sequitur* as one could

---

[163] See 'The Logical Form of Action Sentences' and 'Causal Relations' in Davidson 1980.

[164] So as to avoid begging the question, a logicist would also have to determine what counts as an *argument* and what counts as *an* argument – without appeal to logical form. Mark Wilson draws attention to yet another source of additional complexity: 'we are familiar with the ambiguous drawings where two figures can be imposed upon the same bundle of lines – a young lady's profile or the hooded face of a crone. Linguistic analogues exist where a given language can be seen as simultaneously structured by two completely different syntactic patterns. With these distinct grammars come considerably different patterns of semantical assignment, which validate in turn divergent rules of inference' (Wilson 1994, pp. 519–20). He defines 'apparent grammar' as 'the syntactic components of "logical form", as well as the additional determinations to which orthodox linguistics usually considers itself responsible', and describes 'working grammar' as emerging from speakers' gradual realisation that '. . . previously unrecognised syntactic categories now become salient as the keys to deductive validity' (p. 520). Wilson's major conclusion then reveals an important connection with the problem of argument-identification: 'a working semantics tries to validate the basic integrity of the major large-scale chains of reasoning, possibly at the cost of cancelling or reparsing the local "logical" links accepted in apparent grammar' (p. 527).

desire. It is no good to protest that its form is 'really' '$(\forall x)(Ax \supset Mx)$; As; $\therefore$ Ms': 'all animals are mortal; Socrates is an animal; therefore Socrates is mortal' *is* 'really' invalid – that is, invalid by the rules of the sentential calculus. This is not to deny that the predicate calculus representation conforms better to our *pre*-formal convictions about the inferential powers to be accorded reasoning formalisable on this pattern; thus, Haack recommends defining 'optimal formal representation' as '. . . the one which reveals the least structure consistently with supplying a formal argument which is valid in the system if the informal argument is judged extra-systematically valid'.[165] That, however, is no reason to admit that the predicate calculus representation enshrines the argument's *unique* form: there is none.[166] Strawson's *Introduction to Logical Theory* contains an early and suggestive protest against the presumption of unique form:

> . . . as if a statement could never have more than one kind of formal power; as if statements could, in respect of their formal powers, be grouped in mutually exclusive classes, like animals at a zoo in respect of their species. But to say that a statement is of some one logical form is simply to point to a certain general class of e.g. valid inferences, in which the statement can play a certain rôle. It is not to exclude the possibility of there being other general classes of valid inferences in which the statement can play a certain rôle.[167]

A natural-language argument is valid if there is some valid logical form which it instantiates – and then *that* will be the form in virtue of which it is valid. And it does not matter that it will also instantiate many other logical forms which are invalid. Again, allowing all this does not commit one to saying that the natural-language argument is *really* of the validating form, if that is supposed to imply that it is not equally of the *non*-validating forms. The relativists keen on these comparisons can hardly take advantage of *pre*-formal convictions to select one and only one formalisation, the procedure Haack so neatly describes. Such convictions inevitably build on factors outside the linguistic structures which 'guidance and constraint' may properly cite as responsible for logical differences between languages. We cannot assess languages' relative logicality without deciding how to formalise sample arguments in those languages; but we cannot reach such decisions without appealing to precisely what linguistic relativists

---

[165] Haack 1978, p. 24; cf. Guttenplan 1986, p. 111.

[166] 'Since there are as many formalisms as logicians and others might dream up, and there is no obvious limit to what at least the others might dream up, there is no obvious limit to the structures an argument of natural language can be made to exhibit' (Richard Davies, 'What do we learn when we learn logic?' (unpublished MS)).

[167] Strawson 1952, p. 53; cf. pp. 55–6. Lemmon neatly suggests that '. . . perhaps it would be better not to speak of the logical form of sentences at all, but only of the logical form of arguments in which sentences are used' (Lemmon 1984, p. 167; cf. Kirwan 1978, p. 43).

must ignore, if they are to remain true to the proposition that *fundamental* linguistic structure determines logicality.

The adherent of logicist 'guidance and constraint' might complain at the last ditch that what *really* motivates his thesis that languages differ as regards relative logicality is the unimpeachable conviction that there is a difference between the logically salient features of a stretch of language expressing an argument and features of that stretch of language irrelevant to the argument's validity; so it is bound to be the case that different languages can – and do – differ as to how perspicuously they exhibit the logically salient characteristics. Anyone not sharing such a belief thereby forfeits any claim to be taken seriously in argument about logic, since such a conviction is an essential precondition for the construction of any *formal* logic. I parry the complaint by returning to what a 'guidance and constraint hypothesis' worth taking seriously must be like; as I have continually emphasised, it must appeal to what is linguistically fundamental, often by citing certain basic aspects of syntax. Of course there are logically irrelevant features of a language, but we can have no reason to assume *a priori* that *any* syntactical feature is logically irrelevant. The undeniable distinction between the logically salient and the logically irrelevant fails to rescue logicist 'guidance and constraint'. The syntactical data which are at once legitimate material for potential exploitation by such a theorist and of *potential* logical significance will not yield any set of agreed formulae for inter-linguistic comparison and evaluation. In the course of discriminating between the logically relevant and irrelevant, one will be obliged to make decisions about the argumentative powers lurking within, say, a given piece of Chinese; and these decisions will again inevitably rely on considerations which a 'guidance and constraint' theorist cannot legitimately consider and avoid question-begging.

The choice between formalisations is hardly likely to be either free of metaphysical injections (for the reasons indicated by our cautionary tales) or independent of *pre-formal*, logical 'intuitions' of validity. If, therefore, what is given representation in a formula is what we may as well keep on calling 'logical form' (i.e. structural features of natural language necessary, and perhaps sufficient,[168] for the determination of validity), *there can be no unique assessments of the relative logicality of different languages.* Admittedly, the pre-formal 'intuitions' can themselves be modified by our recognition of features of formulae. As Haack remarks: 'one uses intuitive judgements of some arguments to construct a formal theory which gives verdicts, perhaps some quite unexpected verdicts, on other arguments; and one might eventually sacrifice some of the original judgements to considerations of simplicity and generality'.[169] I am entirely in accord with Resnik's verdict:

---

[168] See n. 138 above.   [169] Haack 1978, p. 33.

... formalisation is not simply a matter of considering candidate symbolisations in the light of our linguistic intuitions, but rather more a matter of applying broad linguistic, logical, and metaphysical theories. When there are competing candidate symbolisations, deciding between them may involve choosing between pervasive theories having different advantages and disadvantages on a variety of dimensions. Meaningful comparisons of competing proposals might prove elusive.[170]

Not only will ancient Greek and ancient Chinese score differently in different tests; in one and the same test, there might very well be conflicting results, depending on entirely defensible variation in our choice of formal representations. And that is why, to return briefly to our earlier polemic, it is best to eschew the term 'translation' when formalising, given the wealth of misleading implications with which it is burdened, and given, too, the weighty historical fact of early analytical philosophy's doomed pursuit of the grail of unique logical form.

7 Case-study 3: being

The blandishments of 'guidance and constraint' are never more in evidence than when the formidable and apparently inexhaustible topic of being arises. Graham maintains that 'the *dependence* of Western ontology on the peculiarities of the Indo-European verb "to be" is evident to anyone who observes from the vantage point of languages outside the Indo-European family'.[171] The story goes that Western philosophy is usefully viewed as the history of thinkers first succumbing to, and then, with Arabic help, struggling free from the temptation to confuse the existential verb with the copula.[172] The original culprit is the Greek 'to be', εἶναι, whose multiplicity of senses misled all Greek philosophers, Aristotle excepted. Since Graham so rightly advocates that generalisations about Chinese language and thought must have a firm grounding in adequate grammatical knowledge, it is only fair to point out that his simplistic conception of εἶναι as either copulative or existential and his utterly erroneous *ex cathedra* assertion that 'in Greek, εἶναι is primarily existential'[173] fall to the ground before the ample documentation in Charles Kahn's contribution to the *Foundations of Language* series on the verb 'to be' (for which Graham himself provided the Chinese monographs),[174] a contribution which he cites repeatedly in his bibliographies.[175] But Graham believes that modern Western philosophy has, at long last, cast off the crippling linguistic *impedimenta* which did so much damage to ancient Greek philosophy:

---

[170] Resnick 1988, pp. 85–6.   [171] Graham 1989, p. 406; my italics.   [172] *Ibid.*, p. 407.   [173] *Ibid.*
[174] '"Being" in Classical Chinese' (Verhaar 1967–Part 1) and '"Being" in Linguistics and Philosophy' (Verhaar 1967– Part 5).
[175] Verhaar 1967– ; Kahn's monograph is *The Verb 'Be' in Ancient Greek* (1973).

being has vanished altogether in symbolic logic, which has distinct signs for the existential quantifier and for several copulae . . . The abstract noun 'being' remains of course as freely manipulable in philosophical discourse as any other noun; but one may well ask in what sense Western thinkers, however confidently they may talk of Being, may still be said to retain a concept which no longer has a place in either their natural or their artificial languages.[176]

There is some irony to be discovered in the fact that the West's greatest champion of ancient Chinese philosophy subscribes so wholeheartedly to the analytical programme I sketched earlier, a programme fundamentally inimical to the recognition of the range of problems and attacks on them which preoccupy ancient Chinese philosophers.

It may be noticed that in the functions here discussed Classical Chinese syntax is *close to symbolic logic*: it has an existential quantifier 有 (*yu*) ['there is'/'there are'] which *forbids* mistaking existence for a predicate and is distinct from the copulae (which come to include a special copula for identity), and it has no copula linking subject to predicative adjective and no common symbol for them all.[177]

One could not wish for a purer example of the 'guidance and constraint hypothesis' in the form of beneficent constraint.

But an even more precise genealogical claim suggests itself:

an important consequence of the theory of descriptions is that it is meaningless to say 'A exists' unless 'A' is (or stands for) a phrase of the form 'the so-and-so'. If the so-and-so exists, and *x* is the so-and-so, to say '*x* exists' is nonsense. *Existence, in the sense in which it is ascribed to simple entities, is thus removed altogether from the list of fundamentals. The ontological argument and most of its refutations are found to depend upon bad grammar.*[178]

This must certainly be the historical stimulus for Graham's confident dismissal of existence from the realm of philosophical propriety. Note, however, that even in 1924 Russell's rejection is limited to 'existence in the sense in which it is ascribed to simple entities'. There is also a much more venerable philosophical antecedent for Graham's diatribe against 'to be':

and as we use the Verbe *Is*; so the Latines use their Verbe *Est*, and the Greeks their Ἔστι through all its Declinations. Whether all other nations of the world have in their severall languages a word that answereth to it, or not, I cannot tell; but I am sure they have not need of it: For the placing of two names in order may serve to signifie their Consequence, if it were the custome, (for Custome is it, that gives words their force,) as well as the words *Is*, or *Bee*, or *Are*, and the like.[179]

---

[176] Graham 1989, p. 408.   [177] *Ibid.*, p. 412; my italics.
[178] Russell 1956, p. 328; my italics.   [179] Hobbes 1973, part IV, ch. 46, p. 368.

This is Hobbes inveighing against (his conception of) scholastic Aristotelianism, urging, in particular, a nominalistic rejection of substantial forms; by replacing his admission of ignorance about the languages of 'other nations of the world' with a Sinological education, we get the China syndrome *in embryo*.

Has 'being' vanished? Not at all. It is true that old-guard analytical philosophers, notably C. J. F. Williams, who draws polemically on Graham's work,[180] would broadly approve of his outlook, but the situation is hardly so simple. The status of essential individuating properties and their relation to existence for some given natural kind is one of the most hotly debated questions in contemporary Western philosophy. The debate draws freely on a range of symbolic representations employing the signs to which Graham refers, but cannot be resolved just by inspecting the regimentations favoured or even imposed by some particular script, as we learnt in the preceding section.

When he explicates 'Chinese concepts comparable with Being', Graham adduces the phrase 無鬼者 (*wu kuei che*), 'there are no ghosts' (*Mo.* 31/6), in support of the contention that:

> an important difference from existential 'be' and from 'exist' itself is that while 'ghosts' is the subject of the verb in English, 鬼 (*kuei*) is the object of the verb in Chinese. The existence of a thing is affirmed by saying that the cosmos has it as itself it has shape, colour, sound. Since in verbal sentences the nominalisation of a verb generally shifts the reference from action to agent, nominalised 有 (*yu*) 'having' and 無 (*wu*) 'not-having' become 'that which has (shape, colour and other characteristics)' and 'that which does not have', which however *logically implies* also being had by the cosmos or not being had . . . One may see 有 (*yu*) as *illustrating* the Chinese tendency to divide down from a wider whole, 'is' and 'exists' our own tendency to start from the thing itself.[181]

In *Later Mohist Logic . . .* , Graham initially expresses this thesis somewhat more diffidently: '. . . or, if one *prefers* to translate 有(*yu*) by 'have', the world has the horse, which has shape and colour (or the horse exists and shape and colour exist in it)';[182] but he then returns to the predictable theme of the essence–existence distinction as a product of Indo-European 'guidance and constraint':

> in Chinese however the word 是 (*shih*) 'this', being a demonstrative, simply picks out one thing from others as the one in question; there is no 'essence', merely the

---

[180] From his *What is Existence?*: 'it has been suggested that the concept of being is something that has no significance outside an Indo-European culture, that the problem of being is a little local difficulty [citing Graham's ' "Being" in Linguistics and Philosophy'] . . . The spirit of the claim, if not the letter, is one with which I sympathise' (Williams 1981, p. ix).
[181] Graham 1989, p. 411; my italics.   [182] Graham 1978, p. 26; my italics.

existence (有) (*yu*) of the thing with all its properties. The world has a certain object, and if the object has, for example, four legs, teeth, a tail, colour (white, black), no horns, it fits the name 'horse' . . .[183]

In Graham's ancient Chinese, 'dog' or 'ewe' apparently means the same as 'horse'. More important, his evocation of cosmic 有 (*yu*) is reminiscent of original Whorfian theorising: 'every language contains terms that have come to attain cosmic scope of reference, that crystallise in themselves the basic postulates of an unformulated philosophy, in which is couched the thought of a people, a culture, a civilisation, even of an era'.[184]

Speaking as a philosopher, Graham is convinced that locutions like 'there are' and 'exist' do not function as predicates. Speaking as a descriptive linguist, he rejects the so-called 'Aristotelian principle' that all sentences are of subject–predicate form. Doubtless in 'ghosts do not exist', 'ghosts' is the grammatical subject of the grammatical predicate 'exist'; but, as I have been at pains to emphasise, that does not entail that they are the expressed existential proposition's logical subject and predicate. Not that I am now executing a *volte-face* and implying that the 'real' form of 'ghosts do not exist' is not of logical subject–predicate form; rather, I am endorsing the familiar *argument* that we are well advised to formalise the sentence as a negated existential generalisation just in order to avoid the Parmenidean dilemma of apparently affirming the existence of ghosts (by meaningfully using the word 'ghosts' as subject) in the very course of denying their existence. For all I have said so far, Graham's case has a certain limited plausibility; nevertheless, in English there is a perfectly good equivalent for 'ghosts do not exist' (namely, 'there are no ghosts') which would seem, from Graham's perspective, to exert a beneficent constraint on Anglophone philosophising by at least partially neutralising the maleficent encouragement to confusion radiating from the verb 'to exist'. The logicist friends of Chinese might respond that at any rate in ancient Greek there is no substitute for saying οὐκ ἔστι μορμώ, and that in such a sentence μορμώ, by serving as the subject of ἔστι, sets Indo-European philosophy off on altogether the wrong track. But anyone interested in confuting Graham's generalisation that εἶναι prompted Greek thinkers to 'confuse' the existential verb with the copula is faced by an *embarras de richesses* in the philosophical literature.[185]

What about Graham's explication of 有 (*yu*)? The argument is that since nominalisation shifts reference to the agent, and when 有 (*yu*) is nominalised a particular agent is not specified, its nominalisation 'logically implies' that 'everything' or the 'cosmos' is to be understood as agent, thus 'illustrating' ancient Chinese holism in the Whorfian spirit.

---

[183] *Ibid.*   [184] From 'An American Indian Model of the Universe' (Whorf 1967, p. 61).

[185] Particularly vivid counter-evidence is supplied by Plato, *Sophist* 251B, *Philebus* 14C–D; Aristotle, *Physics* I.2; and Plutarch, *Against Colotes* 22–3.

Can this really be so? It is precisely the obliteration of the subject that characterises existentials *generally* across languages: *il y a*, *es gibt*, ἔχει (in modern Greek), etc. All take a complement (the 'existent') and lack any but an expletive subject; since such an expletive subject is *manifestly* non-referential, why should it be taken to be 'the cosmos' in ancient Chinese, or in any other language? (Chao avoids Graham's Whorfian error: 'There is no "there is"; there is only "has" . . . But who has? What has? . . . Suffice it to say here that frequently a Chinese sentence begins with an impersonal verb, which needs no subject. If the speaker is pressed for an answer as to *what* has, he is apt to give the place, time, or circumstance as the subject.'[186]) And who is encouraged by 有 (*yu*) 'to divide down from a wider whole'? I take it that the average ancient Chinese peasant did not either explicitly assert or tacitly suppose that when he said 'there is no pork', he was talking about a local modification of the cosmos. Graham's appeal to 'logical implication' indulges in a proclivity for projecting certain metaphysical and logical doctrines onto a linguistic culture which was blissfully ignorant of them.

8 Case-study 4: truth

Inevitably, those sufferers from the China syndrome who deny ancient Chinese a semantics powerful enough for it to be a language at all will have no truck with what they castigate as the most tyrannical of all Western semantic concepts, 'truth': 'it may certainly be argued that classical Chinese has no word or phrase that translates as "truth" '[187] and '. . . not only is there no appreciable distinction between truth and reality as such, there is also no distinction among the events encompassing a subjective knower, an objective reality known, and the description of this relationship as truth'.[188] Hall and Ames's rendering of Chinese 'truth' as '. . . speech and deed that *effects* an intended consequence'[189] complements Hansen's theme that 'we can best understand all developments in classical Chinese philosophy against the background of a pragmatic theory of language'.[190] Elsewhere Hansen explains, no more plausibly, that 'the pragmatic function of language is not describing or representing reality, not stating truths, but guiding actions and co-ordinating social interaction'.[191] He is aware that his approach

---

[186] Chao 1955, p. 37. Harbsmeier also makes interlinguistic comparisons ('der Begriff der *Existenz* wird im AC häufig durch ein subjektloses transitives Verb HABEN ausgedrückt . . . (Man vergleiche *il y a* sowie das deutsche *es gibt*)' (Harbsmeier 1979, p. 224)), and then implicitly forbids Graham's 'cosmic' construal: 'der wesentlich subjektlose Gebrauch von HABEN zum Ausdruck von Existen-zaussagen muß deutlich vom Gebrauch des Wortes HABEN mit allgemeinem unausgedrücktem Subjekt *unterschieden* werden . . .' (pp. 225–6; my italics).
[187] Hall and Ames 1987, p. 343, n. 48.   [188] *Ibid.*, p. 58.   [189] *Ibid.*, p. 57.
[190] Hansen 1987, p. 322.   [191] Hansen 1989, p. 85.

opens him up to an accusation of linguistic determinism (in his phrasing, '. . . the currently unfashionable Whorf–Sapir hypothesis that language constrains thought makes certain thoughts unthinkable [*sic*]'),[192] but protests that '. . . the conclusion is not about what can or cannot be said in classical philosophical Chinese, but about what was said';[193] thus he is an advocate of 'guidance and constraint', only not the 'hard-core' variety. All Hansen's theses are roundly refuted by Harbsmeier's 'Marginalia Sinologica'. He supplies a very full catalogue of ancient Chinese phrases from pre-imperial and Han texts which, so Harbsmeier argues, employ 'the semantic concept of truth'. Not that he imprudently ascribes a foreshadowing of Tarski to ancient Chinese culture: 'there is a crucial distinction between the question of whether the ancient Chinese did or did not apply semantic truth predicates like "is true" to sentences on the one hand, and on the other hand, whether they developed, defined, or discussed a theoretical concept of truth'.[194]

But, despite Graham's forthright dismissal of Hall and Ames's appalling 'Chinese is a list' argument for the absence of truth from ancient Chinese, he propounds one of his own:

> Let us say that to have the concept [of Truth] implies having a word the meanings of which have the same range of family resemblances as 'true'. We use the word 'true' in the first place of such matters as whether the money, as you told me, is already in the bank. Outside such factual issues, on which we confront the Chinese and everyone else as inhabitants of the same world, we speak of the logical truth of tautologies, of the truth to life or nature of a fictitious narrative, of metaphysical truths, of the moral truths in the Sermon on the Mount, extending the word along chains of similarities linking to the factual. Finally 'true' comes to be not much more than the word by which we assent to any kind of utterance to which we attach a certain importance. Such words as 然 (*jan*), 有 (*yu*) and 信 (*hsin*) would not be expected to, and do not, have the same metaphorical spread as 'true'. . . . That [Chinese philosophers] have no concept of Truth is to be taken for granted, but is trivial.[195]

Here Graham emphatically denies the existence of an objective semantics for 'true'. Whatever the attractions of a redundancy theory of truth might be – and I judge them to be considerable – that is assuredly not quite what, or perhaps not all, that Graham is proposing. Despite the introductory Wittgensteinian fanfare, by the end of the passage 'true' has degenerated into a sort of 'enthusiasm-operator'. Given the remoteness of philosophical topics from the starkly factual centre of Graham's semantic web (never mind how problematic his idea of unproblematic fact is), it follows that he cannot consistently suppose that Chinese and Greek philosophers are alike engaging in some

---

[192] Hansen 1985, pp. 492–3.   [193] *Ibid.*, p. 493.   [194] Harbsmeier 1989, p. 126.
[195] Graham 1989, p. 396.

fairly determinate, common activity by virtue of addressing questions which share identical, true answers; or even, rather more plausibly, questions yielding feasible altern- ative answers of incompatible truth-value.

This is nothing short of a disaster. Graham is adamantly committed to the thesis that at least certain pre-Ch'in thinkers are best described from the Western perspective as 'philosophers', and wisely insists that what is common to their and, say, Greek philo- sophy must be defined in methodological terms, by way of semi-formal conditions on disputation 辯 (*pien*). But then, given his denial of the concept of truth to the ancient Chinese, it is genuinely enigmatic from which vantage-point this methodological definition is to be applied. It cannot, obviously, be done from the perspective of the ancient philosophical participants, Chinese or Greek. On the Chinese side, if there is a dispute over match between name and object, then there is an argument about what it becomes very difficult to avoid calling the *fact* of the matter, easily expressible in Chinese as 然不然 (*jan pu jan*, 'so or not so'). Many readers might wish to be excluded from this particular realist camp. The fact remains that whether or not the Chinese ever progressed beyond asking whether there is a good match between name and object or not, the very form of the dispute is enough to justify, perhaps even to compel, *our* ascribing a conception of objective truth to them, while abstaining from the inflation of this conception into an embryonic theory on the Chinese side accounting for objectiv- ity.[196] The only alternative is to ascribe to the Chinese a criterion of pure social utility for belief evaluation such as Hansen's, which is anathema to Graham. I am not arguing that *Hsün Tzu*, ch. 22, for example, advocates a single and simple procedure of name rectification deploying a criterion of straight factual match: obviously it does not, and it is noteworthy that the varying standards invoked are not subjected to any rigorous stratification. The point I need and have is that whatever the standard in play, however its relation to the others is conceived, the author is manifestly committed to a match *really* being preferable to a mis-match, whether on grounds of clarity, beauty or social propriety.

From a Western point of view the striking feature of Chinese rectification discussions is actually not so much the nature of the criteria used, but rather the disposition, that of a sort of mirror – *Cratylus*, to bring things back into conformity with their right names, rather than the other way round. Roy Harris displays his customary pithy brilliance on this point:

> . . . things are conceived of as conforming to the natural order not in themselves, but in virtue of corresponding to their names. When things for any reason fail to correspond to the essence represented by their names, disorder ensues; and this

---

[196] Cf. Harbsmeier's disclaimer (see p. 56 above).

can be rectified only by bringing things back into correspondence with what they are called, and hence what they should be.[197]

But his further characterisation of rectification gives one pause:

> here we glimpse the possibility of a totally logocentric view of reality: that is, a view according to which words hold the key to things, and language provides the patterns to which reality must conform. Its antithetical counterpart is a reocentric view of language: that is, a view according to which things hold the key to words, and reality provides the patterns to which language must conform.[198]

Harris explicitly denies that the term 'logocentric' in his usage has the same sense as in Derrida's. He ascribes to 正名 (*cheng ming*) a full-blown representational theory – but, in accordance with his nice antithesis, words themselves are now paradoxically the *significanda*, as it were. What is true and important is that the exclusively normative thrust of 正名 (*cheng ming*) is not mediated by semantic theory, even Harris's inversion of semantic theory. When things deviate from their (authentic) names, the deviation must be corrected, not because the rectification theorists subscribe to 'logocentrism' or anything like it, but rather because the original meaning of the true word derives from the *wisdom* of the ancient Sage-Kings, a wisdom best characterised in sociopolitical rather than linguistic terms (to the limited extent that such a distinction can be sustained in the ancient Chinese context).

Since for Graham 正名 (*cheng ming*) is not an objective matter in the sense I have delineated, he must both reject the Chinese philosopher's self-conception as deluded (while of course substituting another) and explain how the apparent appeal to reality in deciding if a name fits is merely apparent. Needless to say, on the Greek side, where philosophers enthusiastically engage in the construction of explicit, often impressive semantic theories, Graham's task would prove even more formidable. The unreflective semantic presuppositions of the actors in this scenario, including ones involved in the metaphysical and ethical claims mentioned by Graham, are robustly realist. His disquisition on what he regards as the provincial concept of truth clearly labels him a spectator. I think little of its merits. But even if we were to endorse it for the sake of argument, the result would be an unhappy one for Graham. His greatest achievement is the substantial and powerful presentation of Chinese *philosophy* as just that, where 'philosophy' is not to be construed relativistically. But if Western dialectic and Chinese 辯 (*pien*) are distinct filaments in a semantic web, albeit both linked to the common core of 'factual' talk, then there is no reason to think – no reason for Graham as his sort of anti-realist to think – that they intersect. If they do not, then much of his comparative work is radically

---

[197] Harris 1980, p. 48.   [198] *Ibid.*, pp. 48–9.

undercut. I prefer to believe that Graham has fallen prey to one aspect of the seductions of 'the guidance and constraint hypothesis', despite his resistance to others.

9 Case-study 5: nouns and ontology

'The guidance and constraint hypothesis' has a strong impact not only on the relativistic treatment of existential concepts, but also, more generally, on philosophical projects which move between a language's fundamental structure and the ontological commitments of its speakers. To broaden and clarify our appreciation of the philosophical issues at stake, let us once more approach the China syndrome indirectly by examining an ultra-Whorfian argument of Ian Hacking's.[199] Hacking mounts what he insists is an *empirical* refutation of Strawson's famous thesis that the ontological category of substantial particulars is essential to the conceptual endowment which makes us human. Exploiting the work of Sapir and Boas on the Amerindian languages Nootka and Kwakiutl, Hacking claims that although these are *real* 'feature-placing' languages, they are not inferior in expressive power to, say, English.[200] The principal evidence he adduces falls into four groups.

First, Kwakiutl pronominal suffixes do not suffice to establish reference to individuals;[201] instead, they are strongly analogous to predicate calculus variables.[202] But if this is factually correct, all it establishes is that reference to particulars, if it occurs in Kwakiutl, is not marked, *not* that it does not occur.

---

[199] Hacking 1968.

[200] *Ibid.*, p. 185. A 'feature-placing' language, as defined by Strawson, is one whose imaginary speakers are capable of saying, e.g., 'there is snow here' but not 'there is a drift of snow here': that is, they lack the resources necessary for reference to individuals. Nevertheless, feature-placing is not far removed from individual reference: '*though feature-placing sentences do not introduce particulars into our discourse, they provide the materials for this introduction.* Suppose we compare a feature-placing *sentence* ("There is snow here") with a *phrase* ("This (patch of) snow") in the use of which an individual instance of the feature is mentioned. It seems possible, in this case, to regard the notion of the individual instance as something logically complex in relation to the two simpler notions of the feature and of placing' ('Particular and General', in Strawson 1971, p. 38).

[201] Harbsmeier comments: 'Hacking ist lediglich zu der Anmerkung berechtigt, daß die einzigen referierenden Ausdrücke in Kwakiutl anscheinend die Pronomina sind. Von einer Aufhebung der Prädikation im Kwakiutl kann nicht die Rede sein, höchstens von einer Begrenzung der Subjekte auf Pronomina' (Harbsmeier 1979, p. 101). But this misses the point: Hacking is banking on a claim concerning the ontological category of that to which the pronouns refer, a claim which Harbsmeier fails to address.

[202] 'Fortunately for anyone trying to follow a Kwakiutl sentence, pronouns are inflected according to the sex and shape of the features they "stand for". "Stand for" is a misnomer, for though in English you can often replace a pronoun by the name it stands for, you can no more do this in Kwakiutl than you can replace variables by predicates in the predicate calculus: the pronouns are place markers, just as in the predicate calculus' (Hacking 1968, p. 179).

Moreover, Hacking never explains how it could be that his Kwakiutl Indians are feature-placers, yet suffer no diminution in expressive power. This obscurity carries over to Hacking's second purported piece of major evidence, the claim that plurals in these languages are merely 'distributive'. For instance, one would pluralise 'cat' only if presented with qualitatively distinct cats, say a Burmese and a Persian – but then, so Hacking argues, one might be referring, not to particular cats in the plural, but rather to discriminated Burmese and Persian features.[203] Again, all that emerges is that 'distributive' pluralisation alone is marked, not that it alone is available for these speakers. Third, Hacking is impressed by the supposed absence of lexical classes in the Amerindian languages; our consideration of the claimed repercussions of this absence in Chinese will leave us unimpressed.[204] Fourth, Hacking finds the localising expressions used to designate places highly suggestive. He reads them, not as names, but as spatio-temporal discriminators that are *not* noun-like, since they merely specify features.[205] To maintain his thesis he must deny that they are *names* of times and places, but only on the weakest of grounds. Hacking concedes that one could readily argue that such geographical 'descriptions' (e.g. 'last-one-on-the-ground') are, in actual use, leached of their descriptive content, and so are really functioning as names of geographical particulars. At this juncture he takes refuge in translational indeterminacy: if he cannot decisively prove this is not so, his sceptical opponent cannot prove that it *is*.[206] The manœuvre fails, however, since the principle of charity dictates that in the absence of hard evidence to the contrary, we should not attribute diminished descriptive resources to the Indians, and Hacking has only stated, not argued, that denying them names does not reduce their expressive power. The moral is not far to seek: efforts to read a culture's metaphysics (even supposing it has such a thing) off from the structure of its language are liable to come to grief unless one grants the strong and unmotivated premiss that a detailed isomorphism obtains between language and ontology, so that absence of a morphological marker, say, *automatically* corresponds to an ontological gap.

The comparable move from Chinese language to Chinese metaphysics focuses on certain alleged peculiarities of Chinese nouns. Chad Hansen is responsible for the

---

[203] 'Distributive plurals are plurals which do not embody our distinction between "same one again" and "another one" . . . Thus it is only a so-called *true plural* which a feature-placing language need lack – a plural in which one speaks of cats if and only if different cats are in question' (*ibid.*, p. 172).

[204] *Ibid.*, p. 178. Harbsmeier cogently remarks: '. . . wenn es in einer Sprache überhaupt keine lexikalische Unterscheidung zwischen Verben und Nomina gäbe, dann könnten wir immer noch nach syntaktischen Merkmalen für nominale oder verbale Wortfunktion in dieser Sprache suchen' (Harbsmeier 1979, p. 102).

[205] Hacking 1968, p. 183.

[206] *Ibid.*, p. 183. Harbsmeier is quite rightly intolerant of this comfortable evasion (Harbsmeier 1979, p. 102).

'mass noun hypothesis', according to which Chinese words corresponding to Indo-European count nouns behave more like our mass nouns: ' "of what is 馬 (*ma*) 'horse' the name?" has a natural answer: the mereological sum of horses. "Horse-stuff" is thus an object (substance or thing-kind) scattered in space-time.'[207] It has been pointed out frequently that direct application of this hypothesis to ancient Chinese is worse than dubious, since it lacks modern Chinese's regular supply of measure words (comparable to '*pails of* water') for the conversion of what look more to us like mass nouns to what look more to us like count nouns.[208] Furthermore, Hansen has remained curiously unresponsive to Harbsmeier's devastating, apparently definitive refutation of the mass noun hypothesis.

Nevertheless, Graham, for his part, is content to embrace Hansen's conclusion, which he describes as 'the insight . . . that the tendency of Chinese thought is to divide down rather than to add up, to think in terms of whole/part rather than class/member'.[209] But then he opens up the throttle: 'it remains acceptable that Western philosophising in languages with number termination starts from the adding up of particulars, leading at two of its limits to the reduction of cosmos and community to aggregates of atoms and of individual persons, while the Chinese operating with generic nouns think in terms of variously divisible Way, pattern, 氣 (*ch'i*), and kind of thing'.[210] (Generic nouns are those which itemising number phrases can precede, but which cannot yield an individual enumeration; where '*x*' is a numeral and 'a' is a generic noun, '*xa*' means '*x* kinds of or varieties of or types of a'.[211]) So Graham in fact advocates replacement of the (discredited) mass noun hypothesis with the generic noun hypothesis. But is this intended as a 'guidance and constraint' hypothesis? The quotation is pretty non-committal: it advises that the opposition between 'philosophising in languages with number termination' and 'operating with generic nouns' is 'acceptable', without according that opposition a determining rôle in setting the mode of philosophy adopted.

[207] Hansen 1983, p. 35.
[208] 'If such classifiers had been obligatory or at least common in Classical Chinese, the interpretation of Chinese count nouns as mass nouns might at least have had some initial plausibility' (Harbsmeier 1991, p. 66: the entire essay repays careful study).
[209] Graham 1989, p. 401.
[210] *Ibid.*, p. 402. Atomistic extremism is not the only philosophical sin to which Indo-Europeans are prone, as the following remarkably robust passage of 'guidance and constraint' excess reveals: '[in Chinese] there is none of the tendency towards hypostatisation of thinking in Indo-European languages, where inflection converts verbs and adjectives into abstract nouns, in varying degrees assimilated to ordinary nouns by number, gender and the article, so that it is difficult to deal with any concept except on the analogy of a nominal concept' (Graham 1978, p. 29).
[211] Harbsmeier lays out the distinctions between ancient Chinese count, generic and mass nouns in 'Marginalia Sino-logica', pp. 157–60.

Likewise, Hansen's credentials as a committed 'guidance and constraint' theorist are dubious, since the explanation of his strategy, which derives the whole tenor of ancient Chinese philosophy from the mass nouns he attributes to it, settles for cautious correlation rather than ambitious causation:

> essentially, I contend that a one–many paradigm *goes along with* a count noun (nouns to which the many–few dichotomy applies) syntax. Chinese language, during the classical period, *tends toward* a mass noun syntax (based on nouns to which the much–little dichotomy applies). Mass nouns *suggest* a stuff ontology and what I call a division or discrimination view of the semantic function of words (terms and predicates).[212]

In any case, Graham's characterisation of Chinese and Western philosophy is a crude travesty. Even leaving to one side his blanket description of the *Tao*, his reduction of Western philosophy to a process of adding up particulars terminating in physical and political atomism is an unacceptable caricature. But suppose we object that Graham's characterisation hardly fits Platonist philosophy of any description. The rejoinder would come back that it is only within a linguistic framework disposed to show up countable particulars as peculiarly prominent that the Western emphasis on prior unity (transcendent or not) could emerge to attack that very prominence. In other words, Graham's generalising sweep obliges us to talk like Hegelians loftily diagnosing Neoplatonic strategies, a conversation which leaves me restive, if mildly amused. For such a rejoinder, from the side of those committed to 'guidance and constraint', in effect concedes that absolutely any philosophical development can be explained by appeal to linguistic features, even where the philosophy in question labels those very features misleading or incoherent. 'Guidance and constraint' has thus altogether lost its explanatory bite.

10 Conclusion

Pioneering forays into what Graham aptly described as 'the no-man's land on the common borders of linguistics, philosophy, and Sinology' are brave and helpful, and fully deserve the respect of argumentative response rather than incurious neglect or uncritical acceptance. This first chapter of *Aristotle in China* might have produced the impression that I see nothing but harm in employing linguistic approaches when studying the history of philosophy, ancient or modern, Chinese or Greek. Far from it. The great pity is rather that wanderers in this no-man's land have devoted their efforts to seeking superficially stupendous but ultimately delusive philosophical rewards in the analysis

---

[212] Hansen 1983, p. vii; my italics.

of fundamental linguistic structure. I have every confidence that the study of language does indeed have a vital contribution to make, so long as we widen our gaze to take in not only the lessons of pragmatics and socio-linguistics, but also the field of rhetoric broadly conceived as the interpretation of persuasive strategies sensitive to an entire spectrum of cultural stimuli.[213]

Two profound but as yet unanswered questions can serve to illustrate the need for constructive linguistic treatment, on the enhanced understanding of 'linguistics'. Graham's Derridean contrast of East and West in the matter of logo- versus phono-centrism is punctuated by his conviction that ancient Chinese philosophers conceive of words as spoken rather than as written:[214] 'the philosophers teach orally, always say "I have heard . . ." not "I have read . . .", theorise about names in terms of sound, not graphs . . .'.[215] (Elsewhere Graham says that the ten Mohist triads are '*transparently* records of oral tradition . . .'[216] and that 'this impersonality [of the later Mohist *summa*] is unusual in pre-Han philosophy, when the most interesting examples of disputation tend to be (or to have been dramatised as) actual face-to-face debates . . .'.[217]) On the other side, Harbsmeier justifiably denies that there was any real parallel in China to the dialectical competitions which were so important in Greek intellectual history. Yet he backs up this denial with the opinion that ancient Chinese logicians or sophists, call them what one will, were 'marginal' figures.[218] Certainly they were effectively marginalised in philosophical doxography from Han times onwards: but that is a far cry from establishing that they were marginal in the context of living Warring States disputes.

If Graham is right, there are indeed potentially fascinating comparisons and contrasts with the Greek experience. But where is the evidence? He rests his case on the

[213] Arthur Wright's 'The Chinese Language and Foreign Ideas' (in his 1953) reports some superb anecdotal material from the missionary period which forces on one's attention the magnitude and complexity of cultural factors truly at work as foreign languages and modes of thought combine and collide, in contrast to the relatively sparse, simple linguistic phenomena which fascinate champions of 'the guidance and constraint hypothesis'. Roy Harris issues a manifesto to which I happily subscribe: 'the alternative to a linguistics which concerns itself exclusively with "the language" is a linguistics which takes as its point of departure the individual linguistic act in its communicational setting. Only by such a change of perspective will it ultimately be possible to do justice to the facts concerning the renewal of language. Any theoretical account which abstracts from the phenomena of communication in such a way as to ignore these facts can have no serious claim to be a theory of the human activities and capacities which we customarily subsume under the term "language"' (Harris 1981, p. 166).

[214] Graham 1989, p. 228. [215] *Ibid.*, p. 390.

[216] Graham 1978, p. 5, n. 7; my italics. [217] *Ibid.*, pp. 24–5.

[218] E.g. 'those who, like the Later Mohists, to a certain extent tried to detach the theoretical considerations of objective truth from their political, social, and personal contexts, were doomed to a marginal place in Chinese intellectual history' (Harbsmeier 1998, p. 208; cf. p. 414).

standard use of formulae in the sources suggesting spoken discourse, but that is hardly
satisfactory, since the Greek tradition reveals how long a dialectical format, originating
in face-to-face verbal combat, can survive in vastly different intellectual circumstances
which nonetheless preserve the forms of oral dispute as fossilised literary artefacts.[219]
Of course, vivid instances of the denigration of writing and reading, extolling the
virtues of the spoken word as the medium of expression of sincere thought, are not hard
to come by;[220] but note that these denigrations are themselves expressed in the written
medium, just as is Plato's celebrated dismissal of writing in the *Phaedrus*, and thus
cannot yield any unambiguous results. So how, if at all, does its purported orality make
itself felt in Chinese disputation, 辯 (*pien*)?

Second, to a specialist in ancient Greek philosophy perhaps the single most exciting
development in the ancient Chinese tradition is the possible later Mohist conception of
a sentence as more than a string of names, as expounded in *Names and Objects*:

> throughout the *Canons and Explanations* a sentence is assumed to be simply a
> name or string of names, and 謂之牛 (*wei chih niu*) 'call it ox' is used where we
> should choose the wording 'say it is an ox' (B35); the difference was first appreci-
> ated by the author of *Names and Objects*. One might say that this distinction,
> which Western logic could take for granted from the beginning, was the last and
> most difficult of the Mohist discoveries . . .[221]

(Someone arbitrarily beginning the history of Western logic after Plato's *Sophist* would
still be hard-pressed to show that even the most basic propositional structure is then
'taken for granted'.) What, according to Graham, made the discovery of the proposition
so comparatively arduous for Chinese philosophy was, for once, the *advantage* conferred
on Indo-European thinkers by 'guidance and constraint': 'the distinction between word
and sentence, term and proposition, is much more obvious in inflected languages than

---

[219] Schenkeveld 1992 convincingly demonstrates that in later Greek the formula ἤκουσα Χ λέγοντος
('I have heard X saying . . .') is often equivalent to 'I have read in X' without the slightest implication
of orality: '. . . very often we should interpret statements of this kind as simple indications that someone has read something in a book by X, e.g. Plato. I shall also argue that this expression is the proper
Greek idiom for "I have read in (e.g.) Plato that . . .", at least from the end of the Hellenistic period
onwards' (p. 129). One infers that the explanation of the idiom is to be found in the fact that reading
aloud (either to oneself or to members of an audience?) was far more common than silent reading in
the ancient West. This passage, in which the late commentator Ammonius is speaking of Andronicus
of Rhodes, who lived in the first century BCE, is telling: 'he was the eleventh in succession from
Aristotle, and heard him call thoughts "affections" in the preface to this book [*De Interpretatione*]'
(*In Int.* V.5.28ff., cited by Schenkeveld in n. 26, p. 134).
[220] E.g. *Han Fei Tzu* 21.15.1, *Chuang Tzu* 13.6.   [221] Graham 1978, p. 25.

in a purely analytic language such as Chinese'.[222] What is so tantalising about the Mohist discovery (if that is what it was) is that in ancient Greece Plato's parallel achievement in the *Sophist* emerges from a mature context of earlier and contemporary speculation about false statement which fuels and directs the course of his work. In striking contrast, the Mohist theory stands largely bereft of the context necessary for us to gauge many of its implications.

Obviously our ignorance is in some considerable measure the consequence of the appalling state of this portion of the ancient Chinese evidence. Indeed, there are real grounds (quite apart from Hansen's unsuccessful critique) for querying Graham's conclusions. His first piece of evidence for a revolutionary analysis of the 辭 (*ts'û*) supposedly emerges from *Names and Objects* 3: 'the recognition that mental pictures are variously interpretable is perhaps the Mohist's crucial step in his discovery of the proposition . . . The author of *Names and Objects* understands that a proposition affirms that something is a catch of game, or is a pile of dead birds; it does not present a mental picture which might be interpreted as either.'[223] This cryptic argument is extremely difficult to understand, let alone judge. First, Graham adduces no convincing reasons for rendering 意 (*i*) as '*pictorial* idea'. There is no basis for importing anything as specific as mental imagery into the passage. But second, perhaps Graham does so because he supposes that imagery is indeterminate between a choice of propositional 'labels', and so we will necessarily select one or another of the propositional options for purposes of identification. This argument fails even on its own terms. All it could establish is that to identify a pictorial idea, we should have to give it a particular 'label', not that that 'label' need be of any given degree of semantic complexity. For example, 十 (*shih*) is a picture of the Cross or the Chinese graph designating the number '10' or . . .; but recognition of the need for imagistic labelling does not of itself demand choice between the *names or descriptions* 'picture of the Cross', 'the Chinese graph designating the number "10"', and the *propositions* '(this token of) 十 is a picture of the Cross', '(this token of) 十 is (a token of) the Chinese graph designating the number "10"'. Finally, if, as we ought, we reject any connection here with mental imagery, then we

---

[222] *Ibid.*, p. 25. His findings have been contested by Chad Hansen (in, e.g., Hansen 1989), but his counter-arguments lack all credibility: 'pre-Han writers wrote characters vertically on bamboo strips or on silk. They used no punctuation and thought of strings of characters as precisely that – strings. In theory there seemed to be no notion of words playing generalisable syntactic rôles in some specifiable string structure – for example a sentence' (Hansen 1989, p. 77). This, I suppose, is a sort of *technological* 'guidance and constraint', and submits to an obvious refutation by analogy: ancient Greek writers wrote horizontally (sometimes in opposite directions alternately) on papyrus strips. They used no (or very rudimentary) punctuation and thought of strings of letters as λόγοι . . .

[223] Graham 1978, p. 473.

ought to infer that what *NO* 3 concerns is the distinction between 智 (*chih*), conventionally rendered 'knowledge', and 意, *i* ('idea' *tout court*). What it says about the difference between these cognitive states is obscure, to say the least, but would seem to have no bearing whatsoever on the claimed discovery of the semantic complexity of the 辭 (*ts'û*).

Graham's second piece of evidence, however, while still, inevitably, very speculative, demands the most serious consideration: 夫辭以故生，以理長，以類行者也 (*fu ts'û i ku sheng, i li chang, i lei hsing che yeh*), 'the proposition is something which is engendered in accordance with the thing as it inherently is, becomes full-grown according to a pattern, and "proceeds" according to the kind' (*NO* 10; trans. Graham). Graham himself remarks that the 'organic metaphor' is 'odd',[224] but fails to acknowledge that this image is in fact his only evidence for a new conception of the 辭 (*ts'û*) (he misleadingly suggests that the author's grasp of the difference between name and proposition is 'clear').[225] In truth Graham's exciting claim hinges on nothing more than the connotations of 理 (*li*), 'pattern, arrangement', and the plausible guess that the organic metaphor was intended to imply that the 辭 (*ts'û*) possesses a functionally diversified structure, as the parts of the plant or animal are articulated. Thus we have good reason not to dismiss Graham's interpretation, despite his exaggeration of the evidence, while admitting that even on the most optimistic reading, pushing the comparison of the Mohist's 'odd' metaphor to the intimidating argumentation of the *Sophist* would be to play a mug's game. Again the prospect beckons of further research aimed at enriching our understanding of the Mohist dialectical milieu.

Our study of logical form has brought home the message that the lines of mutual influence between concepts of formal and of informal validity are multiple and complex; still, talk of 'validity' both formally in logic and informally in 'natural' reasoning hardly trades on a mere homonym, and the formalisation of an argument involves both descriptive and prescriptive[226] decisions in subtle and varying proportions. The message for sufferers from the China syndrome must be that they should never have hoped that a neutral inspection of samples of Chinese could make them yield up logical forms

---

[224] *Ibid.*, p. 481.   [225] *Ibid.*, p. 480.

[226] Such modest normativity is deeply traditional, and easily discovered in the 'traditional' logic whose exaggerated, wholesale rejection was prompted by Fregean and post-Fregean anti-psychologism. I cull the following claims from a little handbook precisely because its humble, pedagogical character helps to convey how commonplace the old prescriptive conception was: 'our object in studying Logic is to ascertain and describe the general forms of thought, which we must employ so long as we reason correctly . . . A Science teaches us to know and an Art to do: ∴ Logic is both, because (1) it investigates the principles and forms of thought, and (2) it frames rules for our guidance in reasoning correctly' (Hawkins 1893, p. 7).

deviating more or less radically from English or ancient Greek forms.[227] Rather, attribution of a distinctively 'Chinese' logic to the Chinese would have to be precipitated by a process of interpretation which, Quine and Davidson notwithstanding, did not blench at saddling another culture with an exotic, perhaps even exotically inferior, quasi-rationality. With the demise of 'the guidance and constraint hypothesis', it is hard to see on what grounds such an enterprise could recommend itself.

All comparativist projects, the naive no less than the self-conscious, have a guiding methodology, although the naive are more prone to build blindly on rickety assumptions. One might deduce that theorists who succumb to the China syndrome combine defects to produce the worst possible comparativist strategy: despite their methodological self-consciousness, their 'guidance and constraint hypothesis' is the flimsiest of linguistic foundations for viable work. But this would be unfair, and in conclusion I wish to turn to the defence of these theorists' aspirations, if hardly of their practice. It might be suggested[228] that Hansen's mass noun hypothesis, say, if its scope be sensibly restricted to nouns designating certain philosophically significant items, such as 氣 (*ch'i*), is much more plausible and potentially useful. 氣 (*ch'i*) functions logically like a stuff, and with Yin and Yang is the most important of all Chinese cosmological concepts. Furthermore, it delivers a neat contrast to most ancient Greek cosmological concepts in not being subject to a ruling formal element.

Just where does this leave us? The simple act of pointing out the contrast, no matter how important it might be, gets us nowhere, since we have failed to address the question *why*. Restriction of Hansen's hypothesis to philosophical mass nouns robs it of all interest: in its original form, it insisted that the prominence, or absence, of certain features in Chinese metaphysics and philosophy of language is the direct consequence of certain linguistic features – the hypothesis was causal.[229] In its restricted form the hypothesis has lost its teeth, and in fact reduces to the simple observation that the conceptual repertoire of Chinese cosmology is dominated by mass concepts – but that has nothing

---

[227] Eli Hirsch has devoted an entire book to what he calls 'the division problem': 'can we clarify and justify our intuition that there are rational constraints on how the words of a language ought to divide up reality . . . ?' (Hirsch 1993, p. 7). It might seem as if Hirsch's interesting work on classification and individuation is immediately relevant to the China syndrome; but since he restricts the problem to lexical properties rather than ranging more freely over what I have designated 'fundamental linguistic structure', and explores imaginary alternatives to the way 'we' (human beings) divide reality rather than considering how 'they' (e.g. the ancient Chinese) supposedly do it, his study does not in fact intersect with our own.

[228] This idea was in fact suggested to me by Nathan Sivin in conversation, but he is not responsible for its development here.

[229] As we saw, Hansen actually hedges his bets; but I am using his hypothesis only *exempli gratia*, and many of the other theses which we have examined would do as well for the sake of the present argument.

whatsoever to do (necessarily) with the structure of the Chinese language. If wrong –
disastrously wrong – the original hypothesis at least ventured a comparativist *explana-*
tion, and to that extent is preferable to any mere marshalling of contrastive data, no
matter how meticulously accurate. That is why 'guidance and constraint' hypotheses
are worth taking seriously; if, as I have argued, their influence is baleful, they deserve
respectful attention nevertheless for attempting the only comparativist tasks worth the
effort.

   In the second chapter of this book, 'Aristotelian Whispers', I shall make the move
from philosophical theory of translation to a translation of philosophical theory. The
transition is not abrupt, since the translated theory concerns the structure of reality,
thought and language; one might almost say that the success of the 名理探 (*ming li t'an*)
as a translation of the *Categories* has a bearing on the success of the *Categories* as a
theory with linguistic implications.

2

Aristotelian whispers

And thus it was from the Greeks that philosophy took its rise, whose very name refuses to be translated into foreign speech.   Diogenes Laertius I. 4

1 Introduction

Readers of 'The China Syndrome' might well feel inclined to complain of a glaring omission in its consideration of 'guidance and constraint'. A moderate sceptic about the hypothesis could readily concede that the case-studies of the first chapter are effective against Sinological relativism, yet suggest that I have ignored the most massive presence in the history of philosophy: Aristotle. The contention is that his thought is permeated throughout by a variety of linguistic influences rarely recognised as such by Aristotle himself. Nowhere is this clearer than in the *Categories*. Although the *Categories* stands in the first rank of the Western philosophical tradition, its students ancient and modern are in doubt over its status. Is it (primarily) a work of dialectic; of semantics; or of ontology? The sceptic contends that this chronic perplexity is no accident. The *Categories* puzzles us because it, and much later philosophy in its wake, has indeed been guided and constrained by language. The moral of 'The China Syndrome' is that we should fight shy of formulating too specific a hypothesis concerning just how Greek (or Indo-European) leaves its mark on Aristotelian doctrines. We should nevertheless remain confident that a deep imprint is there, even without a detailed explanation of how it was made. Had there been a Chinese Aristotle, his categories would have been shaped by Chinese, and so would have been strikingly different from the Greek ones.[1]

---

[1] This is precisely the assumption governing the thought-experiment in which Angus Graham constructs a scheme of Chinese categories: 'that people of another culture are somehow thinking in different categories is a familiar idea, almost a commonplace, but one very difficult to pin down as a topic for fruitful discussion. The most promising approach would seem to be to identify the question forms in the language which are answered by grammatically distinct sentence units. It has long been noticed, and demonstrated in detail by Benveniste, that Aristotle's categories do largely coincide with Greek

I answer with a historical fact which, if not massive, is at least intriguing: Aristotle's *Categories* was translated into literary Chinese, so disputants in the 'guidance and constraint' debate can appeal to an actual text in support of their claims, rather than making up hypothetical competitors to Aristotle. The great merit of Sinological relativists lay in their engagement with real languages, rather than with imaginary philosophical constructs. Historians of philosophy can do even better by engaging with the 名理探 (*ming li t'an*), a version of the *Categories* prepared by the Chinese *literatus* 李之藻 (Li Chih-tsao) in collaboration with the Jesuit Francisco Furtado (傅汎濟, Fu Fan-chi) and published in Hangchou in 1631.[2]

It seems too good to be true. In the 名理探 we have not merely a sample of philosophical translation, but also a rendering into Chinese of that very philosophical text which has been castigated as the classic instance of inflating quite parochial linguistic traits into general features of reality itself. One might infer that insofar as the 名理探 works well as a translation, its theory is free from any bias imparted by the original language in which it was composed; but that its failure in Chinese might call into question the validity of the *Categories* in any language. If category theory is valid, then it ought to be indifferent to the language in which it is expressed. If it does betray differential sensitivity to languages, then Aristotle was indeed working within the confines imposed by ancient Greek, whether he realised this limitation or not.

To a degree it is too good to be true. The 名理探 could function as the ultimate test-case for linguistic relativism only on condition that any instances of mis-translation it might contain could be immediately and confidently attributed to quite general Chinese characteristics, rather than to particular features of this special exercise in translation. For example, a Whorfian obviously does not want to draw any conclusions from sheer incompetence: nothing follows from a given Chinese individual not knowing Latin well (this is to be distinguished from the claim that Chinese people systematically do badly at

---

grammatical forms, not all of them shared by modern languages' (Graham 1989, pp. 414–15); and 'no Chinese thinker classifies categories. But in Chinese too we can find correspondences between interrogative words or phrases, the sentence units, and vernacular categorical words of the type of our own "thing", "characteristics", "action" ' (p. 415). Graham is forcibly struck by the oft-remarked fact that, for example, 'quantity' in Aristotle's list is the translation of a Greek word, ποσόν, which functions as both an interrogative ('how much?') and an indefinite adjective ('so much'). (The issue of the relation between the categories and interrogatives is directly addressed below in section 8, 'How Many Questions?'.) But he seems to have been unaware of the existence of a real experiment in categorial translation.

² Three copies of the original are known to have survived, and have been preserved in Beijing, the Bibliothèque Nationale in Paris and the Vatican. Although the Italian copy has some extra material (including an additional preface), I have elected to refer to the 1965 Taipei reprint (identical to the Beijing and Paris exemplars), since it contains everything pertinent to our enquiry, and is relatively accessible.

Latin, which would be of potential interest to a relativist). It is not true that simple inspection of the 名理探, no matter how scrupulous, could help us to adjudicate the 'guidance and constraint' debate. We should also require criteria for discriminating between those phenomena arising from the sorts of factor at issue in the debate and the host of idiosyncratic peculiarities evident in all translations, and such criteria would inevitably be *parti pris*. Therefore the hope that the Chinese *Categories* might help us resolve the controversy is misplaced, if it rests on the assumption that the 名理探 could be assessed quite independently of prior convictions about the relation between language and thought.

Furthermore, as we have seen, proponents of 'guidance and constraint' refer almost exclusively to the pre-Ch'in language, not to Ming-Ch'ing Chinese; but there is every reason to think that seventeenth-century literary Chinese might well be a more subtle instrument for conveying new ideas than the pre-Ch'in. Moreover, in the course of translating Buddhist texts into Chinese some logical terminology had already been invented,[3] and it is plausible to suppose that this tradition might well have constituted at least a partial context in which Chinese *literati* might situate Western logic. Nevertheless, a distinction must be made which bears heavily on the pertinence of the 名理探 to the 'guidance and constraint' controversy. That Ming-Ch'ing Chinese could encompass what was beyond the resources of the pre-Ch'in language is undeniable, undeniable, that is, when what is in question is the 'evolution' of Chinese as a translating medium in consequence of centuries of *cultural* change. If, however, the suggestion is that seventeenth-century literary Chinese possesses enhanced expressive power in the sense dear to relativists, it is strongly to be resisted on the basis of now familiar considerations.

Not that these inevitable restrictions rob the 名理探 of its considerable fascinations. As soon as we begin to probe the complexities of the original Greek *Categories* and the Latin version translated into Chinese, as we consider the motivations and intellectual backgrounds of Li Chih-tsao and Furtado, we shall find that the notion that the Chinese categories might supply unproblematic evidence swiftly becomes ludicrous. But we shall also discover that the 名理探 provides highly suggestive, if hardly definitive, materials pertinent to 'guidance and constraint', and that its significance extends far beyond the linguistic relativism debate, important as that is. The intrinsic interest of the 名理探 as a unique artefact in the history of inter-cultural communication is undeniable. Students of Aristotle, of late Ming society, and of the transmission of Western classics to the Chinese all have much to learn from these curious Aristotelian whispers.

Categories are very slippery fish indeed. What is a category? And how might a category theory achieve legitimacy? Orthodoxy has it that Aristotle in the treatise appropriately

---

[3] Now see Frankenhauser 1996.

entitled *Categories* introduces categories to the Western tradition: 'of things said without any combination, each signifies either substance or quantity or qualification or a relative or where or when or being-in-a-position or having or doing or being-affected' (1b25–7). Despite what his phrasing might easily be (and often has been) taken to imply, Aristotle plainly intends to refer, not to linguistic items, but rather to their referents.[4] Thus his sentence might be paraphrased 'of things to which we can refer in uncombined (i.e. syntactically simple) language, each is . . .', and it enumerates all the types of *being* there are: substances, such as human beings; quantities, such as three feet long; qualities, such as red; and so forth. There are immediate negative implications for Graham's relativistic interpretation of Aristotle, which, despite his disclaimers, is startlingly extreme.[5] His reading presupposes that Aristotle proceeded in blinkered ignorance of the (alleged) fact that his native language variously stimulated and inhibited his tendency to propound ontological doctrines. But inspection of his works amply demonstrates that Aristotle is acutely aware of the linguistic traps into which philosophers are prone to fall. After all, in large measure the goal of the *Topics* is to alert us to such dangerous possibilities, and Aristotle's exercises in linguistic analysis often reach a pitch of extreme sophistication. In the *Sophistici Elenchi* (*Sophistical Refutations*) V (166), arguments running *counter* to the suggestions of grammar are discussed.[6] This is not to say that gauging the impact of language on category theories is fruitless: only that they must not be reduced to paltry impositions of fortuitous linguistic structure onto a world left untouched by such strictly local projections.

But although his manner of expression is in one clear sense misleading, it should not be deplored or dismissed as merely something like a trivial confusion of material and formal modes of speech. Rather, here, as so often elsewhere, Aristotle is moving from

---

[4] Cf. '. . . it is important to recognise from the start that the *Categories* is not primarily or explicitly about names, but about the things that names signify . . . Aristotle relies greatly on linguistic facts and tests, but his aim is to discover truths about non-linguistic items' (Ackrill 1979, p. 71); and '. . . Aristotle tends to think of predicates as the non-linguistic items introduced by predicate-expressions' (from 'Categories in Aristotle', Frede 1987, p. 35).

[5] E.g. 'since modern languages lack equivalents to the Greek middle and perfect, the two corresponding categories [Posture and State] have lost their significance for us' (Graham 1989, p. 415).

[6] Passmore concludes that 'Aristotle is suggesting a purely syntactical division of predicates, one based on their grammatical form, need not correspond to a philosophical categorisation' (Passmore 1961, p. 122). Frede's similar argument explicitly sets aside the view of Benveniste, which Graham unfortunately takes as authoritative: 'nor does it seem that Aristotle arrives at his list of categories by grammatical considerations as has been proposed again recently by Benveniste. It is true that Aristotle thinks that certain grammatical forms tend to go with certain categories; the active form of verbs, e.g., naturally goes with the category of doing and the passive with the category of suffering. But he also is aware of the fact that grammatical form in this respect can be quite misleading, and he thinks that a large number of fallacies are due to this' (Frede 1987, p. 47).

what we would regard as features of language to features of the world without so much as signalling any recognition that there is a transition to be made (the relativist claim is that these particular moves are made only, or at least most easily, in Greek).[7] Nor does he explain how he arrived at his list, or why one should feel confident that it is accurate and comprehensive.

To complicate matters further, there are compelling grounds for the belief that, despite the venerable tradition, the genera of being with which the *Categories* deals are not (Aristotelian) categories, at least in their original guise.[8] The word which we transliterate 'category' is employed by Aristotle to mean 'predicate' or '(type of) predication', so that a 'category theory' ought to be a theory of predication, not of being. And in a relatively unfamiliar text, *Topics* I.9, this is just what we do find. After saying that the types of predication must be distinguished, Aristotle provides a list identical to that in the *Categories* – except that the first item is not 'substance', but 'what it is' (103b21–3). In the *Categories*, individuals such as Socrates are substances pre-eminently, and species such as human being are substances secondarily: in the *Topics*, in contrast, colour is the 'what it is' of red no less than human being is the 'what it is' of Socrates.

What the *Topics* delivers, then, is a theory of predication according to which the predicates which can characterise any subject whatsoever will fall into ten ultimate kinds. Again, defence of this list in particular (or of the possibility of constructing *any* non-arbitrary, correct list) is lacking; but reflection on why the *Topics* was written

---

[7] '. . . the real interest of the Aristotelian notion of a category seems to lie in the fact that we are supposed to have one set of notions, or, perhaps, two or three very closely related sets of notions, which do needed work in logic, in grammar, and in metaphysics' (from 'Categories in Aristotle', Frede 1987, p. 48). Exactly: but why and how is this supposed to be so? For Montgomery Furth the purpose of the *Categories* is '. . . nothing less than to offer a logical/semantical analysis or "philosophical grammar" for the entirety of *predicative being* – that is, for every state of affairs in the world that ordinary language (the immediate object-language of the theory is of course Greek of the mid-fourth century, but we may for our purposes pass rather freely between that medium and our own) casts into the form *X is Y* for any subject *X*, and any predicate *Y* ' (Furth 1988, p. 9). Furth does not explain how philosophical grammar does or can modify what ordinary language says about states of affairs in the world. Aristotle blithely assumes that the fabric of the world is accessible to us, disclosed by the range of predications people, at any rate those of a philosophical disposition, have been inclined to make; he mounts no argument for the reliable accuracy of predication.

[8] Michael Frede's 'The Title, Unity, and Authenticity of the Aristotelian Categories' (in Frede 1987) is the magisterial exposition of the account relating the *Categories* and *Topics* which I have adopted. He maintains that '. . . it is not as if the contents of the treatise are about categories in the Aristotelian sense. When I speak of categories in the Aristotelian sense, I am assuming that we need to distinguish between categories (that is, kinds of predication in a special, technical sense which we find in *Topics* I 9), genera of being, and categories of "being" (i.e. kinds of predication of "being"). In terms of this distinction, the first part of the treatise, at least in the form in which we have it, deals with the genera of being and not with the categories' (Frede 1987, pp. 16–17).

might make the absence of this defence considerably less shocking, albeit at the cost, ironically enough, of undermining the status which the categories of the *Categories* have historically enjoyed. The *Topics* as a whole comprises prescriptions for the classification and analysis of a vast array of the sorts of argument then current in Greek philosophy. The intention is combative as well as constructive: Aristotle also teaches how to detect and dismember what he considers varieties of fallacious reasoning; and prime among these is ignorant or malicious exploitation of confusion in manner of predication. For example, what is good about food? That it does something – it produces pleasure. What is good about human beings? That they are 'of a certain quality, such as temperate or courageous or just' (*Topics* I.15, 107A). So, if viewed as a digest of types of predication already familiar from the practices of Greek dialectic, the categories of the *Topics* require no defence beyond reasonable fidelity to the range of predicates actually found in the typical dialectical repertoire. In particular, there need be no presumption that predicational categories rooted in philosophical practice will correspond to a significant, let alone universal, ontological classification.[9]

This is not to say that predicational and ontological categories are unrelated. Because Aristotle moves with disconcerting freedom from language to the world, he takes it for granted that predicate-expressions do usually, without the possibility of radical misrepresentation, refer to real entities. So a scheme of predicational categories might indeed suggest at least the outline of a corresponding ontological scheme, one justified in detail and scope precisely to the extent that the original classification of predicates, and its extension, are well founded. If this is the right story about how these theories developed in Aristotle, what, in particular, prompted the substitution of ontological 'substance' for predicational 'what it is'? Perhaps the governing idea of the *Categories* is that substance alone can serve as the subject in which items from other categories inhere: for instance, Socrates, but not his height, is pale-skinned, and can properly be said to be pale-skinned.[10] Therefore the design of the treatise is to convince us that at its

---

[9] Cf. 'the actual use made of the categories in the *Topics* very much suggests that the crucial distinctions are picked up one by one and that it is long experience with arguments and the analysis of fallacies which will put one into the position to produce one list of such distinctions, filled up and completed by a general consideration of what kinds of things one can say about something, to arrive at a complete list of the various kinds of things one can say about something. For there does not seem to be any one problem whose solution requires the complete list of categories, nor is there any sign of a systematical derivation of the categories, e.g. in terms of a set of formal features' (from 'Categories in Aristotle', Frede 1987, p. 47).

[10] Frede makes a related point: 'the old category of the what it is collects disparate items insofar as statements of the what it is of non-substantial items presuppose statements of the what it is of substances, and, what is worse, they presuppose statements concerning substances in the other categories. To take account of this secondary and, in a way, parasitical nature of these statements, we restrict the category of the what it is to substances' (from 'Categories in Aristotle', Frede 1987, p. 46).

deepest level ontology is marked by a crucial asymmetry between substantial and non-substantial being, quite possibly in a spirit hostile to the elevation of Platonic Forms, which so far from being most real, would figure as no more than non-substantial, parasitic things. If so, a further irony is that the *Categories* was intended to establish a metaphysical thesis essentially independent of the grand classificatory ambitions with which it came to be historically associated. In the event the philosophical tradition which, from late antiquity on, was dominated by the followers of Aristotle elevated the ontological categories into a system uniquely capable of displaying the lineaments of what is.

True, it is not as if later Aristotelians simply ignored the issue of what the categories are categories of. Because the *Categories* was incorporated into the *Organon* – which came to be the traditional logic course, culminating in the analysis of arguments – some interpreters were indeed inclined to the position that the *Categories*, which began the course, ought to deal with the simples from which propositions making up arguments are constructed, and so favoured the identification of categories with words.[11] Other strands in the tradition preferred a realist interpretation, while nevertheless asserting that a strong isomorphism obtains between the structures of the world, our concepts, and the words in which we express ourselves.[12] Still, even philosophers sensitive to the question 'what are categories categories of?' neglected the gulf which might separate our conceptual and linguistic resources from what really is. Such isomorphism is viable only if premissed on the assurance that an impersonal teleology (as in Aristotle himself) or divine providence (as in his Christian followers) secures and protects the fit between us and the world. Modern Western thinkers have lost that confidence: it remains to be seen how alien it might have appeared in the Chinese context.

But the remarkable text which emerged in that context is not a translation of Aristotle's *Categories* plain and simple. During the early seventeenth century the Jesuits of the Portuguese University of Coimbra issued a major series of commentaries on the Aristotelian corpus[13] (many of the Jesuit missionaries to China emanated from Coimbra, among them Francisco Furtado, Li Chih-tsao's co-worker). *In Universam*

---

[11] 'The order of this collection [the *Organon*] clearly suggests the view that in logic we first deal with terms, then with propositions, and finally with arguments, a view still current in modern times. And the ordering of the treatises in the collection thus suggests that the first treatise, the *Categories*, in providing us with a doctrine of categories provides us with a theory of terms. Hence a traditional tendency to regard the categories as classes of terms or expressions rather than as classes of entities' (from 'Categories in Aristotle', Frede 1987, p. 30).

[12] As we shall see, this 'isomorphic' interpretation is vividly presented in the Coimbran commentary on the *Organon*.

[13] Readers can pursue further details in *The Cambridge History of Renaissance Philosophy* (Schmitt and Skinner 1988).

Dialecticam Aristotelis, which was the work of Sebastian Couto (published 1607), contains a Latin version (by the Byzantine scholar Johannes Argyropulos)[14] of selections from the entire *Organon*, accompanied by voluminous philosophical and philological comments. Despite the vast length of the commentary, the treatment is extremely uneven: the *Topics* and *Sophistici Elenchi* are dispatched very briskly indeed, and a modern reader will be surprised to discover how relatively little attention is accorded the *Analytics*.[15] It is important to note that *In Universam Dialecticam* begins not with the *Categories*, but rather with the *Isagoge* (literally 'introduction') of Porphyry, an early Neoplatonist, which is itself a commentary on the *Categories*. Porphyry raises, without answering, a series of existential questions about categories: do they exist apart from the understanding? Are they incorporeal? Do they enjoy independence from sensible particulars? Boethius' translation of the *Isagoge* together with the *Categories* and *De Interpretatione* created the pattern which the commentarial tradition, including the Coimbran volume, would follow: Porphyry sets out the agenda of problems which Aristotle's *Categories* is understood to have settled.

Any attempt to extract the Aristotelian text from its commentarial environment would be a profound error. *In Universam Dialecticam* comes replete with overwhelmingly compendious citation of the tradition stretching from the ancient world through the Middle Ages and Renaissance to scholars active shortly before the composition of the commentary.[16] The format is: the Latin text of Aristotle, printed in a distinctive font; a chapter summary; commentary; and then an elaborate series of thematic articles, further subdivided into questions, all set off with *marginalia*. We assume very much at our peril that what Furtado communicated to Li Chih-tsao disregarded the immense armature of the commentary in favour of what we regard as authentic, if Latinised, Aristotle: Furtado gave Li a version of the tradition, with all that that entails.[17]

---

[14] Not that the work is devoid of very specific references to the original, e.g. 'in Greek it is λέγονται in the third person, as Argyropulos, Boetius and Perionius translated' (*In Universam Dialecticam*, p. 483). Elsewhere the commentary even corrects the Argyropulos rendering, e.g. 'the sense of the definition adduced is that relatives are those things, that is, entities, which are what they are, or, agreeing more closely with the Greek text, those very things they are, that is, according to their natures and essences, of other things, or are said to be related to something in another manner . . .' (p. 445).

[15] Despite what might strike us as the monumental quality of *In Universam Dialecticam*, at various junctures (e.g. p. 41, p. 50) we are advised that certain matters are glossed over as inappropriate either to the subject-matter (dialectic) or to the readers (relative beginners). But so far as I have been able to check, all such references to limitations of the discussion seem to have disappeared from the Chinese version.

[16] Although St Thomas is singled out as 'the prince of scholastic theology' (*In Universam Dialecticam*, p. 7).

[17] There is at least this difference between Aristotelian text and commentary in the Chinese: the text both falls into stylised rhythmical units of a set number of characters and on occasion employs strikingly archaistic graphs (e.g. 厥 (*chüeh*) as a demonstrative), presumably to lend Aristotle the appearance of an ancient classic. In the sequel we shall see how the 名理探 in fact synthesises the *Categories* and what the Latin commentary teaches is the correct way to read the *Categories*.

Quixotic as it may seem to us, Jesuit missionary policy as formulated by Matteo Ricci and carried forward by his immediate successors on the whole dictated that the key to converting the Chinese to Christianity lay in gaining the allegiance of the *literati*, and that the key to gaining the allegiance of the *literati* lay in intellectual collaboration.[18] At its crudest but perhaps most effective, this approach could result in Ricci's attempt to impress the emperor with the marvel of a Western chiming clock, a device beyond the ingenuity of indigenous Chinese technology. Thus one might hazard the guess that at least at one level giving the *Categories* to the Chinese is like giving them a fancy time-piece: it is simply meant to impress. But in fact the case for undertaking the translation is over-determined.[19] The *Ratio Studiorum* of the Jesuit order (1585) obliges them to promulgate Aristotelian philosophy in general and his logic in particular, and the obligation is complete in their *Constitutiones*: 'the teaching of Aristotle is to be followed in logic, natural and moral philosophy and metaphysics'.[20] Thus if the Jesuits were to teach the Chinese anything, at least in these areas, they were from the outset officially committed to starting with Aristotle. Furthermore, the logical works are referred to as the *Organon* because that means 'instrument', and philosophers with an Aristotelian background conceived of logic as an instrument for thinking: so, again, if the Chinese are to learn to think properly, they had better learn some Aristotle. *In Universam Dialecticam* explains why this logic book has been published after the other volumes in the series, physical and metaphysical:

> because in Logic, like the many-headed hydra, nearly all the difficulties are to be combatted, which are found scattered throughout philosophy in its entirety. Accordingly we erected a building neither flimsy nor without mortar, but rather attacked the difficulties one by one, as is the custom with seasoned generals, so that we could fight them at last, after they had been tried and overthrown by many blows already, with the single sword of Dialectic.[21]

---

[18] Only 'on the whole': Longobardi, for example, completely disagreed with this policy. Furthermore, such intimacy between Jesuits and *literati* was a relatively short-lived phenomenon: 'in late Ming China, an interesting group of scholars joined the Jesuits in their pattern: they were interested in science, philosophy, morality, and the knowledge of Heaven. But as the seventeenth century progressed, Chinese scholars who continued to be interested in the westerners' investigation of things were no longer interested in their way of fathoming principles, although they continued to fathom principles in a Chinese way' (Standaert 1994, p. 419). Descriptions of the Jesuit programme are to be found in Mungello 1989, Gernet 1985 and Etiemble 1988. The reader should be warned that the fate of the Chinese mission continues to excite considerable passion, and that while all three authors are well worth consulting, their accounts of both policy and implementation thereof are strictly incompatible.

[19] Wardy 1992, which is the forerunner of this book, suggests a somewhat different rationale for the translation project.

[20] *Monumenta Paedagogica Societatis Jesu*, I, p. 299.

[21] From 'To the Reader' (unpaginated). It also explains that the style of this volume is distinctive because the study of dialectic requires 'scholastic terms'.

Finally, because Roman Catholic theology is dominated by Aristotelian philosophy, educated converts could not begin to make proper sense of the teachings of the Church without an Aristotelian training.[22]

We also require information about the receiver of the message and about the translating relationship.[23] Li Chih-tsao met Ricci early, and on account of his geographical interests was excited by Ricci's famous map of the world.[24] He was also involved in the design and construction of scientific instruments, and collaborated with Ricci himself on the translation of Euclid and of Clavius' *Arithmetica*.[25] For a time at least he was in bad odour with the other Jesuits, since, while he readily accepted Roman Catholic doctrine, he was loath to give up his numerous concubines, heavy boozing and inveterate gambling, but he later fell into line, was baptised as 'Leo', and indeed became one of the so-called 'Three Pillars' of the Church in China.[26] Li took charge of Ricci's funeral, and on his return to Hangchou in 1611 he established a chapel and residence there for the missionaries, and was thus largely responsible for Hangchou's eventual rank as a great Christian centre.[27]

At this time the Imperial Board of Astronomy had miscalculated an eclipse (which actually occurred on 15 December 1610). A memorial suggested that the Westerners

---

[22] All these reasons are, at least most obviously, reasons for Furtado rather than for Li Chih-tsao. One sees without any difficulty why a thinker of his talents and predilections would have taken to the translation of mathematical, geographical or cosmological works with alacrity: but Aristotelian dialectic may well have been a different matter. One must concede the possibility that Li was told by the Jesuits that his duty was to help translate what struck him as appallingly rebarbative material. I should very much prefer to believe that he derived both pleasure and profit from his great labour on the 名理探, just as I have from perusing his translation.

[23] I rely heavily on Hummel 1943 for the details of Li's biography.

[24] Peterson's account is the best: 'Li's fascination in 1601 was with the new model of the world rather than with the geography of the countries of the world. It was not so difficult for him to accept that there were many countries not previously known in China. The world map, or, more specifically, the two-dimensional rendering of a sphere the missionaries called the earth, directly challenged the prevailing Chinese assumption that the earth was a relatively flat square under a canopy or an encapsulating heaven. This is what Ricci meant when he said that Li easily grasped what others found so difficult to believe. Li stressed in his 1623 preface that after seeing the map in 1601 he made calculations to confirm that the earth was a sphere the size Ricci said and that it was a sphere located in the midst of the great sphere of the heavens' (Peterson 1988, p. 141).

[25] Hummel writes that 'Ricci dictated several works to Li who put them into acceptable Chinese . . .' (Hummel 1943, p. 452): in the sequel we shall have occasion to question whether this standard view of the translating relationship, according to which the Chinese collaborator is very much the passive partner, should go unchallenged.

[26] 'Why was it that Li Chih-tsao was so tardy in converting? Of course his having concubines was the reason. But in February 1610 he fell ill in Beijing, and accordingly Ricci persuaded him to proceed with his baptism' (Fang Hao 1967–73, p. 116).

[27] Mungello 1994 covers the later history of the mission.

and their contacts be enlisted to help with calendar reform, Li among them. In 1613 he presented his own celebrated memorial, which enumerated achievements of Western learning unknown to the ancient Chinese. In 1621, when the Manchus were making deep incursions into China, Li was head of the Department of Waterways and Dykes in the Board of Works,[28] and he arranged for the delivery of Western artillery from Macao to Beijing to aid the military effort. The explosion of two of the four cannon in the capital resulted in the death of several people and (to put it no more strongly) occasioned renewed criticism of the Christians.

Li retired to his garden in Hangchou, where he occupied himself entirely with translation.[29] The 名理探 itself was preceded by a Chinese version of the *De Caelo et Mundo*, the 寰宇詮 (*hüan yü ch'üan, The Explanation of the World*), dated 1628 and with a preface by Li himself.[30] This preface contains a moving personal comment on the enormous challenge posed by the translation of Aristotle: 'because the language was so rarefied, thorns have come into my throat, and several times on account of difficulties I have set aside my pen'.[31] He died in 1630, and the 名理探 was published posthumously in 1631.[32]

> This Leo, besides that he was a quick and vivacious wit, had a most eager and intense desire of knowledge; by which means he did the more engage himself to an inward friendship and conversation with the *Father*, being allured thereunto by the solidity and novelty of our *Sciences*, and in particular by the delight he tooke in some maps and other curiosities; so that he could have been willing to have lived alwaies in his company. In the meane while, together with humane *Sciences*, the *Father* did instruct him in the heavenly wisdome of the *Law of God* . . .[33]

[28] Father Fang Hao transmits an amusing anecdote testifying to Li's administrative astuteness and rectitude: 'his staff calculated the tax-rate, but there was much peculation; Chih-tsao inspected the records of cases so as to rectify them according to Western mathematics; the whole lot were amazed and yielded' (Fang Hao 1967–73, p. 116). Did the Jesuits teach double-entry book-keeping as well as algebra?

[29] 'The reason why Chih-tsao excerpted and summarised in one out-of-the-way locality was that he declined social appointments, so as solely to translate books at his convenience' (*ibid.*, p. 212).

[30] The second preface to the 名理探 insists that Chinese and Western cosmology 'can easily be fused' (p. 8).

[31] 惟是文言夐絕，侯轉棘生，屢因苦難閣筆。

[32] Li and Furtado had laboured for five years, during which Li lost the vision of one eye. Li's son-in-law, the author of the second preface to the 名理探, has this to say of the co-workers: 'different seas, matching heart. If the tallies match, how could there be duplicity giving rise to obstructions?' (p. 8: a reminiscence of Lu Chiu-yuan's (twelfth century) declaration, 'the sages of the Eastern and Western Seas have the same heart and the same principle' (同心同理, *t'ung hsin t'ung li*)). I am unaware of translations of *In Universam Dialecticam* into modern European languages, so the reader without Latin must either take advantage of the Chinese, or rely on my English translations of selections from both Latin and Chinese versions.

[33] Semedo 1655, p. 240.

Geography, instrumentation, mathematics, philosophy: it is hardly an exaggeration to claim that were we to reveal Li Chih-tsao's intellectual adventures fully, we should thereby cast a very bright light on the nature of early modern contacts between China and the West.

Our final preparatory information – or rather, sadly, lack of it – concerns readership. As for Li Chih-tsao's audience and how they received his efforts, we unfortunately know nothing. The 名理探 was discreetly printed in Hangchou, presumably to avoid the dangers involved in publicly disseminating any Christian work at that time, and all my efforts to discover how many copies were printed, where they were lodged, and who might have read them, have come to nothing.

We do, however, possess two original prefaces.[34] The composition of prefaces is an ancient and very rich Chinese genre. Such works vary widely in size and substance, sometimes substantial and exact, at others purely ornamental. The prefaces to the 名理探 are allusive and mannered in the extreme, but at least they provide us with some exiguous knowledge about how sympathetic native scholars attempted to represent the translation, presumably with an eye to winning it a readership. The first and far more interesting one[35] was composed by Li T'ien-ching (李天經), a prominent official in the Calendrical Bureau and advocate of Western astronomical methods. He proclaims:

> This generation is excessively loquacious about nothings,[36] and brags about the supernatural and the exotic. Consequently knowledge is not necessarily thorough, and laws and symbols are all rejected. Recognition and understanding are completely swept aside. People hope for sudden enlightenment[37] as their authoritative teaching, and stray into exaggerated absurdities. As for their distance from truth, are they not remote indeed from its great way! The Western scholar Dr Furtado has not only explicated the world,[38] he has also expounded the ten books of the investigation of the theory of names.[39] The general purpose was that he wanted other people to be clear about this theory of reality (實之理, *shih chih li*), and he had intelligence as the means and argument (推, *t'ui*) as the ladder. When you read the gist would seem obscure, but when you savour it, the principles are all true, and it would really seem to be the great original source for investigating things and exhausting principles![40]

Li T'ien-ching is expressing entirely predictable dissatisfaction with contemporary moral degeneracy: perhaps his anti-Buddhist slurs disclose pro-Christian bias, but they

---

[34] Yet a third is to be found in the Roman copy, but it does not contribute further material pertinent to our immediate concerns.

[35] The other does stoutly maintain, however, that 'virtuous education goes straight back to Confucius and Jesus' (名理探, p. 7).

[36] An anti-Buddhist pun.   [37] Buddhist 悟 (*wu*).   [38] The *De Caelo et Mundo*.

[39] The *Categories*.   [40] 名理探, p. 3.

might well pass instead as a conservative Confucian reaction to Buddhism's other-worldly tendencies. Does he have any conception of what the function of logic ('this theory of reality') could be? The opening complaint about vain chatter might just possibly suggest that the Western antidote will help to regulate talk, but nothing in this passage demonstrates more than the vaguest acquaintance with the theories developed in the translation.

Later his claims become relatively specific:

> Understanding the theory of reality is not easy. Perfect clarity enjoys perfect blessings: this only resides in celestially blessed sages. Our class, which occupies this inferior region and is restrained by its endowment of *ch'i* (氣), is incapable of perfect clarity, but it is possible for us to understand the starting-points (端, *tuan*), and to regard this as the source from which perfect clarity arises. As for this way, but for reasoning (推論, *t'ui lun*), there is no means to progress.[41]

Here it is tempting to detect a syncretistic rationale for the study of logic. The 'celestially blessed sages' most certainly are Confucius and other Chinese culture heroes, but perhaps also include the Christian saints, who enjoy a beatific vision of the Godhead, while our benighted state in this life is surprisingly attributed not to the Fall, but rather to faulty 氣 (*ch'i*), the standard native term for the universal component of physical bodies. If this is so, then Li T'ien-ching is suggesting, casually or not, that training in argument is the royal road, or even the only path, to beatitude. This, of course, would constitute a powerful, if unacceptably heterodox, motive for pursuing dialectical studies.

Finally, we read something which seems to connect more or less directly with the traditional Western understanding of logic:

> How could those investigating theories have avoided being covered by their fallacies and errors, if they did not establish regulations on inferential discussion (推論之法, *t'ui lun chih fa*)? They were able not to confuse what was being examined. Regulation on inferential discussion is the investigation of the theory of names. If one dispenses with the investigation of the theory of names and conducts inferential discussion in some other way, one is inevitably incapable of successfully evading confusion by seeking out reality. Therefore the ancients likened the investigation of the theory of names to the sun. The sun transmits its light to the moon and stars. They rely on sunshine to produce their brightness. The investigation of the theory of names lies in the midst of the whole multitude of studies: it also spreads illumination. It causes the absence of dissension and delusion. The multitude of studies rely on it so as to return to reality. Is this function not certainly serious and great?[42]

---

[41] 名理探, p. 4. [42] *Ibid.*

'Inference' for 推論 (*t'ui lun*) is justified by its regular employment in the body of the 名理探 to mean just that, in the technical sense of the word: which is not to say that Li T'ien-ching could be conveying anything so precise to someone opening the book for the first time. When the Jesuits and their Chinese collaborators undertook joint mathematical or cartographical work, the *literati* came to the project with the benefit of a schooling in the impressive native traditions in these fields. But there is no analogue in the case of the translation of the *Categories*. The magnificent but lonely achievement of the Mohist logical canon more or less totally disappeared until interest in it revived in the nineteenth century, largely under the stimulus of exposure to Western logic and science, so neither Li Chih-tsao nor his potential audience could have had anything like a familiar context in which to place this book of logic. But it is certainly the case that educated Chinese would respond strongly to the promise that herein lies a method for the elimination of 'dissension and delusion' (舛迷, *ch'uan mi*): although they might well feel bemused on discovering that the regulations to be imparted are strictly ratiocinative, rather than ethical and political.

Collaborative translation was not a novelty for the Chinese in the late Ming and early Ch'ing. After all, their Buddhism came from just such joint exercises undertaken by missionary monks from Central Asia working with Chinese scholars on the rendering of the Buddhist scriptures. That experience stimulated considerable recognition of the dangers inherent in pressing established Chinese philosophical or religious vocabulary into use for the representation of foreign ideas, although it would seem that the Christian missionaries and their Chinese associates typically employed the relatively unsophisticated procedure of one-on-one collaboration, a far cry from the large efforts involving organised teams in which the Buddhists engaged. How was responsibility shared between the Jesuit and the Chinese scholar in the case of the 名理探? The message printed at the very beginning of the *Categories* is explicit: 'Furtado translated the meaning; Li Chih-tsao rendered it into acceptable style.'[43] It would be at least mildly disappointing were the division of labour so clear-cut. In particular, if Li's contribution were limited to stylistic correction, then we would have before us an impressively bilingual European's attempt to put Aristotle into Chinese, rather than the work of a native speaker, with an obvious consequent loss of interest so far as relativism is concerned. But surely we should not be convinced. Reports of Jesuit linguistic expertise are impressive – especially Jesuit reports thereof – but we have no *a priori* grounds for the belief that Furtado could conduct a fluent, highly technical conversation in even fumbling Chinese, while Li Chih-tsao was utterly ignorant of Latin (oral or written). Unfortunately we also lack any *a posteriori* grounds for separating the

---

[43] 傅汎際譯義李之藻達辭 (名理探, p. 289).

contributions of the two men: we have only the 名理探 itself, and must assess it purely on its merits.

What does not get translated can be fully as important as what does: only the translation of the first Coimbran volume, consisting of the *Isagoge* and the *Categories*, was published. One section of Ferdinand Verbiest's uncirculated 窮理學 (*ch'iung li hsüeh*) of 1683, entitled 理辨之五公稱 (*li pien chih wu kung ch'eng*), is in fact the 名理探 translation of the *Isagoge*, attributed, however, not to Li Chih-tsao and Furtado, but rather to Verbiest himself.[44] Another section, entitled 理推之總論 (*li t'ui chih tsung lun*), contains a fragmentary translation of the *Prior Analytics*. In his preface to the second edition (1639), Li Chih-tsao's son, Li Tsu-pin (李次霦), declares that the 名理探 comprises thirty 卷 (*chüan*), but the Jesuits' *Annual Letter* of 1637 explains that only ten were published. To complicate the picture yet further, there is a copy of *In Universam Dialecticam* preserved in the Beitang Library containing an anonymous table of correspondences between the Latin and Chinese texts; and this table includes the *Posterior* as well as the *Prior Analytics*.[45] Thus we have good reason to believe that Li Chih-tsao and Furtado produced a more or less complete Chinese *Organon*, but that only the *Isagoge* and the *Categories* went into circulation. Moreover, a very rough estimate is that no more than three-quarters of the book was put into Chinese. Some of this shortfall is simply the consequence of Chinese concision. Repetitive summaries tend to be cut,[46] and the very extensive cross-referencing of the original to works within and outside the Aristotelian corpus is lost:[47] when *In Universam Dialecticam* refers to another Aristotelian text, the Chinese has 'Aristotle says', whereas cross-references internal to the *Categories* are preserved.[48] Most, but not all, Western names are left out.[49] Not quite

---

[44] 'This, is, however, not a simple case of plagiarism. From Western sources and Verbiest's memorial presenting 窮理學 we know that he reworked texts, and more specifically, that he left out the examples directly relating to the divine law. A comparison between *li pien chih wu kung ch'eng* and *ming li t'an* reveals that this has indeed been the case: Verbiest repeatedly omits or changes sentences in which the term 天主 (*t'ien chu*) occurs' (Dudink and Standaert, n.d.: I am extremely grateful to the authors for sharing the fruits of their researches).

[45] Verhaeren 1935, pp. 426–7.

[46] This impression is corroborated by Peter Engelfriet's work on the translation of Euclid into Chinese (see Engelfriet 1993 and 1998).

[47] There is, however, a reference to the availability of a more detailed account in 超形性學 (*ch'ao hsing hsing hsüeh*) which, just as in Latin or English, is ambiguous as it stands between the field 'metaphysics' and the book *Metaphysics* (名理探, pp. 365, 370).

[48] E.g. p. 346.

[49] On the other hand, quite apart from Aristotle (frequently), Plato (e.g. pp. 1, 349, 369, 437, 439) and St Thomas (frequently), more obscure characters such as Archytas (pp. 289, 349: but with different graphs), Xenocrates (p. 349) and St Damascene (p. 369) do make it into Chinese. I can discern no obvious principle of selection at work: e.g. the list of earlier category theorists (p. 349) is randomly abbreviated.

all of the text of the *Categories* itself, as distinct from the commentary, is translated. And the losses – or changes – are far from exclusively quantitative. The Latin insists on an extremely tedious regimentation of arguments into syllogistic (occasionally, pseudo-syllogistic) form: the Chinese eliminates all such often useless formalism, instead employing sensible formulae such as 'and how does one prove that?'.[50]

In Universam Dialecticam is quite capable of scathing sarcasm. For example, in the course of elucidating Aristotle's division of substances into primary and secondary ones, it cites the view of an influential Neoplatonic commentator: 'the first opinion is that of Ammonius, who commenting on this passage denies that any division is made here, but rather a sort of enumeration of those things which are in the category of substance, as if the Philosopher is numbering substances existing in the category, like someone accustomed to count the listeners at his lecture'.[51] Doubtless we are meant to ask ourselves whether someone capable of propounding so foolish an interpretation would not have been just the type to scan his dwindling audience anxiously. The Chinese version runs: 'the first explanation says that Aristotle is not here effecting an analysis, but rather counting up how many items are located in the category of substance'.[52] This is perfectly adequate as a translation of the doctrine; but when Ammonius' name disappears, and with it the withering remark about counting heads, the register alters dramatically.[53] Again, when discussing earlier philosophers whose categories did not sum to the full ten, the Latin version states that 'the number three was missing, but Valla chose it, so as to sing among the swans'.[54] In Chinese this becomes 'Valla divided them into three.'[55] The general result is that while *In Universam Dialecticam* displays a refreshingly argumentative disrespect towards a collection of quite august authorities, the tone of the 名理探 is altogether more muted and neutral.

There is also the question of how the different versions establish contact with the student – or fail to do so. In the Latin we find a very personal, and shifting, second-person form of address. *In Universam Dialecticam*, having formulated a potential objection, may declare: 'the response should be . . .', using the impersonal *dicendum*;[56] but it might equally insist that 'in response to this objection, you will say' (using *dices*, the second-person singular future indicative), and thereby take the tractability of the reader

---

[50] 何以證之 (*ho i cheng chih*), 名理探, p. 347, translating *In Universam Dialecticam*, p. 360.

[51] *In Universam Dialecticam*, p. 391.

[52] 名理探, p. 374.

[53] Modern scholarship has reassigned the commentary on the *Categories* that went under Ammonius' name to Philoponus, so that even were the vitriol of the Coimbrans justified, it was misdirected.

[54] *In Universam Dialecticam*, p. 362.

[55] 名理探, p. 349.

[56] Instances of *dicendum, putandum, negandum*, etc. occur too frequently throughout the work to require referencing.

for granted.[57] Occasionally a statement introduced by *diximus*, 'we have said', anticipates, expounds and dismisses a potential problem. There are even formulae along the lines of 'it will occur to you to object so-and-so; but in answer we declare this; and, on reflection, you will agree'. All this gets flattened out in the Chinese: there are plenty of injunctions on the pattern of 'one should know', 當知 (*tang chih*), but the remarkable expressive range of the Latin is lost. On one occasion the Latin pairs 'you will say' with 'I respond':[58] in Chinese this is reduced to 或曰 (*huo yüeh*, 'some say') and 曰 (*yüeh*, 'one says').[59] It is not as if the Latin reader is given any great degree of intellectual liberty: on the contrary, he is constantly dictated to, coaxed, bullied and generally told not merely what he should believe, but also just why he should believe it. The contrast is not between Western freedom and Chinese constraint, but rather between quite intense scholastic engagement in perennial controversies and a certain impersonal detachment from the debate.

Another sort of omission can be detected, with regard to the extensive discussions of transubstantiation in the Latin. Such discussions are just what one would expect: the Eucharist is the most important of the sacraments, and the *Categories* is of paramount *theological* significance because it provides the conceptual scaffolding for making whatever sense can be made of transubstantiation. The *Categories* explains the metaphysical difference between substance and accident, and the official doctrine is that while the accidents of the bread and wine remain unchanged, the substance miraculously alters. Yet extensive references to the Eucharist have been excised from the Chinese translation.[60]

Why? This brings me to my final introductory point: we cannot be altogether sure what type of book the 名理探 might be. Cannibalism is, unsurprisingly, offensive to Chinese proprieties,[61] and that is what the Eucharist has always sounded like to hostile non-Christians, ancient Western pagan philosophers and late Ming Buddhists alike. So if the 名理探 is intended for circulation among learned unconverted Chinese, then the reason for the abridgement is glaringly obvious. Now if they were indeed the intended readership, then the translation must be judged a spectacular failure, although not on grounds of either inaccuracy or inconsistency: on the contrary, as we shall learn, the

---

[57] E.g. 'ad primam obiectionem negandum est . . .' ('in response to the first objection one should deny . . .') can be followed by 'ad secundam obiectionem dices . . .' ('in response to the second objection you will say . . .') (p. 397). Second-person singular imperatives also occur.

[58] 'Dices' and 'respondeo' (*In Universam Dialecticam*, p. 358).

[59] 名理探, pp. 344 and 345 (cf. p. 346).

[60] E.g. the Latin formulates two apparent objections to the comprehensiveness of the division of being into substance and accident: that the definition of 'accident' does not fit the 'accidents' of the Eucharist; and that the scheme cannot accommodate creation *ex nihilo* (*In Universam Dialecticam*, p. 340). The corresponding passage in the 名理探 excises the Eucharist objection (p. 329).

[61] Not universally offensive, however, if there is any truth in the reports that Hangchou itself once boasted eating-houses in which human flesh (whether of men or women, young or old) could be ordered.

Chinese *Categories* positively bristles with a purpose-built, forbiddingly technical vocabulary. But what this trivially entails is that the book would be little better than gibberish, at least *in extenso*, for learned Chinese unschooled in the newly created philosophical jargon.[62]

So let us assume an alternative *primary* audience: insiders, Chinese converts, who would have had the benefit of preparatory schooling covering theological and philosophical rudiments. References to the Eucharist are still repressed, since the book might well come into the hands of sympathetic yet unconverted readers, or even be seized by hostile Buddhists; in the first instance, however, the 名理探 is meant to be studied by those who will be actively helped in their reading,[63] and so might conceivably cope with the rigours of full-blown, uncompromising Aristotelian logic. This hypothesis is doubly attractive because *In Universam Dialecticam* itself is not quite a modern book. One is not supposed to be able to come to it cold and make any progress. It is to be used in the teaching of philosophy, which at that time remained very much a matter of live disputation couched in an esoteric vocabulary picked up in the schools. The Jesuits would never have assumed that anyone, Portuguese or Chinese, should be expected to acquire the conceptual equipment required for philosophy through solitary reading.

But then, if the Jesuits realised that that was the situation, why bother to translate? Realistically, the Chinese could learn to dispute successfully only with full access to the Latin tradition, only, that is, if they could, ultimately, read all the authorities for themselves and react accordingly. With this end in view, it would have been much easier

[62] But nevertheless better than sheer nonsense. In 1603 Ricci had published the 天主實義 (*t'ien chu shih i*, in Latin, the *Coeli Domini Verax Explicatio* or *De Deo Verax Disputatio*, that is, *The True Doctrine of the Lord of Heaven*): the second edition of 1607, published in Hangchou, was revised by Li Chih-tsao himself, who was responsible for various terminological and stylistic modifications (see Melis 1994, p. 66, n. 4). The 天主實義, written in the form of a dialogue between a Western *literatus* (西士, *hsi shih*) and a Chinese *literatus* (中士, *chung shih*), introduced its readership to basic Aristotelian concepts, terminology and patterns of argument; since it enjoyed very wide circulation amongst the *literati*, converts or not, we have every reason for confidence that the 名理探 would not have been met with blank incomprehension. For example, the 天主實義 briefly expounds the doctrine of the four causes (Melis 1994, pp. 72–4), although its identification of the material cause with 陰 (*yin*), the formal cause with 陽 (*yang*) is far from happy. There is also an exercise in philosophical taxonomy referring to both categories and species as 倫 (*lun*) and 類 (*lei*) respectively, thus establishing the obvious precedent for Li Chih-tsao and Furtado's rendering of these cardinal terms.

[63] This hypothesis gains plausibility when one reflects on active Jesuit involvement in the so-called 'learned conversations' which were a mainstay of *literatus* society: 'operationally, Ricci and his confrères proceeded with the work of proselytization by cultivating individuals or small groups of *literati* with learned conversations and discussions rather than by public preaching. The latter would all too easily attract unfavourable attention or lead to breaches of the public peace in the late Ming milieu, while learned conversations were an accepted part of *literati* culture and of the philosophical tradition' (Luk 1988, p. 174; cf. Holzman 1956).

– if still fantastically difficult – just to teach them Latin and have done with it. (Perhaps, however, the obstacles to Chinese Latinity, even from the most visionary perspective, were far more formidable than I am allowing.[64]) To exaggerate for the sake of a neat formula, the dilemma is that the 名理探 appears to be either trivially incomprehensible or well-done but partially ill-motivated. Of course, it might be that the translation was an unstable compromise between various complex and not entirely compatible motives.

'The China Syndrome' discussed Angus Graham's contention that forcing Indo-European words and concepts for being, *esse* or εἶναι, into Chinese, at best produces bad Chinese, un-Chinese Chinese.[65] Evidently the 名理探 had very little impact on Chinese culture. But when translations are influential – for example the translation of Greek philosophy into Latin, the Bible into the Greek Septuagint or the English King James version, or indeed Shakespeare into German – they are quite capable of profoundly changing the languages into which they are put.[66] People all too unreflectingly conceive of the language into which the translation is made as a fixed system to which the alien matter must conform, if it is to earn acceptance. On the contrary, the act of translation can effect a real transformation of the target language. I am not insisting that this was the case with the 名理探, even with regard to the esoteric discourse of the tiny community of Jesuit and *literatus* making their way together through the intricacies of the *Organon*; but I do insist that their work does not deserve automatic dismissal as an awkward novelty.

2 What's in a name?

The preface to *In Universam Dialecticam* begins with a passage on the discovery of the arts which, although not translated into Chinese, indicates what the – or, less rashly, a – Jesuit attitude to foreign cultures might have been. The arts in general are under

---

[64] Not that an impressive institutional base was lacking in Li Chih-tsao's native city: 'the Church of the Savior was part of a Christian college or complex of buildings that included a seminary, a dormitory, a library, and a separate chapel for women called the Church of the Blessed Virgin. In 1624 Hangchou was chosen for establishing a seminary because of its central location in China. The seminary continued to function for approximately seventy years, from the time of Fr. Aleni to the death of Fr. Intorcetta in 1696' (Mungello 1994, p. 34).

[65] See p. 5 above.

[66] Cf. 'the import, of meaning and of form, the embodiment, is not made in or into a vacuum. The native semantic field is already extant and crowded. There are innumerable shadings of assimilation and placement of the newly-acquired, ranging from a complete domestication, an at-homeness at the core of the kind which cultural history ascribes to, say, Luther's Bible or North's Plutarch, all the way to the permanent strangeness and marginality of an artefact such as Nabokov's "English-language" *Onegin*. But whatever the degree of "naturalisation", the act of importation can potentially dislocate or relocate the whole of the native structure' (Steiner 1992, pp. 314–15).

consideration because, as will become clear, both dialectic's standing as an expertise and its relation to other technical fields are problematic: their discussion will introduce a plethora of knotty methodological issues new to the Chinese but debated in the West almost from the inception of Greek philosophy.

In the West there is a venerable literary *topos* of 'the first discoverer', which assigns an inventor, human or divine, legendary or (semi-) historical, to cultural acquisitions ranging from cookery to philosophy.[67] Since this genre was originally Greek, it is not entirely surprising to find that Greek names tend to predominate in most of the ancient lists of 'first discoverers'. But under the influence of the Renaissance vogue for 'wise barbarians', the Coimbran commentators resist any such bias. Despite Greek pretension to 'the name and fame of wisdom as if it were their own property',[68] the Babylonians take precedence by many centuries, and some of the sages claimed by the Greeks as their own were in fact 'barbarians' (i.e., in an unpejorative sense, not Greek: Thales was Phoenician, Mercury, Egyptian). 'Just as in other matters, so in this as well Epicurus raved, when he said that no one is capable of philosophising unless he is Greek.'[69] Accordingly no reason is so much as suggested to fear that the prospects for doing philosophy in Chinese are poor.

However, the sequel establishes that no human nation, Eastern or Western, really deserves to be awarded prizes for cultural innovation: 'if we wish to be fair judges of things, we shall state that the arts were first discovered by neither the Greeks nor the barbarians, but that their origin was far more ancient and noble'.[70] It was not fitting for 'the first members and authors' of the great human family to receive an empty soul, as it were a *tabula nuda*, like ours: instead God equipped Adam and Eve with 'clear cognition of things not only divine, but also human and natural', so that the stream of learning 'flowed from God as from the primal font' through Adam and his children to all the nations of the earth. 'Hence the Assyrian and Persian magi, the Egyptian priests, the Bactrian Shamans, the Indian Brahmans and Gymnosophistae, the Druids of the Gauls, the sages of the Greeks, the doctors of the Latins, and others, heaped with special praise for science, flourished.'[71]

---

[67] Since the Chinese have a parallel *topos* (to select one of myriad examples, Shen-nung, the inventor of agriculture), the passage cannot have remained untranslated on account of any intrinsic strangeness: often there simply seems no accounting for omissions in the 名理探.

[68] *In Universam Dialecticam*, p. 1.

[69] *Ibid.*; cf. 'Epicurus contrariwise supposes that only Greeks are capable of philosophising' (Clement of Alexandria, *Stromateis* I.15); and according to Epicurus 'a wise man could not come to be from either every bodily constitution or among every people' (Diogenes Laertius X.117: both texts are in Usener 1887, fr. 226).

[70] *In Universam Dialecticam*, p. 1.   [71] *Ibid.*, p. 2.

It is of course a great pity that the Chinese here fall anonymously under 'and others'. However, the fact that the Jews are also missing should remind us that this sort of list is itself an updated ancient *topos*, so that the same characters will tend to recur: hence, perhaps, the exclusion of the Chinese, since India and Gaul were once perceived as the true limits of the world. But what follows – an objection and a response to it – is at least suggestive: one might be tempted to reject 'this almost hereditary transmission of the sciences from the first origins of the world'[72] because the *topos* of 'the first discoverer' is so well entrenched, and thus unlikely to be simply false. The answer is that since many arts were either seriously injured or indeed nearly extinguished with the passage of time, and through human laziness, many notable figures who mended the damage are wrongly celebrated as the inventors, rather than the repairers, of the arts.[73] Thus Zeno, who is remembered as the founder of dialectic, in fact restored a discipline of divine origin, our common birthright as the descendants of Adam. Not that the Coimbrans are unwilling to concede that certain auxiliary improvements are genuine later discoveries: 'should we also wish to speak of those arts which are employed in manufacture in the last stages of the work, it is well known that not a few previously completely unknown have been discovered by later ages, such as copper-printing and that which introduced gun-powder'.[74] Although the extent of early modern European recognition of borrowings from the East remains unclear, there must be a tolerable chance that a reference to the Chinese lurks close to the surface here (although one should admit that the mention of a later time rather than another place perhaps implies invention rather than importation).

A Coimbran reader might therefore extrapolate from this story to the hypothesis that access to the 名理探 could help restore the Chinese nation to some fragmentary portion of our *shared* Prelapsarian heritage of comprehensive wisdom. If the Chinese are intellectually unfortunate, this is due not to any innate logical inferiority, but rather to the geographical accident of Zeno's coming from Elea rather than, say, the state of Lu (just as they are not to be blamed if the Gospel message only penetrated the Far East 1,600 years after its enunciation in Palestine). If on a first reading Aristotle strikes them as a startling novelty, that is only because no equivalent Chinese thinker repaired their remnant of Adamic logic: but surely our common descent from those who enjoyed the

---

[72] *Ibid.*

[73] Some of this material is later inserted into the translation: 'the arts of the first men were not acquired gradually: God produced and bestowed them. They were perfectly good and without defect.' But they were injured in transmission, 'whereupon there were many capable scholars who created new arts so as to repair them. They themselves regarded them as new, and did not know that they were all possessed in the beginning' (名理探, p. 10).

[74] *In Universam Dialecticam*, p. 2.

gift of a pristine rational discipline ensures that they will eventually come to see dialectical training as anything but a foreign imposition.

The preface to the 名理探 begins in a very different fashion:

> In the West the study which loves knowledge is called 'philosophy': it is actually
> the general name of all studies which investigate principles. The translation of the
> name is 'addiction to knowledge'. The translation of the meaning is 'knowledge'.
> Of old there was a king of a country who enquired of a great sage: 'I have previ-
> ously heard that your knowledge is profound, but I do not know what to call the
> study you are profound in.' He replied: 'I am incapable of knowing: I just love to
> know . . . Therefore not venturing to use the name "knowledge" I have selected
> the name next in order, "loving knowledge".'[75]

This arresting introduction has no exact correspondence with the Latin, but might
plausibly be linked to a later passage:

> φιλοσοφία thus means the same in Greek as the Latin 'love of wisdom'. And
> φιλόσοφος means the same as 'lover of wisdom', by which descriptions some
> have defined philosophy and philosopher; but they are interpretations of the
> words, rather than definitions of the subjects. For philosophy regards the intellect,
> not the will, and those who are now called Philosophers by the word invented by
> Pythagoras previously used to be called σοφοί, that is, wise men; and what is now
> called φιλοσοφία was previously called σοφία, that is, wisdom. But wisdom, as
> the dignity of the name precisely conveys, is perfect cognition of things, which is
> judged perfect when it introspects both a thing and its cause.[76]

How might a Chinese scholar previously unacquainted with 'philosophy' react to
this description of 愛知學 (*ai chih hsüeh*)?[77] As remains common Chinese translational
practice to this day, the phrase is a calque, and especially on first reading would retain its
full semantic value, 'the study which loves knowledge'. But is such love not characteristic of all disciplines? Perhaps the assertion that any exploration of *principles* is 'philosophical' saves the term from vapidity, since 理 (*li*, 'principle'), if hugely polyvalent, at
least narrows 'philosophy' down to some type of fundamental investigation. The dual
scheme of translating 'name' and 'meaning' is a routine procedure in the 名理探 when

---

[75] 愛知學者。西云斐錄瑣費亞 [= *philosophia*]。乃窮理諸學之總名。譯名。則知之嗜。譯義。則
言知也。古有國王問於大賢人曰。汝深於知。吾夙聞之。不知何稱之學為深。對曰。余非能知。
惟愛知耳…古不敢用知者之名。而第取愛知為名也 (名理探, p. 1).

[76] *In Universam Dialecticam*, p. 39; the 名理探 also has an abbreviated version of this passage at the corresponding point in the Chinese (p. 16). A number of other Jesuit writings had already introduced
'philosophia', e.g. Giulio Aleni's 西學凡 (*Hsi hsüeh fan*) of 1623, which includes a short discussion of
the subject-matter of Western logic.

[77] The glossary of technical terms collects an illustrative sample of the Chinese rendering of the Latin's
specialised philosophical vocabulary.

rendering notable and unusual Latin phraseology: the nominal translation is intended to be what we would call 'literal', while the translation of the meaning is supposed accurately to convey the original signification. But employment of the scheme here creates a problem, since identification of philosophy with 知 (*chih*), 'knowledge', is strictly inconsistent with the import of the following anecdote, which evidently exemplifies 'philosophy' as literally and truly addiction to *unpossessed* knowledge. So is there more in the name 'philosophy' than Li – or, indeed, Furtado – understood? Is the epigraph to chapter 2, which insists that philosophy's 'very name refuses to be translated into foreign speech', thus vindicated? A decision on this matter has a bearing on whether the conception of 'philosophy' presented by the 名理探 recommends a practice capable of mounting a legitimate challenge to received ideas. Chinese history does of course teem with self-proclaimed experts anxious to redeem the empire; what are missing are knowledge-addicts threatening to undermine conventional beliefs and mores just because their enquiries are inconclusive and open-ended (Chuang-tzu, of course, does undermine convention, but cannot plausibly be represented as addicted to 'knowledge' in any obvious sense).

Inspection of the Latin passage reveals that if the Chinese signals are confused, that is not the result of the manifest untranslatability of 'philosophy', whether through narrowly linguistic or broadly cultural factors. The comment that describing philosophy in terms of love of wisdom is mere verbal interpretation, rather than 'definition of the subject', is reminiscent of the Chinese division between translations of the name and of meaning; and locating philosophy in a wisdom which is 'perfect cognition of things' amply justifies the suggestion that what 'philosophy' really means is 知 (*chih*). However, the beginning of the 名理探 both omits the vital detail that cognition is perfect 'when it introspects both a thing and its cause' and excises the Latin objection to the etymological account of 'philosophy' that desire, whether for knowledge or anything else, pertains to the will, while philosophy belongs to the intellect. The later matching Chinese passage (名理探, p. 16) will state that philosophical knowledge is aetiological, but is still missing the objection to the mention of desire in the explanation of 'philosophy'. What this means is that, if anything, confusion in the translated signals is fruitful: it remains easier for the Chinese reader to focus on the anecdote and keep alive the possibility that knowledge-addicts love what is not (yet?) within their grasp.

The anecdote is fascinating on a number of counts. First, the anonymous sage's denial that he is capable of knowledge helps us to identify its ultimate source. Some Western traditions view the philosopher as an aspirant to wisdom without concluding that such knowledge will necessarily remain permanently inaccessible: but the Chinese says that the philosopher cannot know. That denial puts us in mind of Pythagoras. *In Universam Dialecticam* suggests that Pythagoras' imposition of the names 'philosophy'/'philosophers' (φιλοσοφία/φιλόσοφοι) on what had been called 'wisdom'/'wise men' (σοφία/σοφοί) was little more than a temporary *linguistic* aberration leaving the underlying reality of 'perfect cognition' unaffected. The allusion is to Diogenes Laertius' famous account of Pythagoras' contribution to the development of philosophy. The doxographer claims that the first person who employed the term 'philosophy' and designated himself a 'philosopher' was Pythagoras, on the grounds that god alone is wise; but it quickly happened that philosophy (φιλοσοφία) came to be called 'wisdom' (σοφία), and only the learner was a 'philosopher' (D.L. I.12). The historical veracity of this account is of no importance to us: what does matter is that it retails Pythagoras' original denial of wisdom and the admission that the denial was temporary, but does not substantiate the innuendo that Pythagoras left a permanent *status quo* untouched.[78]

Second, Pythagoras is not represented in Diogenes Laertius as coining 'philosophy' in response to questions from a king. But elsewhere Diogenes recounts another anecdote, according to which Pythagoras likened life to a festival where the best sort attend as spectators: thus philosophers, the most privileged of human beings, are hunters after the spectacle of the truth (D.L. VIII.8; it is not said in so many words that philosophers do not know, but their ignorance might be implicit in the claim that they *hunt* the truth). Furthermore, the anecdote has it that Pythagoras produced his comparison in response to Leon, the tyrant of Phlius, who had asked him who he was. (Pythagoras is also talking to Leon in D.L. I.12, but the topic of conversation remains unspecified; only in VIII.8 is he asked to identify himself.) However, there is a parallel doxography preserved in the fifth book of Cicero's *Tusculan Disputations* which, on the authority of Heraclides Ponticus, relates a version of the question and answer much closer to what we find in the 名理探: 'and Leon after wondering at his talent and eloquence asked him to name the art in which he put most reliance; but Pythagoras said that for his part he had no acquaintance with any art, but was a philosopher'.[79] It would seem that the 名理探 has fused Diogenes Laertius with the *Tusculan Disputations* to create its own unique synthesis.[80]

---

[78] At least some aspects of Platonic thought preserved a heavily modified version of the Pythagorean idea and transmitted it to later philosophical traditions (if, that is, the idea is indeed Pythagorean, rather than an invention of the fourth-century Platonist Heraclides Ponticus). *Republic* 475B–C emphasises the true philosopher's insatiable appetite for all learning: and, of course, one only learns what is not yet known. More closely connected to Pythagoras is *Symposium* 204A–B, which teaches that none of the wise philosophise, since the philosopher desires to *become* wise.

[79] 'Cuius ingenium et eloquentiam cum admiratus esset Leon, quaesivisse ex eo qua maxime arte confideret; at illum artem quidem se scire nullam, sed esse philosophum' (*Tusculan Disputations* V.8). Pythagoras duly proceeds to compare life to a festival to explain who the 'philosophers' are.

[80] Since the Chinese anecdote is not in Latin, three possibilities for its manufacture present themselves: either Furtado brought along copies of Diogenes, of Cicero, or of both; or he more or less vaguely

The West does not lack its own literary *topos* of the encounter between enquiring ruler and questioned sage. But a typical feature of such stories is that the frequently despotic ruler is shown up, if not rudely rebuffed, by the fiercely independent philosopher (for example accounts of Diogenes the Cynic's withering replies to Alexander the Great – a personage shortly to appear in the pages of the 名理探). Thus what is arresting in the Chinese anecdote concocted by Li and Furtado is that it subscribes to a Chinese literary convention instantly familiar to any reader of Mencius: king enquires of sage. The etymological analysis of 'philosophy' has been partially domesticated. Chinese readers encountering here their own *topos* would also presumably infer that the 'philosophical' sages of the West must have *something* of practical, political benefit to impart to the receptive ruler. Much Western philosophy has traditionally promised just that, but relatively few – and certainly not Aristotelians – have professed to enhance government by the direct, let alone exclusive, application of dialectic – which is all the 名理探 has to offer.

From 'philosophy' to the Philosopher: the 名理探 furnishes a potted biography of Aristotle once again absent from the Latin.

> Aristotle's (亞利, *ya li*) reputation spread throughout the world. King Philip invited him to act as tutor (師, *shih*) to the heir-apparent Alexander. The king often declared that 'God uses the heir-apparent to favour me: His grace is great! And he uses Aristotle's being the heir-apparent's tutor to favour me: this grace is outstandingly great!' Alexander was profoundly affected by Aristotle's teaching. He often said: 'I love Aristotle like my father. For my father gave me life, but Aristotle gave me justice and principles to live with.'[81] Stagira was Aristotle's birthplace; its walls had succumbed to disasters and were in ruins. When Alexander had been established as king, he renewed them for Aristotle's sake: they were made even stronger than they had been.[82]

What impression would this *curriculum vitae* make on the Chinese? Aristotle's successful relations with powerful rulers (although it would be hard to pass Alexander off as 'the conqueror of the known world' to this audience) and the pious restoration of his birthplace would be easily recognised as a canonical portrait of the worthy sage; and, if

---

remembered books he almost inevitably would have read in the course of his education; or the story was lifted directly from another Coimbran volume (*In Universam Dialecticam* (p. 39) mentions that the preface to the *Physics* commentary – which I have not been able to examine – deals in depth with the nature of philosophy). In the present state of uncertainty over which Western books were conveyed to China, when they arrived, and who might have had access to them, we cannot speculate any further.

[81] 亞利。與我以義理而生也。

[82] 名理探, pp. 1–2. Düring 1957 demonstrates that the Stagira story is found throughout the various strands of Aristotelian biography, but I have found no exact parallels for the sayings attributed to Philip and Alexander (the closest is Plutarch's *Life of Alexander*).

in Alexander one can be made to see a Western imperial unifier, in this respect Aristotle does very much better than Confucius himself, who consistently failed to win a permanent position of political influence.[83] Since Alexander's expression of gratitude speaks of 'justice and principles', a Chinese *literatus* would also feel reassured that Aristotle must preach a moralistic doctrine much more closely akin to orthodox Confucianism than cold-blooded Legalist advice on the efficient maintenance of power.

> King Alexander himself having already received education in ethics and politics,[84] desired to investigate the nature of the myriad things,[85] and dispatched a number of men to travel all over the world. They enquired after rare and unusual kinds (類, *lei*) of plants, trees, birds and animals . . . Aristotle availed himself of this all the more to exhaust the knowledge of the natures of living things and animals and explain them. He was inseparable from the king.[86]

Is it desirable for a ruler to pass beyond the indispensable attainments of ethics and politics to a preoccupation with natural science? The research into exotic flora and fauna conducted under Alexander's patronage would again seem familiar, in the light of the encyclopaedic projects supported under many Chinese regimes. But by the same token, involvement in botany and zoology would be unlikely to count as top-flight scholarly activity: the biography's recurrent attribution to Aristotle of the highest political success combined with thoroughgoing empiricist commitments might well have struck an odd note.

> Aristotle then went to the great city Athens, where he established a school. He lived there for thirty years. The high scholars of the entire state received his instruction.[87]

Nearly all Western biographies of Aristotle emphasise his precarious status as a 'metic', a resident alien debarred from participation in the political life of the city, lacking the privileges of a citizen, and vulnerable to attack as a foreigner; and, in Aristotle's case, these disadvantages were exacerbated by his intimacy with the Macedonian regime. Nearly all of them also quote the words he is said to have uttered on the occasion of the Athenian rebellion against the occupying power, that he thought it prudent to withdraw from the city 'lest Athens sin a second time against philosophy' (adding his death to Socrates'). No such unsavoury stuff is permitted into the Chinese. In fact

---

[83] The Chinese reader is subsequently assured that 'later kings desired even more to benefit the world with his education, and spread Aristotle's teaching abroad' (名理探, p. 2: in the West it was in fact widely acknowledged that numerous statesmen emanated from the Lyceum, Aristotle's school).

[84] 修身理國之教 (*hsiu shen li kuo chih chiao*).

[85] Cf. Pliny the Elder, *Natural History* VIII.44, where Alexander, said to be ambitious 'to know the natures of animals', dispatches collectors far and wide.

[86] 名理探, p. 2.   [87] 一國高士皆受其訓。

Aristotle's school, the Lyceum, was a private institution, tolerated but in no manner endorsed by the public authorities. But the assertion that he trained 'high scholars', 高士 (*kao shih*), encourages the impression that Aristotle had charge of advanced, official education, and himself doubtless held an exalted position: Chinese readers would never suspect that in the ancient West there had existed numerous polities jealously guarding their autonomy and excluding from the citizenship all but their 'own'. Although both Li Chih-tsao and Furtado would have been all too aware of the pressing need to cultivate the powers that be, they were not, after all, translating Aristotle's *Politics* (although their colleague Vagnoni was: the Jesuits' unrealised ambition was to translate the entire Coimbran canon). Thus there is every reason to suspect that neither the Chinese translator nor his prospective readership would possess more than a remote analogue to the very concept of 'citizen' which shapes traditional Western philosophical biography (not that one should assume too confidently that a seventeenth-century Jesuit would be alive to the original repercussions of 'citizenship' either). Aristotle has been transformed from an ambivalent intellectual outsider to a paragon of the thriving scholar-official.

> Afterwards he desired to investigate deeply the names and principles of the world. He emigrated to Chalcis in Euboea and lived on for a few more years. The tide of the Euripan sea advances and recedes seven times daily.[88] Aristotle wanted to investigate the reason; he strove to investigate and ponder. For years he did not become weary, but in old age he contracted an illness. When it was about to reach its crisis he still prayed very earnestly to the Creator: 'the very first reason for things being as they are – take pity and tell me!'.[89] Then he died.[90]

The 名理探 ascribes Aristotle's emigration from Athens to his inveterate curiosity about natural phenomena. Several ancient Western biographies tesify to the legend of Aristotle's overwhelming interest in the Euripus,[91] but they all go on to speak of his

---

[88] Aristotle himself does not give an exact number, but does refer explicitly to the tides' changing direction (*Meteorologica* II.8, 366ª23); it is clear from the *Nicomachean Ethics* (IX.6, 1167b6–7) that the Euripus was proverbial for its inconstancy.

[89] 萬所以然之最初所以然。幸憐而啟我。   [90] 名理探, p. 2.

[91] Collected in section 48 ('Hellenistic Fabrications') of Düring 1957. Cf. Chroust, from the chapter entitled 'The Myth of Aristotle's Suicide': '*Il Vita Aristotelis Syriaca* maintains that "Aristotle withdrew to Chalcis on Euboea and there ended his life watching (studying) the ebb and flow of the Euripus." Similarly, the *Vita Aristotelis Arabica* of Al-Mubashir narrates that Aristotle "withdrew to Chalcidice [should read, Chalcis] . . . in order to study the ebb and flow of the gulf [should read, straits] of the Euripus close to Euboea, and in order to write a book about this phenomenon." It is possible, indeed, that during the last year of his life, that is, when he was sixty-one or sixty-two years old, Aristotle was still interested in, and preoccupied with, scientific studies and investigations . . . What is disturbing in this account, however, is the fact that this particular tradition, which credits Aristotle with having studied the tides of the Euripus shortly before his death, is apparently of a fairly late date, late enough to be possibly classified as a piece of Hellenistic fabrication' (Chroust 1973, pp. 177–8).

chagrined death – usually self-inflicted – brought on by failure to crack the problem.[92] The Chinese text[93] does not altogether rule out the possibility that Aristotle was striving all that time to solve the riddle of the tides, but nor does it demand such a reading; and it is difficult to square the deathbed cry to God for 'the very *first* reason' with an exclusive absorption in the Euripus. But perhaps the train of thought is that Aristotle's failure to account for the tides, despite his prolonged researches, brings home to him his intellectual limitations, so that *in extremis* he throws himself on divine mercy for enlightenment.[94]

In truth Aristotle's god, the Prime Mover, is neither a creator nor a supernatural being to whom one prays for help, even for philosophical illumination. (One does, however, pray to the Neoplatonic One and to Mind: which is why Christianity needed Neoplatonic help in absorbing Aristotle.) Therefore this final anecdote presents Aristotle, 亞利, to the Chinese as a type of saintly quasi-Christian magus – who nevertheless achieved analytical supremacy:

> Of the natures of many things and the principles of many natures, there were none which he did not thoroughly analyse. The teaching he established necessarily delivers transparent meanings and principles of names.[95] He would wait for scholars of towering ability who love learning to go over what is unclear and difficult to interpret. He would tell the obtuse and idle to specialise in some other branch of learning, and did not want them to waste his time.[96]

Despite its profundity, Aristotle's 'transparent' teaching must be easy to understand. What need, then, for exceptional scholars fitted for the task of exegesis? At this juncture the contrast with the original text is very telling. The Latin freely concedes that

---

[92] See Düring 1957, p. 347. Chroust records that 'this particular account, which by no means is above suspicion, also records that Aristotle was unable to solve this problem and, in a fit of despondency over his failure, either took his own life or died of a "broken heart" ' (Chroust 1973, p. 178: he provides references to Justin Martyr, *Cohortatio ad Graecos* 34B (Migne VI.305); Gregory of Nazianzus, *Oratio* IV.72 (Migne XXXV.597); and Procopius VIII.6.20). His concluding remark is most judicious: 'it may be well to remember that Greek tradition abounds with stories of wise men and philosophers either deteriorating physically or ending their own lives after having experienced some unsupportable personal chagrin' (p. 178).

[93] 經年不倦。老而有疾。

[94] In some Western versions Aristotle despairingly throws himself *into* the sea: 'mediaeval authors seem to know that Aristotle drowned himself in the Euripus exclaiming: "quia non possum capere te, capias me" ["since I can't take you, take me"), or "quoniam Aristoteles Euripum minime cepit, Aristotelem Euripus habeat" ["since Aristotle entirely failed to capture the Euripus, let the Euripus have Aristotle"]. This would indicate that the story of Aristotle's alleged suicide persisted into the Middle Ages' (Chroust 1973, p. 386, n. 8). The 名理探 prayer might risk offending Chinese sensibilities, as it does mine. I have not encountered it elsewhere. It is obviously a bizarre variation on the standard Euripus anecdotes; but I do not know whether it originated in one of the plentiful mediaeval Alexander romances recounting episodes from his tutor's life, or was fabricated by Li and Furtado.

[95] 物物之性。性性之理。無不備解。其設教。必務透名義理。   [96] 名理探, p. 2.

Aristotle is a deeply obscure writer, but insists that the impenetrability of his works is a deliberate effect. He endorsed older reasons for concealment, the wish to defend philosophical *esoterica* from vulgar contempt and to ward off the dim-witted (distantly echoed in the Chinese Aristotle's rejection of 'the obtuse and idle'?); 'as a result he followed Hippocratic brevity in the terse and concise Acroamatic style'.[97] The Coimbran book makes an ingenious, if implausible, addition: 'sometimes also he argues the more obscurely the more difficult the controversies are, since, because it is not sufficiently clear on which side the truth stands, as it would be to a skilled and insightful intellect, he would take pains to wrap his own opinion in verbal confusion'.[98] So much for the oriental Aristotle left puzzling about 'the very first reason for things being as they are', let alone about the tides. Perhaps the Chinese translation falters badly here through mere inadvertence. Or perhaps, because the 名理探, unlike the Latin, now makes a direct transition to the topic of dialectic, it decides to forgo the valiant rationale of motivated obscurity and bring Aristotle's practice into line with his theory of lucid discussion:

> Because human knowledge and strength have limits, Aristotle first wrote this book to introduce men to the clarification of the understanding. He has distinguished right/true and wrong/false, and banished all deluded error so that we might return to the road of unique correctness: it is called 'logic'. This speaks of inferential discussion and the principles of names. Its great purpose lies in inferential progression . . .[99]

I have rendered 是 (*shih*) as 'right/true', 非 (*fei*) as 'wrong/false', to alert English readers to the fact that while both these extremely common graphs occur with either meaning, the ethical sense is uppermost, and often a choice between them is difficult, or even ill-advised. Of course context does frequently dictate that one sense should be adopted to the exclusion of the other; and one might have thought that a dialectical context, where 'logic' will shortly be distinguished from 'ethics', is doubtless one in which 是 (*shih*) is precisely equivalent to 'true', and 非 (*fei*) to 'false'. And surely the statement that logic is predominantly concerned with inference clinches the case, since the 'great purpose' of formal logic from its Aristotelian beginnings has been to isolate those patterns of reasoning which will always lead from *true* premises to a *true* conclusion, never to a falsehood. Traditional logic specifies the further condition that the inferences studied by the dialectician should ideally make real contributions to knowledge by generating new truths: dialectic conveys the reason 'for declaring the unknown on the basis of things which are known'.[100]

---

[97] *In Universam Dialecticam*, p. 7.   [98] *Ibid.*, pp. 7–8.

[99] 亞利因人識力有限。首作此書。引人開通明悟。辨是與非。辟諸迷謬。以歸一真之路。名曰絡日伽 [*logica*]。此云推論名理。大旨在於推通 (名理探, p. 2).

[100] *In Universam Dialecticam*, p. 17.

Nevertheless one should place no confidence in this line of thought, since it overlooks how unprepared for such cues the new Chinese reader would be on encountering this passage so early in the introduction. I have translated 推論 (*t'ui lun*) and 推通 (*t'ui t'ung*) as 'inferential discussion' and 'inferential progression' respectively because that is what they will come to mean in the 名理探, because Li and Furtado employ them consistently to render *illatio* and other Latin terms for 'inference'; but this usage will become (slightly) clearer to the Chinese dialectical novice only when he has won through to the end of the translation. At this point he would assuredly assume that the Western sage 亞利, like the great figures in his native tradition, distinguishes 是(*shih*) from 非(*fei*) to make the world right (again): and how could that salvation reside in rules of reason alone? The lofty phrase 'the road of unique correctness' trumpets the very Chinese idea of a return to ancient rectitude (albeit in combination with the very un-Chinese idea that such rectitude is to be found only in the Catholic faith): the shock, immediate for us, delayed for the perceptive Chinese reader, is the nonchalant explanation that 'it is called "logic"'.

3 Disputation, discrimination, inference

Since the introduction intends to convince us of dialectic's importance in the general scheme of the sciences, it goes on to establish that logic plays a unique rôle as an instrumental art. As a preliminary, 'art', itself a term of art, is defined for us: 'an art involves much habituation; its goal is necessarily correct; it is necessarily unified; and it necessarily brings about benefit to men'.[101] Assessment of this definition requires consideration of some Latin glosses left untranslated. First, 'involves much habituation' renders 'is a collection of many comprehensions'; and 'comprehensions' is expanded into '*intellectual habits which are not erroneous*'.[102] Second, 'it is necessarily unified' comes from 'de una re', 'of one thing', it being explained that an authentic art can be no mere random assemblage of habits or propositions, but must derive its integrity from the objective unity of the art's field of study or operation.[103] Third, 'it necessarily brings about benefit to men' translates 'with some end useful to life'. The Latin provides two explanations. First, maleficent arts such as magic are to be excluded;[104] but second, and far more importantly, one should understand this clause in a relaxed sense embracing purely speculative sciences, which are initially said to have *no* potential utility.[105] However, 'the good could without incongruity be called useful in the proper and specific sense, which is brought

---

[101] 藝也者。括有多許習熟。其所向。必真。必一。必致益於人者也 (名理探, p. 3, corresponding to *In Universam Dialecticam*, p. 11).

[102] *In Universam Dialecticam*, p. 12, my italics.   [103] *Ibid.*, pp. 12–13.   [104] *Ibid.*, p. 13.

[105] *Ibid.*, pp. 11–12.

about by the speculative sciences, namely the perfection of the mind and its rescue from error and ignorance'.[106] Hence the Chinese are being introduced to something whose claims to utility are painstakingly hedged about in the original – but not in the translation. The loss of qualifications is all the more noteworthy when one remembers that the 名理探 is providing an introduction for its *Categories*, whose 'benefit to men' is anything but practical. Will Jesuit, Christian *literatus* and Chinese reader assume all too rapidly that however else their vocabularies might differ, at least they must share a universal concept of utility?

The arts can be divided on the basis of their subject-matter into those concerning real objects or states of affairs and those occupied with discourse; and the latter then split into grammar, rhetoric and 'the art of discrimination/disputation: in the West it is called "logic"'.[107] 辨 (*pien*) means 'to tell apart, to distinguish, to discriminate', and is cognate with 辯 (*pien*), 'to argue, to dispute': I have provided alternative English renderings because although the 名理探 prints the discriminatory 辨 (*pien*), the graphs are readily interchangeable, and in a logical translation we should not happily relinquish the argumentative 辯 (*pien*).[108]

As in the previous instance, here too there is a significant absence. The Latin further subdivides the arts of discourse into the 'external, by means of which we speak with others and communicate the senses of the soul, and internal, by means of which the mind itself reasons by itself'.[109] With this passage omitted, the Chinese are left unaware

---

[106] *Ibid.*, p. 12.

[107] 三曰辨藝。西云絡日伽 [*logica*] (名理探, p. 6). The elaborate classification of branches of knowledge presented by the 名理探 was at least partially anticipated by Aleni's 西學凡 (*Hsi hsüeh fan*, 'A Summary of Western Learning') of 1623, where the dialectical subdivision of philosophy is designated as 明辯之道 (*ming pien chih tao*, 'the method of clear disputation'). See Luk 1997 for a helpful study of the 西學凡.

[108] I have already remarked on the suggestive difference in register between original and translation: the stock formulae of *In Universam Dialecticam* are considerably more pugnacious than their Chinese analogues (see pp. 84–5 above). In his preface to Aleni's 西學凡 (*Hsi hsüeh fan*), Yang Ting-yün (楊廷筠) reflects on the emphasis which Western learning places on 'disputation' (辯, *pien*) and refutation (駁, *po*), and concludes that 'while Chinese prefer flattering words and consider refutation as shame or a great difficulty, Westerners dispute and refute continuously and do not appreciate blind or silent acceptance of their words'. Cf. Liang Yün-kou's (梁雲搆) preface to Vagnoni's 斐錄答彙 (*fei lu ta huei, Philosophical Compendium*) of 1636: 'the educational system of various countries in the Far West is divided into six disciplines, one of which is the discipline of 理 (*li*), or philosophy ["philosophy" is represented phonetically] . . . A large number of scholars are brought together who interrogate one another concerning different types of puzzles and questions, and in a detailed and systematic manner they discern and advance proofs. Only those more frank than the famous Chu Yün (朱雲) or more fluent than the famous Tai P'ing (戴憑) can become officials.' I borrow these fascinating references from an unpublished paper by Nicholas Standaert, 'Classification of Sciences and the Jesuit Mission in China', which he delivered to the conference 'Europe in China III' in April 1998.

[109] *In Universam Dialecticam*, pp. 16–17.

of the prevalent Western conception, stemming from Plato, of thought as silent, internal speech.[110] The absence disguises the fact that logic is the discipline of private ratiocination, no less than of interpersonal discussion. Perhaps, however, reflection on the possible meanings of discriminatory 辨 (*pien*) and argumentative 辯 (*pien*) will be of help here. The Chinese would have readily acknowledged that the *Topics* and the *Sophistici Elenchi* present an art of *discourse* (however inscrutable or unacceptable that art might be). But without the entire *Organon* translated into Chinese, the connection between discourse and the 'logic' of the *Isagoge* and the *Categories* would be largely concealed.[111] On the other hand, a reader approaching the 名理探 with argumentative discrimination primarily in mind might avoid disappointment. The *Categories* in its traditional guise of grand metaphysical taxonomy might well pass muster as delivering the precepts of an esoteric technique allowing the adept to discriminate, to articulate, the structure of the world: and that idea could be expressed by discriminatory 辨 (*pien*).

Explanations follow of various orderings, genetic, educational and evaluative, of technical disciplines. It is not as if epistemic taxonomy, albeit largely limited to bibliographical organisation (always implicitly, if not explicitly, normative), is unknown in China, e.g. the divisions into canons, histories, philosophical works, etc.; but this particular taxonomy would rudely disconcert the Chinese.

> The annals of Augustine state that the art of talking (譚藝, *t'an i*, 'grammar') was earliest, and that the art of history followed it. Since the soul of the human heart[112] realised that the arts functioned ingeniously, and also realised that without rules for clear discrimination/disputation[113] they would be hard put to avoid error, they consequently created a doctrine for determining assertion/what is right and denial/what is wrong.[114] Accordingly they went on to ornament a polished phraseology and thus perfected the arts of literature and poetry. They made gradual progress until they attained all the disciplines of astronomy.[115]

The full Latin order of discovery is: basic literacy; grammar; history ('without the colours of oratory'); dialectic; rhetoric; poetry; and finally mathematical studies (on the traditional understanding, which includes astronomy). This is a sequence partially

---

[110] Much later the 名理探 does assert that 'the main business of the investigation of the theory of names lies in the clarification of internal speech' (名理探。則務明內語, p. 28), but without any explanation of what 'internal speech' might be.

[111] I am of course not pretending that the *Categories* really is the first component of a unified course of dialectical instruction: rather that, as I have shown, is how *In Universam Dialecticam* conceives of it.

[112] 人心之靈 (*jen hsin chih ling*).

[113] 明辨之法 (*ming pien chih fa*): subsequently 明辨 is used, like 推論 (*t'ui lun*), for 'inference' (名理探, p. 13).

[114] 是非之道 (*shih fei chih tao*).

[115] 名理探, p. 10, corresponding to *In Universam Dialecticam*, pp. 21–2.

validated by earlier members preparing the way for later ones: in some cases (e.g. literacy and grammar) as relatively simple prerequisites; in the central case, dialectic ('the discipline of disciplines'), as a universally necessary aid. Other things being equal, a later position in the sequence might be taken to imply relative difficulty, and perhaps worth. So even if fully ornamented history comes under the relatively advanced study of rhetoric, its placement before the culmination of mathematics suggests a valuation of types of research seriously at odds with prevailing Chinese opinion.

In the order of teaching, linguistic regulations once settled, 'nothing should take precedence over the investigation of the theory of names'.[116] And, of course, the very book in one's hands is entitled 'the investigation of the theory of names', 名理探, which means 'dialectic'.[117] But it is when one arrives at the order of dignity that Chinese preconceptions would be shattered:

> If one makes a comparison with self-denial (克己, *k'e chi*: or Aristotle's *Ethics*?) and the work of government (齊治之功, *ch'i chih chih kung*: or Aristotle's *Politics*?), then the theory of names is still more valuable. There are two reasons. The first follows from the domain of discussion which each of them concerns. For self-cultivation (修身, *hsiu shen*) and government (治世, *chih shih*) are occupied with regulating the production of all the virtues belonging to the will (愛欲, *ai yü*); but the exploration of the theory of names is occupied with regulating the production of all the disciplines, which belongs to the intellect (明悟, *ming wu*), and the purity (純, *ch'un*) and spirituality (神, *shen*) of the virtues of the intellect exceed those of the will. Hence how could the theory of names not be more valuable when comparing these three studies? The second reason follows from the criteria (規, *kuei*) with which they comply in discussion. The primary work of the exploration of the theory of names lies in sorting out the errors in the mind's inferences.[118] Therefore all its discriminative discussions are manifestly certain. But if one is talking about the disciplines of self-cultivation and government, their work only lies in common mores and customs (習俗風化, *hsi su feng hua*). They concern what should be done, and do not freely explore the reasons why.[119] The exploration of meanings and principles and the manifestation of reasons are certainly more valuable than mere compliance with examples which does not explore the source of their meanings and principles. Hence the exploration of the theory of names must be more valuable than the disciplines of self-cultivation and government.[120]

Acceptance of the first reason for exalting dialectic above ethics and politics depends on endorsing a hierarchy of psychic faculties with which the Chinese were completely

---

[116] 莫先名理 (名理探, p. 11).

[117] 'The name Dialectic is imposed on the entire art of discussion' (*In Universam Dialecticam*, p. 27): informing the Chinese that this branch of learning is occupied with the principles of language correctly reproduces the broad scope of dialectic as it is understood by the Coimbrans.

[118] 名理推之本務。在辨明悟所推或有之謬。   [119] 而不暇推究於其所以然者。

[120] 名理探, p. 12, corresponding to *In Universam Dialecticam*, pp. 24–5.

unacquainted. What is ultimately responsible for this faculty psychology is the Aristotelian preference for the contemplative to the practical life.[121] From early times (e.g. Yang Chu, fourth century BCE) plenty of Chinese thinkers advocate retreat from involvement in public affairs, for either one's own sake or the public weal (and sometimes both). But they do so in the conviction that the life of retirement will protect and promote a self-cultivation entirely unrelated to Aristotle's vision of perfect, uninhibited contemplation of theoretical truth. The claim for the superiority of dialectic clashes with the Confucian commitment to public service, and cannot really be combined with native quietism: the argument adduces a scholastic criterion associating value with incorporeality[122] alien to any but an advanced Christian convert.

The second reason for dialectic's superiority is formal and methodological. The assurance that 'all its discriminative discussions are manifestly certain' assumes too easily that logic can function as a ratiocinative *criterion* – by what independent standard are we to judge logical reasoning which itself delivers rules for reason? – but begs no more questions than does the Latin. Subsequently the Chinese moves beyond the original in a manner which, if anything, exaggerates the demotion of ethics. In Latin the case is developed in terms of dialectic working demonstratively, while moral science 'less frequently' attends to demonstration with truth as its goal.[123] This position does not entail either that ethics is exclusively concerned with 'common mores and customs' or that its practical focus prohibits exploration of 'the reason why': it is rather that those moral principles (partially) verified are not rigorously proved, and that normally the implementation of a right course of action is paramount, rather than the truth that it is right. The Chinese 'mere compliance with examples' fails to do justice to the Latin's 'moral science', since such compliance would, by Western reckoning, be more or less unreasoning, pre-theoretical. Have Li and Furtado deliberately modified the text in a polemical spirit? 'Self-cultivation' (修身, *hsiu shen*) and 'government' (治世, *chih shih*) are not here used as equivalent to the Western practical sciences of 'ethics' and 'politics': rather, we are meant to understand the *Chinese* practices of 修身 and 治世, which are of precious little merit in comparison with the new 名理探.

> In discussing the theory of names everything which belongs to contingency in the West is called 'dialectic'; everything which belongs to the explanation of necessity and cannot not be in the West is called 'logic'. Researchers employ both these

---

[121] *Nicomachean Ethics*, bk. X. Interpretation of Aristotle's doctrine as consistent is fraught with the greatest difficulties, but it is uncontroversial that he does somehow set a higher value on theoretical than on practical activity.

[122] Cf. 'the intellect is much simpler and more immaterial than the will in operation' (*In Universam Dialecticam*, p. 24: cf. 名理探, p. 16).

[123] *In Universam Dialecticam*, pp. 24–5.

names to designate the entire art of inferential discussion. In accordance with this explanation 'logic' is 'the investigation of the theory of names'. It is actually inferential progress from what is already clear to the determination of what is not yet clear.[124]

The translation has been violently compressed at the expense of clarity. The Latin states that many associate the name 'dialectic' exclusively with probable reasoning as expounded in the *Topics*, 'logic' with the necessary demonstration of the *Posterior Analytics. In Universam Dialecticam* eventually approves use of either term interchangeably for the entire art prescribing the criteria governing inferential discussion.[125] Now the significance of this is that in the Latin, where the complete *Organon* is in question, readers can – at least once they have worked their way through the course – make sense of this decision, since they have been introduced to the construction of propositions and syllogisms and to their classification as either probable or necessary. (Lest the modern reader thinks this a lot of pedantic fuss over nothing, remember that such terminological distinctions are intimately bound up with the far from trivial issue of whether reasoning about likelihoods will be accepted as 'proper', albeit non-demonstrative.)

All this lies behind the first three sentences of the Chinese. *In Universam Dialecticam* argues for endorsing the broad acceptation of 'dialectic' and 'logic' on the basis both of cited authorities and of etymological analysis. It is not altogether surprising that Li and Furtado elected to excise that argument, but the effect of their abridgement becomes plain when one arrives at their third sentence. First, without the *Analytics*, the Chinese are denied the background needed for understanding the formal difference between contingent and necessary propositions, and thus the epistemological consequences which Aristotelians attach to this difference: only validly demonstrated, properly organised necessary propositions can constitute a science to be 'known' in the true sense.[126] Presumably then, *faute de mieux*, the hapless Chinese reader deprived of this essential information would vaguely assume that the modal distinctions enunciated here have something or other to do with 命 (*ming*), 'destiny'. Second, if all the Chinese get is the *Isagoge* and the *Categories* entitled 名理探, and they are told that 名理探 is 'logic', they would naturally presume that the following pages will introduce them to the Western inferential art in its entirety. But in fact what the *Categories* on one traditional interpretation delineates is a metaphysical schematism generating a complementary

---

[124] 循所已明。推而通諸未明之辨也 (*hsün so i ming. t'ui erh t'ung chu wei ming chih pien yeh*: 名理探, p. 13).

[125] *In Universam Dialecticam*, pp. 25–7.

[126] An adequate statement of the conditions on demonstration, both in Aristotle himself and his later followers, would be much more complicated than that: the reader should consult Barnes's edition of the *Posterior Analytics* for guidance.

schematism of terms, the basic components of the propositions to be combined into inferences. Thus the sentence 'It is actually inferential progress from what is already clear to
the determination of what is not yet clear' is dangerously misleading, in that it implies
that the book 名理探 contains a whole logic course, not just its first stage.

> The goal of the investigation of the theory of names has both proximate and
> remote domains. Establishing the criteria for clear discrimination (明辨之規, *ming
> pien chih kuei*) is the goal's proximate domain. Compliance with the criteria
> already established and the inferential development of all discussion is the goal's
> remote domain.[127]

This declaration might have a strong impact on the Chinese estimate of 'dialectic'. Its
'proximate domain' would sound like 正名 (*cheng ming*), name rectification, although
of course these new 'logical' criteria are inferential, not semantic, as they are in the
rectification tradition. And the specification of the 'remote domain' would again suggest
that 'logic' is, or should be, implicated in all discourse whatsoever, just as, once names
have been rectified, future discussion had better not tolerate new mismatch between
word and object. Therefore the closest available native analogue to 名理探 makes appropriately ambitious, and appropriately programmatic, claims for its relevance. But a
passage already cited[128] makes a far more substantive claim in response to the question
of whether logic is a proper part of philosophy:

> The translation of the meaning [of 'philosophy'] is the investigation and selection
> of the reasons of all things. It is the wisdom which introduces men to penetrat-
> ing clarification of things and principles: it extends knowledge. In every case
> of finding reasons, it extends the search for sure meanings, and truly discerns
> things and principles. All this falls to the lot of the study which loves to know. The
> investigation of the theory of names is precisely finding reasons, and it clarifies
> sure discussion so as to obtain all the criteria for the myriad forms of inferential
> disputation.[129]

Unlike the extract we analysed from the very beginning of the 名理探, this passage
characterises 'philosophy' not as 'knowledge', 知 (*chih*), *tout court*, but rather as the
wisdom which arises from knowledge of causes and reasons, 所以然 (*so i jan*). 名理探
counts as a proper part of this philosophical enterprise because it finds the criteria for
inferential disputation; that is, it lays out the reasons why philosophy discriminates as it
does in 'reaching the natures of all things and the principles of all natures'.[130] That is – *if*
one has read and understood the Latin text – the Chinese can be read as saying that logic
is the self-reflexive instrument enabling philosophers, those addicted seekers after

---

[127] 名理探, p. 13.   [128] See p. 90 above.   [129] 名理探, p. 16.   [130] 通物物之性。性性之理 (*ibid.*).

reasons, to know both the reasons *why* they seek them and how to achieve this goal successfully. What is open to real doubt is whether one can read the Chinese in that manner without having already grasped what is being claimed for the relation of logic to philosophy.

A later section goes into some detail concerning just what it means to say that the subject-matter of dialectic is inferential discussion. Inference occurs in three modes, definitional (解釋, *chieh shih*), analytical (剖析, *p'ou hsi*) and (narrowly) inferential (推論, *t'ui lun*), these modes corresponding to 'the three things which can be known', i.e. essence (內之義理, *nei chi i li*, literally 'inner meanings and principles'), part–whole constitution (全中之各分, *ch'üan chung chih ko fen*), and affections (情, *ch'ing*) or accidental attributes (依, *i*).[131] Accordingly what dialectic deals with will be either inferential criteria, now identified with definition, analysis and 'narrow' inference; or the constituents of these criteria, propositions (題論, *t'i lun*) and terms (合限, *ho hsien*, literally 'combinatory limits');[132] or things related to the inferential criteria, such as the five predicates (五稱, *wu ch'eng*) of the *Isagoge* and the ten categories (十倫, *shih lun*) of the *Categories*.[133] This is our first, inscrutable hint of what the book entitled the 十倫 (*shih lun*), the only Aristotelian text the Chinese reader will have an opportunity to examine, might contribute to 'logic' as described. But the reader is left to grapple unaided with this impenetrable barrage of technical jargon, as if analytical definition or the distinction between essential and accidental attributes were too obvious to require discussion. This, surely, is the point at which to recollect a warning issued in the introduction to chapter 2,[134] that *In Universam Dialecticam* is not a modern book intended for independent consumption outside school; and that apparently the 名理探 is similarly designed – in part, and perhaps inconsistently – for reading under the guidance of a Western expert. The Chinese reader who could cope with this section was already well on his way to competence in scholastic philosophy.

Finally, the 名理探 introduces some clarification of the *limitations* of logic as a defence against error.[135] A problem is raised:[136] if dialectic was developed for the removal of intellectual mistakes, and such mistakes occur not only in inferences, but also in acts of simple apprehension (直通, *chih t'ung*) or in analysis (斷通, *tuan t'ung*), they too ought to come within the ambit of logic. The answer is simply to insist that

---

[131] 名理探, p. 27, corresponding to *In Universam Dialecticam*, p. 54.

[132] If 'combinatory limits' sounds disconcertingly alien, one should remember that ὅρος or 'term' is indeed a 'limit', so that the translation here is quite precise.

[133] 名理探, p. 27, corresponding to *In Universam Dialecticam*, p. 54.   [134] See p. 86 above.

[135] 名理探, p. 28, corresponding to *In Universam Dialecticam*, pp. 55–6.

[136] *Oppones/respondetur*, 'you will object/one responds', versus 或曰 (*huo yüeh*)/曰 (*yüeh*), 'some say/one says'.

dialectic *is* confined to monitoring inferential error. Angelic intelligences are superior to us in their direct, non-inferential enjoyment of truth, as Ricci's Western *literatus* had already declared in the 天主實義 (*t'ien chu shih i*).[137] Human beings are especially prone to error in making transitions from one thought to another: so, if 'researchers into principles' (窮理之儒, *ch'iung li chih ju*) were to do the best they could to help us to approximate to the angelic condition, they had to concentrate on inference, where error proliferates – hence the birth of logic. 'To sum up, there are some errors in acts of simple apprehension and in analysis, but their control naturally falls to the primary discussion (本論, *pen lun*), and does not lie within the investigation of the theory of names.'[138] This is a lesson familiar to all students of traditional Western dialectic. Logic is designed to weed out fallacious patterns of reasoning; it does not and cannot magically ensure that the propositions featuring in any given, actual piece of reasoning are indeed true (that is, that the argument is not only valid, but also sound). Doing this job is not a logician's speciality: it is for all of us, especially the experts in the various 'primary discussions', to detect and eliminate false propositions. Logic helps us to preserve empirical truths from contamination by inferential error – without, however, producing any extra truths of its own (except for truths about logic itself).[139]

What would be the effect of this defining limitation in an unfamiliar cultural context? It cannot be understood without an understanding of the formal definition of sound inference as the derivation of a previously unknown truth from known truths by means of valid principles of reasoning: and Aristotle's pioneering, partially successful attempt to formulate a theory of inference is set out in the unavailable *Prior Analytics*.[140] Of course, neither orientals nor Westerners had to wait for Aristotle to learn to reason (a denial the Coimbran Jesuits would surely accept, in the light of their thesis that all the arts, dialectic included, come to us from God through Adam). We all can and do reason, more or less imperfectly, without explicit, theoretically motivated reflection on the canons of reason. But we still have grounds to wonder whether a Chinese readership, in the absence of a viable native tradition of formal logic, could seize the full implications

---

[137] See Melis 1994, p. 81.

[138] 名理探, p. 28: it is evident from the context that 'primary discussion' signifies a substantive subject such as metaphysics, as opposed to the formal discipline of logic.

[139] As the 名理探 points out: 'if the operations of inference include acts of simple apprehension and analysis, then they also come within the investigation of the theory of names' (p. 28).

[140] The *Topics* also defines sound inference and gives ample help with sorting good from bad inference. The potential significance of this resource increases when one remembers that some Western commentators read the *Categories* specifically as a prolegomenon to the *Topics*, to the extent that they favoured the alternative title *Before the Topics*. Admittedly, this interpretation fell into disfavour early in the tradition, but certainly shows how much logic could be gleaned without access to the *Prior Analytics*. Not that our final conclusion will change, of course, in the absence of a Chinese *Topics*.

of a doctrine which uses the distinction between deductive validity and material truth to show how logic brings us only so much closer to angelic infallibility.

4 The need for logic

By now the Chinese might well feel bewildered about the pretensions of 'logic'. Quite apart from the decisive question of whether Western claims for its cardinal importance are justified, exactly what is being urged on its behalf? On the one hand, many of the vigorous assertions we have reviewed seem to imply that sure progress in argument and clarity in discussion can only be achieved on condition that 名理探 has been mastered; and that since dialectical competence is a *sine qua non* for subsequent learned accomplishments such as rhetoric, someone unschooled in dialectic will also inevitably fail to speak or write persuasively. But on the other, the restriction of logic to the detection and elimination of formal invalidity, when the explicit idea of deductive validity is itself a challenging novelty, might well seem to weaken the case for logic as an essential discipline. Furthermore, although of course this is not a matter raised in the translation, Chinese *literati* might indignantly reject that case as a deep, grotesque insult to their indigenous scholarly traditions: for the obvious, shaming message is that without logic, the Chinese cannot think straight, talk persuasively, or write proper history or poetry.

The final section of the introduction would assist, if not necessarily satisfy, a confused, perhaps angry, Chinese reader. The section title, 'One Desiring Fluency in all Branches of Learning must first Know the Investigation of the Theory of Names',[141] might seem to formulate the most uncompromising of positions: but it emerges that the necessity in question, and even what is meant by 名理探, moderates the Western stance considerably, if not to the extent that the Chinese might themselves comfortably adopt it.

First, some fundamental technical distinctions are introduced. Absolute necessity (直然之須, *chih jan chih hsü*: e.g. the necessity of God's existence) is to be distinguished from hypothetical necessity (既然之須, *chi ran chih hsü*), where a cause is necessary for the existence of a thing or the obtaining of a state of affairs; and hypothetical necessity further subdivides into instances of efficient causation (作所以然, *tso so i jan*: e.g. the sun necessarily produces daylight) and instances of final causation (為所以然, *wei so i jan*: e.g. using a boat is necessary for achieving the goal of crossing a river). Again, cases of hypothetical necessity involving final causation divide into conditions necessary for obtaining the end in view (e.g. if one is to remain alive, one must have food) and those which, although not necessary for reaching the goal, make success easier (e.g. although one might make a journey on foot, procuring a horse and carriage

---

[141] 欲通諸學先須知名理探 (名理探, p. 32).

gets one to the destination faster and more comfortably).[142] As for dialectic, we are now informed that it too should be divided, into natural and artificial varieties: 'one, the investigation of the theory of names which is naturally perfected, is inferential discussion which is unlearnt and intrinsic; the other, the investigation of the theory of names which is perfected by learning, is inferential discussion only perfected after learning'.[143] Our puzzle concerns the acquired variety of dialectic.

With these distinctions in hand, it is at last possible to formulate the question precisely: when we ask whether artificial dialectic is necessary for competence in all branches of learning, we are concerned with hypothetical necessity involving final causation. That is: if a scholar aspires to mastery of any discipline whatsoever, must he first become a dialectician to achieve his goal? And is dialectic an absolute prerequisite for success in, e.g., history or mathematics, or is it rather the case that a grounding in logic makes progress easier and more secure?

The answer is that although dialectical skill is not an absolute prerequisite, 'in the inferential operation of the intellect it is necessary to avail oneself of it for easy improvements and the evasion of all errors'.[144] Augustine and Clement of Alexandria are cited as authorities for this conclusion, and the latter's simile comparing logic to a fence protecting the garden of learning is also translated.[145] Is traditional Chinese scholarship without logic like a plantation unweeded and unprotected from degradation?[146] First, the text concedes that artificial dialectic is not strictly necessary for scholarship:

---

[142] 名理探, pp. 33–4, corresponding to *In Universam Dialecticam*, p. 62.

[143] 一，是性成之名理探。乃不學而自有之推論。一，是學成之名理探。乃待學而後成之推論也 (名理探, p. 34).

[144] *Ibid.*

[145] 格勒孟 ['Clement'] 云。明辨之規。女學圃之樊。雖不設樊。亦可滋殖。增之以樊。則滋殖尤便也。名理探之為諸學所須也 (*ibid.*).

[146] European readers of Ricci's and Trigault's bestseller *The Christian Expedition to the Chinese* (Latin version, 1616) would assume that the answer must be an emphatic 'yes': 'the only one of the higher philosophical sciences with which the Chinese have become acquainted is that of moral philosophy, and in this they seem to have obscured matters by the introduction of error rather than enlightened them. They have no conception of the rules of logic [*dialectica*] and consequently treat the precepts of the science of ethics without any regard to the intrinsic co-ordination of various divisions of this subject. The science of ethics with them is a series of confused maxims and deductions at which they have arrived under guidance of the light of reason [*natura infundi lumine*]' (Gallagher 1953, p. 30: cf. Semedo's dismissal of Chinese dialectic: 'they have no other rules, but what are dictated to them by the natural light of reason' (Semedo 1655, p. 51). Again I take the references from Nicholas Standaert's unpublished 'Classification of Sciences and the Jesuit Mission in China'). However, 'the most renowned of all Chinese philosophers was named Confucius. Indeed, if we critically examine his actions and sayings as they are recorded in history, we shall be forced to admit that he was the equal of the pagan philosophers and superior to many of them' (Gallagher 1953, p. 30, with the mistranslation of 'multos' as 'most' corrected to 'many').

'because the rules of inferential disputation are perfected by the intellect, a versatile scholar, although unversed in them, will nevertheless be able to infer to and acquire them from his innate resources'.[147] Much turns on the sense in which such a gifted auto-didact can be said to *know* 'the rules of inferential disputation': could this be maintained unqualifiedly without his possessing a science of logic? Would unconscious compliance with such rules suffice? That is apparently the intention: the intellect is naturally capable of an immediate, non-inferential grasp of the defining principles proper to each branch of learning, and full expertise is then acquired through inferences made from these starting-points.[148] Since China has boasted legion 'versatile scholars', the reader might happily conclude that the doctrine of 名理探 is not an affront to his country's learning. Contrast an untranslated piece of Latin: 'the forms of discussion, since they are the proper invention of reason, can without doubt be discerned by a keen intellect, *at any rate rude and inchoate ones*'.[149] In the Chinese we are not told that there are any limits to what versatility may be capable of.

But dialectic is undeniably a necessity 'for convenience and advantage' (便益, *pien i*): all craftsmen perform better with well-prepared tools, and 'the criteria for inferential disputation', 推辨之規 (*t'ui pien chih kuei*), are the instruments of knowledge. Inferential principles are required for testing what we believe we have discovered in the various departmental sciences. Aristotle himself is cited as attributing the errors of ancient philosophers to ignorance of dialectic: might the latterday Chinese be in the unfortunate position of the pre-Aristotelian Greeks? 'Cicero (度略, "Tully") says that even if someone has a superb intellect, if he is not versed in the criteria for disputation, he will lack the means to obtain proofs (證, *cheng*) and certain principles, and it is easy to deceive him on account of his lack of principles.'[150] This Western sage – never mind if one has never heard of him – is saying that no matter how naturally gifted the Chinese might be, their scholarship will remain dangerously fragile unless they study dialectic.

On the best scenario, with what confidence might the Chinese hope to have avoided widespread illogicality in their researches? An analysis of the essential operation of natural, innate dialectic both answers this question and sharpens the case for refining one's logical skills artificially. 'Albertus Magnus says that those who seem to know but do not know why they know cannot be called knowers.'[151] And, as we have been told, to know is to know causes; therefore to know one knows, one must be aware of the causes

---

[147] 推辨之法。既由明悟所成。則穎悟之士。雖未習於辨法。亦自可以推而得之 (名理探, p. 35).

[148] Lurking behind this picture of 'natural' learning is the model of science as an axiomatised deductive system set forth in the *Posterior Analytics* – a scheme not obviously 'natural', to say the least, but taken for granted by the Coimbran Aristotelians.

[149] *In Universam Dialecticam*, p. 63, my italics.

[150] 名理探, p. 35.   [151] 亞利白云。有似知也者。而未知其所以知也者。不可謂知者 (*ibid.*).

of one's knowledge. And when that knowledge is inferential, knowing its causes will be a matter of verifying that the inference is valid. Hence 'were the operating intellect not originally perfected by the spiritual nature and had it no intrinsic prior access to clear principles of names, then its inferential discussions would not have truly sound criteria':[152] natural dialectic is thus essential to the acquisition of any inferential knowledge. Deduction can be verified either completely (詳審, *hsiang shen*) or virtually (照審, *chao shen*). 'For complete verification, the intellect must at the time of inference especially produce an act, additionally checking completely through analysis whether what was concluded in the inference is free from defect or not.'[153] In virtual verification there is no separate intellectual act: we at once draw the conclusion from the premises and attend to *why* the conclusion follows.[154]

So the Chinese, like everyone else, did not have to await the translation of Aristotle to achieve knowledge through proper arguments; and the description of knowing knowers naturally verifying their inferences could just be sufficiently perspicuous and diverting to suggest that formal training in 'dialectic' might be no bad thing. For here is the sting in the tail: 'only the virtual verification of those well versed in the art of inferential disputation is relatively easy (較易, *chiao i*)'.[155] It would be obvious on a moment's reflection that 'virtual' rather than 'complete' verification is standard practice for all reasoners; but if the Chinese are not (yet) 'well versed in the art of inferential disputation', their scholars must be constantly labouring under difficulties of which the 名理探 could relieve them.

If in reaction the Chinese reader is spurred to attempt more self-conscious 'complete' verification, why not take advantage of the immensely and elaborately self-conscious dialectical reflections contained in the book 名理探? Someone named Hieronymus (翁樂) stirringly declares that 'even if the explanations set up by perverse learning appear to have plausibility, the practice of argumentative learning is entirely able to expose and destroy them, as the flame of a raging fire is made completely to subside into ashes'.[156] Moreover, the gains would not stop there: 'the study of inference is beneficial not only for physics (性之識, *hsing chih shih*), but also in metaphysics (超性者, *ch'ao hsing che*)'.[157] 超性者, a perfect etymological calque for 'metaphysics'

---

[152] 用明悟。若非靈性夙成。先自通晰名理。其於推論。非有真確之規 (*ibid.*).

[153] 名理探, p. 36.

[154] 第就所為然此括義者而照之 。後之所收。即從先之所推者而定也 (*ibid.*).

[155] *Ibid.* Once again the Latin is significantly harsher: a virtual judgement concerning logical consequence 'is *insufficient* except in the experienced and exercised, who are perfectly versed in the art' (*In Universam Dialecticam*, p. 64, my italics). The Chinese has the dialectically untrained (including themselves, presumably) in relative difficulties, not starkly incompetent.

[156] 名理探, p. 36.   [157] *Ibid.*

understood as 'the study which transcends nature', is left unglossed; but since Clement proclaims that dialectic can cause the intellect 'to penetrate to metaphysical meanings of supreme remoteness',[158] dialectic would seem to promise to bring us closer to the 道 (*tao*), as all genuine wisdom should. 'The more transcendent a branch of learning, the greater the danger that the intellect will fall into error.'[159] Hence what the Jesuits are offering is special enlightenment combined with an argumentative discipline to ward off error. Regrettably, nothing more of 'the art of inference' was published, but in the text of the 名理探十倫, 'the ten categories of the investigation of the theory of names', the tantalised, perhaps scandalised, Chinese reader would discover an esoteric doctrine utterly unlike the 道 (*tao*) of any Chinese master.

So far we have been occupied with how traditional Western assumptions about the nature and value of logic are transformed, to a smaller or larger extent, on translation for a Chinese readership. Again and again I have had occasion to speculate on how a character named 'the Chinese reader' *would* react to our extracts. This is obviously a dangerous game – especially when 'the Chinese reader' is indeterminately a devout convert, neutrally curious *literatus*, or rabid anti-Christian, dizzied solitary student or member of a guided tutorial – but it is an unavoidable one, if we are to enter the paradoxical state of feeling at home with the foreignness of the *Categories*/名理探. Most of the points discussed turn on the effects of translation broadly conceived: what happens when a strange theory is enunciated in a foreign *cultural* idiom, regardless of translational propriety in more narrowly linguistic terms. Now we come to the 名理探十倫 itself, where examination of the text in the light of 'guidance and constraint' will certainly reinvolve us in the philosophical and linguistic problems of translation theory. But we should nevertheless not lose sight of the cross-cultural questions broached in this introduction to the introduction of the 名理探. The selections are chosen on obvious principles: whether strikingly good or strikingly bad renderings, they are of intrinsic philosophical or anthropological interest, often particularly rewarding for participants in or observers of the relativism debate. Chapter 1 argued that sensitive recognition of the rich contexts in which interpretation occurs should stimulate very robust scepticism about the credentials of linguistic relativism. Since chapter 2 is an essay in such recognition, we must constantly bear in mind that the samples of translated logic and ontology which follow were not generated in an intellectual vacuum. Because Li Chih-tsao and Furtado produced them together, we must make every effort to recreate at least some fraction of what they individually or mutually, in harmony or (unwitting) dissonance, took for granted as the communicative context of the 名理探.

[158] 達於超性高遠之義。 			[159] *Ibid.*

5 Finite and infinite

As the general introduction of the 名理探 began with a double rendering of 'philosophy', so now 'categories' is translated into Chinese: 'as for the Western expression "categoriae", the translation of the name is "appellations"; the translation of the meaning is the positions of all the appellations of all the natures of things, superior and inferior'.[160] The suggestion that the literal meaning of 'category' is 稱 (*ch'eng*), 'appellation' or 'predicate', must derive from a fact already mentioned,[161] that the original sense of 'category' in Greek is 'predicate' or '(type of) predication', so that 'categories' in the Latin text are *praedicamenta* as often as *categoriae*. But 'the translation of the meaning' forestalls any temptation to confine the ten categories, the 十倫 (*shih lun*), to the study of language, since the rôle of the categories in constructing a universal taxonomy must transcend mere linguistic theory. The 十倫 (*shih lun*) seem nevertheless to straddle the boundary between language and reality, since what they rank are not the natures themselves, but rather what the natures are called. The 名理探 therefore broaches the issue of whether the book entitled 十倫 (*shih lun*) belongs to metaphysics, in that it explains nature,[162] or rather to logic, in that it supplies a rational method applicable across all the departmental sciences. The answer is that category theory makes contributions to both metaphysics and dialectic, but from different perspectives.

Three components of dialectic, the direct (直通, *chih t'ung*), the combinatory (合通, *ho t'ung*) and the inferential (推通, *t'ui t'ung*), are relevant to all enquiry and science (尋知者, *hsün chih che*):

> Direct communication directly conveys the meaning of each thing; it deals with the ten categories of position, so as to analyse the direct meaning of every thing. As for combinatory communication, in the West it is called 'Peri hermeneias' [the Greek original of 'De Interpretatione']: it combines and divides. It deals with the combination and completion of a text, so as to complete all propositions. As for inferential communication, in the West it is called 'Analytica' and 'Topica'. It deals with inference and exploratory discussion, so as to complete criteria for all arguments.[163]

---

[160] 西言加得我利亞 ['Categoriae']。譯名。則稱謂。譯義。則凡物性上下諸稱之位置也 (名理探, p. 289).

[161] See p. 73 above.

[162] This might seem incompatible with the earlier representation of metaphysics as 'the study which *transcends* nature'; but here 'nature' is to be broadly construed as ontology in general.

[163] 直通者。直透各物之義。所務在位置十倫。以剖凡物之直義也。合通者。西言伯利爾額默尼亞 ['Peri hermeneias']。合而斷之。其所務。相合成文。以成諸題論者也。推通者。西言。一名亞納利第加 ['Analytica']。一名篤此加 ['Topica']。務在推究討論。以成諸辯之規者也 (名理探, pp. 290–1, corresponding to *In Universam Dialecticam*, pp. 301–2).

Here the 名理探 rehearses the traditional plan of the *Organon*, reproducing the correlation with mental operations and thus linguistic activities intended to justify the ordering of Aristotelian logical books. 'Direct communication' yields meanings, that is, it furnishes us with individual terms: by distributing these meanings correctly among the categories, the *Categories* prepares the semantic foundation for all reasoning. To 'combinatory communication' should be allotted the combination of individual terms into properly formed propositions: but the Chinese description is problematic. A sentence or proposition ought to be produced at this stage; but although we have already had an (unglossed) occurrence of 題論 (*t'i lun*) in this sense,[164] 文 (*wen*) cannot, to my knowledge, mean that:[165] it might be employed to refer to language or literature in general, or to a piece of writing, but not to a single sentence. In any case, without a translation of *De Interpretatione* Chinese readers could not at all easily understand this occurrence of 文 (*wen*) as it must be understood in order to preserve the mental, linguistic and textual sequences. Finally, 'inferential communication' takes collections of these 文 (*wen*) organised into patterns of reasoning and sorts out the valid from the invalid.[166]

Whatever difficulties might beset comprehension of the intervening 'combinatory' stage, the reader is assured that category theory is required for winning through to argumentative criteria,[167] and that 'this book distinguishes genus, species, and d*ifferentia* so as to furnish the resources enabling analysis and definition completed by the intellect. Furthermore, it interprets the nature of each thing and the affections of each nature so as to provide the principles whereby all the disciplines make inferences.'[168] 宗 (*tzung*), 類 (*lei*) and 殊 (*shu*) will not mean 'genus', 'species' and '*differentia*' to the new Chinese reader, and nowhere in the 名理探 are these technical terms explained, but there are sufficient examples of definition *per genus et differentiam*, referred to as such, scattered throughout the work to alert the attentive student to how this jargon might function in scientific and metaphysical taxonomy; and even now he will realise that the 十倫 (*shih lun*) are supposed to be essential for tracing the structure of reality.

But do they capture absolutely everything? *In Universam Dialecticam* tersely announces that 'infinite being' is not included,[169] and says nothing more on the subject.

---

[164] See p. 105 above: notice that 'direct meaning', 直義 (*chih i*), is not similarly associated with the earlier expression for 'terms', 合限 (*ho hsien*).

[165] See chapter 1 for Graham's hypothesis that the later Mohists used 辭 (*ts'û*) in this sense (pp. 65–6 above).

[166] At this point the 名理探 has argumentative 辯 (*pien*) rather than discriminatory 辨 (*pien*), but as remarked (p. 99 above), the graphs are interchangeable, and the variation here must be casual.

[167] 名理探, p. 289.

[168] 蓋其書。分別宗類殊。以具明悟所成能析能解之資。又釋各物之性。各性之情。以具諸學推論 之理也 (*ibid.*, p. 291, corresponding to *In Universam Dialecticam*, p. 302).

[169] p. 339.

The 名理探, however, treats this as an occasion for an extended, very carefully composed contrastive disquisition on being infinite and uncreated (無限而無受造之有, *wu hsien erh wu shou tsao chih yu*), as opposed to being finite and created (有限而受造之有, *yu hsien erh shou tsao chih yu*).[170] In chapter 1 we encountered relativistic arguments denying that 有 (*yu*) is equivalent to any Indo-European 'being' verb, in particular because the restricted use of 有 (*yu*) as an existential quantifier like 'there are . . .' helpfully precludes all manner of Western metaphysical 'confusion'.[171] Here in the 名理探, 有 (*yu*) is a modified nominal, 'the being which is finite/infinite, created/uncreated': does this 'ontological' construction in and of itself pervert the Chinese medium to suit the Latin message?

Creatures do not essentially exist, and only have temporal being. The infinite and uncreated is unique; the creation is myriad. The infinite unites every perfection; each finite nature can enjoy only a single excellence, and so is inevitably defective. Infinite being is necessary; finite being is contingent. 'What is uncreated is without the combination of matter and form and the union of genus and *differentia*, and so achieves pure actuality',[172] while finite entities become actual (為, *wei*) only after having been potential (能, *neng*). Because the uncreated never came into being, it will also never be destroyed. Some of the essential faculties of rational natures (論性之本力, *lun hsing chih pen li*) will escape destruction, but because they came into being, none of them is essentially indestructible. 'What is uncreated achieves psychic perfection without past or present, far or near: there is nothing it does not penetrate',[173] and nothing is outside its government.

Certainly an unaided Chinese reader would be sorely pressed to extract anything more than the surface meaning from this extraordinary philosophical hymn to divinity. Indeed, one may doubt whether Li Chih-tsao himself, even with the benefit of Furtado's explanations, exhausted the import of this passage: only a fully trained scholastic could do that. To follow the catalogue of contrasts between the infinite and the finite – quite apart from acquaintance with Western ideas of infinity – one must know about essentialism, (a)temporality, necessary existence, and the metaphysical perfection of simplicity. The assertion that what never began will never end is merely the conclusion of a venerable argument invented by the ancient Greek philosophers and subjected to prolonged scrutiny and ingenious modification during the Middle Ages; and similarly the thesis that some creatures, even if immortal, are nevertheless destructible descends from Plato's *Timaeus*, via the Neoplatonists, to the scholastics. The limitation that only

---

[170] 名理探, pp. 326–7.   [171] See chapter 1, section 7.
[172] 無受造者。無質模之合。無宗殊之結。乃至純之為 (名理探, p. 326).
[173] 無受造者。至靈全靈。無古無今。無遠無近。無不洞達 (*ibid.*, p. 327).

'*some* of the essential faculties will escape destruction' probably depends on the rather controversial notion that the irrational parts of the human soul do not survive the death of the body, a view which cannot be appreciated without extensive knowledge of the *De Anima* and its major late-ancient and mediaeval commentaries. The uncreated is 'without past or present, far or near' because it exists in a condition of non-discursive contemplative perfection beyond both time and our experience. And so on. But if this text is awesomely demanding, the challenge posed has nothing to do with the use or abuse of 有 (*yu*): it is the sheer mass of accumulated philosophical history which threatens incomprehension. The retort that only a philosophical culture deluded by the vagaries of Indo-European 'being' could ever have earned the dubious distinction of formulating such pernicious nonsense is easily met: so far from exhibiting any telltale relativistic 'strain', the Chinese of this passage moves impeccably, and sometimes elegantly, through its contrasts. The language is lucid; it is the thought which is so fearsomely obscure.

A noteworthy feature of the text is that, while devoted to a systematic exposition of the differences being limited and divine being, it is nevertheless not a foreign, religious intrusion into Aristotelian teaching: it consists of natural theology reliant on philosophical theorising about the divine, not on Christian revelation. Note that the constant reference here is to the neutral 'infinite and uncreated being', 無限而無受造之有 (*wu hsien erh wu shou tsao chih yu*), never to 天主 (*t'ien chu*), the Christian 'God'. Elsewhere we learn that 'the one nature and three ranks are all miraculous substance, and accordingly belong to extrinsic, infinite being which transcends the categories':[174] so the 名理探 is in fact not averse to mentioning doctrines of revealed religion such as the Trinitarian mystery,[175] and it indicates that both the conception of divinity available to the light of natural reason and the miraculous teachings of Christianity elude the categories. The declaration is repeated with variations: Dionysius says that 'God [here 天主 (*t'ien chu*)] transcends all substance and superior being: therefore the substance

---

[174] 一性三位皆自立之妙體。緣屬超然倫外無限之有 (*ibid.*, p. 354, corresponding to *In Universam Dialecticam*, p. 371).

[175] It is a commonplace of seventeenth-century missionary studies that the Jesuits attempted to keep inflammatory doctrines, especially the Crucifixion and the Eucharist, from hostile anti-Christian notice: see, e.g., Mungello 1994, pp. 85–91, who concludes with the telling comment that 'even sympathetic Chinese *literati* found Jesus' submitting to crucifixion as behaviour more appropriate for a slave than for a king or God. Certainly such brutal punishment was viewed with horror by an elite group who regarded their exemption from corporal punishment (secured by their academic degrees) as a precious privilege.' I have already discussed (pp. 85–6 above) the exclusion of all texts dealing with the Eucharist from the 名理探; perhaps this censorship lends some support to the speculation that the book was intended for relatively open circulation. In any case, it is worth remarking that during this period very little of the Bible itself had been translated, and that only a few devotional texts had been produced for converts, so that the excursions of the 名理探 were quite possibly the most sophisticated theological resource 'available' – if that is the right word – in Chinese.

common to God and created things is only equivocal.'[176] Similarly, since God has no extrinsic, accidental attributes, the relations he bears to the creation do not fall under the category of relation: 'the complete discussion is to be found in theology'.[177] But just where is this 'theology'? Is the reference to theological teaching in general, or some specific text or texts? Another such excuse goes further: 'the being which is completely infinite and uncreated is actually the business of metaphysics: *we temporarily set it aside until the primary discussion*'.[178] We have seen that 'primary discussion' signifies a substantive discipline, as opposed to the formal discipline which is dialectic.[179] Therefore the sentence's clear implication is that it is only a matter of time before the Chinese *Metaphysics*, 超形性學 (*ch'ao hsing hsing hsüeh*), is in the reader's hands.[180] The reader of the 十倫 (*shih lun*) comes away from these texts with some confidence that the book will encourage him to master the rudiments of disciplined thought by acquiring a set of categories matching the way the (created) world is. But, as it turns out, full wisdom transcending the 名理探 is only to be found in metaphysics and especially at its summit, theology.

6 The simple and the complex

Since in Aristotle's *Categories* the individual categories are only discussed one by one beginning with the fifth chapter – and indeed the categories are not introduced as a group until ch. 4 – traditional scholarship has been much exercised by the problem of how

---

[176] 天主者。乃超諸自立體而上之有。故天主與受造者所共之自立。惟同此名。不同此義耳 (名理探, p. 372, corresponding to *In Universam Dialecticam*, pp. 389–90). 'Equivocal' and 'univocal' have been introduced, formally defined and commented upon in the translation of ch. 1 of the *Categories*.

[177] 天學有詳論 (*ibid.*). But the 名理探 does not abstain from engaging in theological *argument* where appropriate, although again it never passes the limits of natural theology. For example: 'every particular individual (特一, *t'e i*) taken univocally (一名一義, *i ming i i*) to belong to some particular genus necessarily has other particular individuals similar to it and one common nature: but when it comes to the miraculous being which is infinite and completely perfect, then there is only one. Suppose there were many: how could they be called infinite? Were it necessarily restricted, how could one talk of inexhaustibly pure being? Therefore the creator is not capable of having the same genus in common with created things' (*ibid.*, pp. 372–3, corresponding to *In Universam Dialecticam*, p. 390).

[178] 詳無限而無受造之有。乃超形性學之事。姑置以待本論 (*ibid.*, p. 327, my italics).

[179] See p. 106 above.

[180] As previously noted, 超形性學 (*ch'ao hsing hsing hsüeh*), like the Latin *metaphysica*, is ambiguous between the subject metaphysics and the book *Metaphysics*; but in this context the ambiguity would seem to be resolved in favour of *Metaphysics*. At a pinch one could perhaps argue that the phrase 'the primary discussion' entails only that on some other occasion metaphysics (in general) will be the primary topic, rather than logic, but any such ploy for avoiding a reference to the book *Metaphysics* here is quite desperate.

to account for the contents and organisation of chs. 1–4, which concern the so-called *prepraedicamenta*, always, of course, on the unspoken assumption that the treatise constitutes a rationally ordered unity. Since these chapters contain various semantic and syntactic pronouncements, the traditional solution, duly put into Chinese, is first to remind us that what distinguishes the logical approach to category theory is its linguistic perspective,[181] and then to explain the *prepraedicamenta* as an exercise in isolating all and only those groups of terms which tally with distinct categories. Thus in the second chapter Aristotle 'discusses compound and simple names, with the intention of selecting the simple and rejecting the compound ones'.[182]

The actual translation of the relevant portion of Aristotelian text runs as follows: 'all cases of predicating names are uttered either in combination or on their own. "The horse gallops" and "the man argues"[183] are both uttered in combination. If one says "man" or "horse" or "argue" or "gallop", then these are names uttered on their own' (*Categories* 1a16–19).[184] The Latin *currit* ('runs') and *vincit* ('conquers'), just like the original Greek τρέχει and νικᾷ but unlike the English finite verbs, are unhelpful examples of 'incomplete' lexical items, since in both highly inflected languages, which permit subject pronouns to be dropped, the verbs can stand alone as complete sentences with the subject 'he/she/it' 'understood'. The commentarial tradition was alive to these verbal examples' potential for misleading the unwary: 'Ammonius' in particular was vexed, and went so far as to say that Aristotle would have been better advised to employ infinitives, so that no trouble could arise.[185] None of this controversy is translated into Chinese. 馳 (*ch'ih*, 'gallop(s)') and 辯 (*pien*, 'argue(s)') function without morphological modification as either finite verbs or complete sentences: in Chinese there are no better or worse choices to be made, so far as illustrating the difference between incomplete terms and complete propositions is concerned. It is not altogether unfair to suggest that a proponent of 'guidance and constraint' should feel obliged to conclude that Aristotle would have been best off thinking and writing in English; relatively advantaged, had he been

---

[181] 'In ranking the ten categories metaphysics only discusses the natures of things; but the investigation of the theory of names makes inferences about nature in conjunction with what names signify' (舉其為某名所指者, *chü ch'i wei mou ming so chih che*) (名理探, pp. 341–2, corresponding to *In Universam Dialecticam*, p. 354).

[182] 論合成之名。與不合成之名 。大旨。取不合成者。而置合成之名也 (p. 342).

[183] Substituted for the Latin 'man runs', 'man conquers'.

[184] 凡稱名者。或合而謂。或專而謂。馬馳人辯。皆合而謂。云人云馬。云辯云馳。則專而謂 (p. 314). The quotation marks employed in my English translation are absent from the Chinese, but by the same token Aristotle's Greek also lacks them, while the Latin of the Coimbran translation does not at this point take advantage of its various quotational devices (*In Universam Dialecticam*, p. 330).

[185] *In Universam Dialecticam*, p. 331: the sarcastic Coimbran rejoinder is that only poor old Ammonius (actually Philoponus: see n. 53) is liable to get confused (cf. p. 84 above).

Chinese; but was seriously handicapped in the expression of Aristotelian philosophy, because his language was Greek.

But perhaps the relativist could reply that serious inspection of this stretch of the translation really bears out his suspicions: whatever the relative merits of Graham's and Hansen's arguments over whether the Mohists succeeded in distinguishing 名 (*ming*) from 辭 (*ts'ŭ*),[186] the 名理探 here reveals that the concept of a sentence or proposition is 'unnatural' to a Chinese speaker. The Coimbran Latin runs: 'eorum quae dicuntur, alia cum complexione, alia sine complexione dicuntur',[187] 'of those things which are said, some are said with combination, others without combination'. The phrase 'things said with combination' does not delimit what sort of thing is said; but the use of *complexio* might assist the logically educated Western reader to think of a type of '*combination*' especially appropriate for the following sentential examples. *Complexio* translates the Greek συμπλοκή. Both Greek and Latin words are etymologically related to the English 'plait', and evoke an idea of interweaving more complex than simple juxtaposition. But one can go beyond general connotation: Plato uses the vocabulary of συμπλοκή in the *Sophist* precisely to indicate the complexity of the λόγος or proposition, composed from logically disparate nominal and verbal items.[188] This is the famous insight that the λόγος is to be distinguished from subsentential terms structurally, not just quantitatively; and the Latin 'dicuntur cum complexione' demonstrates that Aristotle preserves that insight.

But the Chinese 'names uttered in combination', 合而謂之名 (*ho erh wei chih ming*), does nothing of the sort. 合而謂之名 means nothing more than 'compound names' or 'phrases'.[189] A further comparison from the translation of ch. 4 should prove decisive. The Latin reads 'of these things which have been mentioned, those said without combination are not, by themselves, said with affirmation or negation, but either an affirmation or a negation comes to be by the combination of these with one another alternately. For it seems that every affirmation is either true or false: but of those things which are said with no combination, none is either true or false: like "man", "white", "runs", "conquers"' (*Categories* 2a4–10).[190] The Chinese reads 'all ten predicates on their own can be said without affirmation or negation, for there is affirmation or negation only on their combination together' (*Categories* 2a4–7).[191] The 名理探 is three lines short because it cuts out the argument that only indicative propositions have a truth-value; and perhaps the lines are cut out because 是 (*shih*) and 非 (*fei*) do not in the

---

[186] See pp. 64–6 above.   [187] *In Universam Dialecticam*, p. 330.   [188] *Sophist* 261E–262C.

[189] Even if, later in the translation of 1b25, 'things said without combination' (不合而謂者, *pu ho erh wei chih*), the supposedly damning 'names', 名 (*ming*), has been dropped.

[190] *In Universam Dialecticam*, p. 338.

[191] 十者皆專稱無是非可論。蓋惟相合成而後有是非 (名理探, p. 326).

Chinese language primarily attach to propositions assessed for truth, or at any rate do not appear to do so to Chinese minds blinded by their language to the logical workings of affirmation and negation in their language.[192] Taken together with the previous section's parallel admission that 文 (*wen*) is totally inadequate as a label for the products of 'combinatory communication', this new evidence establishes that Chinese blinds those who think in it to propositional structure, even when an exercise in translation should encourage them to appreciate degrees of logical complexity.

The relativist counter-objection misfires. Although the 十倫 (*shih lun*) is discussing just those 'deep' semantic and syntactic characteristics appropriate for 'guidance and constraint', once again attention to the language embedded in its full textual and cultural contexts uncovers a far more plausible source for the Chinese renderings. I have already said that traditional commentary tries to interpret these early chapters as systematic preparation for the following category theory. The 名理探 explains:

> If what is designated is single, then the name is uttered on its own. For example, if one says 'man' or 'heaven', they are both names which refer on their own. If what is designated is not single, then the name is not uttered on its own. For example, if one says 'white man' or 'celestial star', they are both names combined so as to be completed.[193]

The lesson is that the unity and plurality in question are semantic, not phonetic, and so must be judged through consideration of the unity or plurality of the words' referents.[194] Even 'names like "without" and "always", although confined to a single sound, should nevertheless be called synthetic designations'.[195] Furthermore, because language's reference to objects is indirect, mediated by 'our concepts of external things' (表物之意想, *piao wu chih i hsiang*), it is also possible to judge whether names are synthetic or not through reflection on our thoughts. The reason it is so important to understand the proper criteria for semantic unity and plurality is that the *raison d'être* of the *prepraedicamenta* is (the Coimbrans assume) the production of the complete list of categories. Because the categories of being are to be 'read off' from linguistic data, it is crucial that ostensibly simple terms do not in fact designate a collection of referents: otherwise we might be deceived into postulating a single ontological category which

---

[192] The 名理探 does say that 'non-synthetic names are of the species exemplified by partial [?] reference to "man", "horse", "argues", "gallops" ' (p. 315), and perhaps 'partial reference', 偏舉 (*p'ien chü*), is meant to suggest the distinction between reference and full-blown assertion, but I am not at all sure of how to take this occurrence of 偏.

[193] 名理探, p. 315, corresponding to *In Universam Dialecticam*, p. 331.

[194] Cf. 名理探, p. 342.

[195] 女無也常也之為名。雖上一言。然皆謂之合稱 (*ibid.*: here 也 (*yeh*) is a quotational device).

actually collects heterogeneous entities.[196] Therefore the whole discussion in both Latin and Chinese is geared towards the detection of complex names, rather than towards accommodating propositions within a scheme of relative logical complexity: who would be tempted into thinking that whole sentences might correspond to basic ontological categories?[197] Warning us off compound nominals is of much more immediate concern.[198] One might even go so far as to say that since the real focus is on *non*-sentential compound expressions, the Chinese translation improves on the Latin original: while 'dicuntur cum complexione' is indeterminate, 合而謂之名 (*ho erh wei chih ming*) much more helpfully drives home the point that compound *names* are the issue. The complexities at play in the Chinese over-translation of 1a16–19 are not a matter of simple illogic, but rather arise from Li's and Furtado's shared assumptions that an Aristotelian classical text must be well unified, and that the Western commentarial tradition transmitted by *In Universam Dialecticam* is organically connected to the *Categories* it expounds.

7 All the things there are

In the remainder of ch. 2 Aristotle introduces and explains a four-way comprehensive division of all there is:

> Of all the things said to be, some are not in a subject but can be said of a subject, as
> man is said of someone, but is not spoken of as in anyone. Others are actually in a

---

[196] One might feel inclined to protest that reliance on referents and conceptual indications of unity and plurality gives the game away: on this procedure how can we pretend to *derive* categories of being from language, when we have all along begged the question by moving outside language to correct our linguistic intuitions? But this is to make a radical mistake about the nature of the exercise. Since *In Universam Dialecticam* – and thus the 名理探 – takes isomorphism between the world and our thoughts and words about it entirely for granted, there are no questions here to be begged; so long as our researches are careful, we can move with impunity from one realm to another.

[197] Aristotle 'ought not to intend only indicative sentences (or only sentences) to count as expressions involving combination. For in Chapter 4 he says that every expression without combination signifies an item in some one category; this implies that an expression like "white man" which introduces two items from two categories is an expression involving combination. Nor should he mean that all and only single words are expressions lacking combination. For he treats "in the Lyceum" and "in the marketplace" as lacking combination (2a1), while, on the other hand, a single word which meant the same as "white man" ought to count, in view of Chapter 4, as an expression involving combination' (Ackrill 1979, p. 73, anticipated by *In Universam Dialecticam*, p. 338: 'this reasoning is not sufficient for proving incomplexity of every sort, since white man and other imperfect utterances are neither true nor false, but nevertheless are complex'). The 名理探 covers both eventualities: in addition to speciously simple words like 'always' or 'nothing', there are also binomes involving no real semantic combination; e.g. 生覺 (*sheng chüeh*), 'animal', is only phonetically complex (p. 315).

[198] Readers who sceptically reflect that in that case Aristotle jolly well should have given us 'white man' rather than 'man runs' are quite right to suspect that the commentarial tradition might be imposing unity on the *Categories*, rather than discovering it.

subject but cannot be said of a subject, as some individual knowledge is actually in soul, and some individual instance of white is actually in body. But the knowledge and white, which are particular individuals without qualification, are not what one can say of a subject. Others are in a subject and can also be said of a subject, as knowledge constitutes a genus, and we say that it is in the soul; but it can also be divided and said of some individual type of knowledge. Others are not in a subject and also are not said of a subject, such as all substances: they are indivisible individuals which cannot depend on a subject, and also are not said of a subject. As for saying that things are in a subject, everything in some thing not as its internal parts, but rather which if separated from it will not escape immediate destruction, is spoken of as being in a subject.   (*Categories* 1a20–b9)[199]

Although the categories themselves will also constitute a comprehensive division of (created) reality, in some respects this prior scheme is of even greater significance. But the text – in Greek, Latin, Chinese or English – is fraught with difficulty, since Aristotle abruptly introduces the vocabulary of 'said of' and 'in' without explaining in so many words that these are technical phrases to be understood in a specialised sense: the quoted passage itself provides all the clarification on offer, by way of exemplification and (partial) definition, as in the final sentence. The reason that this analysis is so momentous is that it at once separates particular individual substances from both substantial universals and all accidents, particular or universal, and proposes that everything else depends on particular substances through being 'said of' or 'in' them. Thus this four-way scheme really divides all there is into two, substance and accident, and suggests that particular substantial individuals – a given man, some horse, we ourselves – are the primary beings, enabling what is in other ways to enjoy a limited and derivative being.

In the West, within the context of ancient Greek philosophy, perhaps the most salient feature of this ontology is its anti-Platonic thrust. The Socrates of the Platonic dialogues had both insisted that the universal and static is more real than the particular and transient and, among universals, favoured non-substantial Forms such as Beauty or Equality, rather than Man: the *Categories* reverses all this, so that Socrates has a greater title to being than the universal Man 'said of him', let alone the Equality 'said of' the instance of equality 'in' his legs. But this reading of the *Categories* is very much the product of twentieth-century historicism; for *In Universam Dialecticam* and its tradition the great

---

[199] 凡謂有者或不在底而能稱底。如人稱某。非謂在某。或實在底不能稱底。如某一識。實在靈性。某一白者。實在形體。但識與白。特一無屬。非能稱底。或在於底。又可稱底。如識為宗。論在靈性。又可分稱。某一種識。或不在底。又不稱底。如諸自立。不分一者。不得賴底。亦不稱底。云在底者。凡在何物。非其內分。但離於物。不免即滅。是謂在底 (名理探, pp. 314–15, corresponding to *In Universam Dialecticam*, pp. 330–2).

value of the doctrine of substance and accident lies not in its polemical implications,[200] but rather in its forming the key-stone for all further theorising about what there is, and about the ultimate organisation of what there is. No pre-modern metaphysical system, however heterodox in other respects, abandons the division between substance and accident, although its interpretation can change radically; recent scholarship is inclined to question the seriousness and permanence of its rejection in early modern philosophy; and contemporary metaphysicians who develop essentialist hypotheses keep alive one or another variant of the original Aristotelian proposal.[201] As has been said, even if the 名理探 suppresses discussion of the Eucharist, what understanding of it there is to be had derives entirely from the theory of substance and accident; and if the divine transcends the categories, that is in part because 'infinite and uncreated being' cannot be analysed into substance and accident. Hence this section of the text and its accompanying commentary show the Chinese the way in to the heart of Western metaphysical speculation and natural theology.

How does the 名理探 handle the translation of this all-important doctrine? It begins with 'of all the things *said to be* . . .', rendering the Latin's 'of the things which are . . .' ('eorum quae sunt'). But one should not jump to the conclusion that the 十倫 (*shih lun*) here betrays the Chinese bent for nominalism. All sides in the relativism controversy agree that Aristotle's movements between things and language about things are unimpeded:[202] the debate concerns whether the things he sees in the world, and how he sees them, are inevitably shaped and coloured by the words in which he thinks of them. Therefore 'of all the things *said to be* . . .' does not change the meaning of the *Categories*, since in this text 'said to be' is not tantamount to 'said to be [and might or might not be]'.

The Chinese for 'said of a subject' is 稱底 (*ch'eng ti*): 稱 certainly summons up verbal ideas of naming or reporting, but so of course do the Greek λέγεσθαι and the Latin *dici* before ch. 2 endows them with a technical sense. Likewise the example 人稱某 (*jen ch'eng mou*, 'man is said of someone') does nothing to distinguish between 'the predicate-expression "man" is linguistically predicated of someone's name' and 'some individual is an instance of the kind "man"'. But the commentary explains that the things which are 'said of' are 'actually things which predicate their categorial placement'.[203]

---

[200] Not that they go altogether unremarked: Aristotle refutes 'Plato's assertion that it is possible for all general natures to be independent things in abstraction from particulars' (凡公性可以脫其賾而獨立者也: 名理探, p. 369, corresponding to *In Universam Dialecticam*, p. 386).

[201] See, e.g., Wiggins 1980.

[202] Remember that in Aristotle context determines whether a 'predicate' is a predicate-expression or the thing or character introduced by that predicate-expression (cf. pp. 72–3 above).

[203] 所云稱底。乃稱其倫屬之物 (名理探, p. 316). Although this section of the Chinese commentary, which expounds the difference between 'said of' and 'in', is not made up out of whole cloth, there is no corresponding exposition in the Latin.

That is: man is 'said of' Socrates; then animal is 'said of' man; and eventually one arrives at a final predication, that substance is 'said of' animal; and these categorial predications establish a taxonomy of being, not of expressions. Again, these items are not 'in' subjects, because 'if one says man of some individual, the inherence of man in the individual is not one which is a combination of accidental attributes, but rather an inherence which is a subtle substantial combination'.[204]

What the commentary is – or, perhaps, should be – getting at is that while 'Socrates is ugly' says something *about* Socrates, 'Socrates is a man' says what he *is*. Were 'Socrates is a man' saying something about Socrates, then it would have to be possible to identify as subject a Socrates which is not a man; but this cannot be done. Practical possibility is not at issue here: the beautification of Socrates might well be beyond us. The point is rather that we can think of Socrates as Socrates without thinking of him as ugly; but we cannot even be *thinking* of Socrates as an unhuman subject qualified by humanity, because Socrates is essentially human. In other words, 'Socrates is a man' expresses a special sort of identity: it tells us what Socrates is, rather than what he is like.[205] How does the Chinese translation cope with these distinctions? It does of course say that an individual man is not *accidentally* a man. But the graph I have translated as 'subtle', 妙 (*miao*), is the same one previously translated as 'miraculous' ('the one nature and three ranks are all miraculous substance').[206] And that is unsettling because the essential identity of Socrates and man, although indeed 'subtle', is anything but supernatural: that natural kinds are 'said of' particular individuals is the great fact which lends the creation its distinctive Aristotelian structure.

Several features of the next division, things which are 'in' a subject but cannot be 'said of' it, deserve attention. The commentary will teach us that these items 'are actually united with the subject in accidental combination';[207] but here for the first time we come to a place where the 名理探 blurs the distinction between text (古, *ku*, 'ancient', short for 'ancient text') and commentary (解, *chieh*). While I have been at pains to emphasise that both the methodology and indeed the typographical layout of *In Universam Dialecticam* discourage neglect of the huge commentary in favour of the actual text of the *Categories*, the Coimbran book is always sure to discriminate between what Aristotle said and what others, no matter how authoritative, had to say about him: the

---

[204] 如以人而稱某甲。人之在某甲。非就依賴者之合而在。但就自立體之妙合而在 (*ibid.*).

[205] Most contemporary Aristotelian scholarship would deny that the theory of the *Categories* can cope with the full implications of the difference between essential and accidental predication, and speculate that the dawning realisation of this fatal inadequacy led Aristotle to abandon or at least alter his original views in major respects. In contrast, the Aristotelian philosophy of *In Universam Dialecticam*, and thus the 名理探, is an unevolving system whose parts are inter-explanatory.

[206] See p. 115, n. 174 above.   [207] 所云在底乃依合之實結乎底者 (名理探, p. 316).

integrity of the Latin version of the *Categories* is never damaged. But the final sentence of the Chinese (quoted on p. 121), which should be the translation of 1a24–5, corresponds to what in the original comes immediately after 'others are actually in a subject but cannot be said of a subject' (in the second sentence of the Chinese passage); furthermore, the Latin '. . . not as a part, so that it cannot become separate from that in which it is' has been expanded into '. . . which if separated from the subject will not escape immediate destruction'. Perhaps the sentence has been moved for the sake of what was considered a more orderly exposition; and if the change *is* intentional relocation rather than accidental dislocation, it makes plain that Li and Furtado had no qualms about tampering with the Aristotelian text. If this seems an exaggerated reaction, remember that a traditional Western philosophical commentator would no more readily introduce even the most minor changes into Aristotle's own words than his theological counterpart would venture to improve on Holy Writ.

What about the inserted gloss? If it is to say what it should say, it must be construed counterfactually: the reader should not be left thinking that, unlike his liver, which if removed survives for some time, Socrates' ugliness immediately disintegrates on extraction. Since this Chinese conditional contains no inferential graphs, a counterfactual reading, although permissible, is not mandatory. It might, however, be possible to account for the alteration as something other than a bad rendering. In the ordinary course of events, when some accidental change occurs, an accident perishes (for example Socrates tans and his pallor disappears), which is why talk of 'extraction' is totally inappropriate. But the *extraordinary* event of transubstantiation is miraculous just because, in this supernatural case, the accidents of the bread and wine have survived replacement of the subjects to which they had belonged by the substance of divine flesh and blood. So perhaps this doctrine, otherwise, as we have seen, carefully ignored,[208] exerts a surreptitious influence on this piece of textual adaptation: even if the Eucharist is not mentioned, the description of natural accidents is a negative extrapolation from the one remarkable exception to the rule of accidental dependency.

The translation '. . . as some individual knowledge is actually in soul, and some individual instance of white is actually in body. But the knowledge and white, which are particular individuals without qualification, are not what one can say of a subject' also calls for comment.[209] This time there is omission and (clarificatory?) relocation. The Latin justifies the supposition that 'this white is in a corporeal subject' with the claim that 'all

---

[208] See p. 85 above.

[209] The trivial substitution of 'some individual knowledge' for 'a certain grammar' must be prompted by a desire to avoid using the novel coinage 譚藝 (*t'an i*), introduced earlier (p. 100 above), for an unfamiliar Western discipline.

colour is in body' (1a28);[210] and the basis of the second sentence in the Chinese comes in the original at the very end of the chapter (1b6–9: 'but nothing stops things individual without qualification and those things which are one in number, although they are said of no subject, from being in a subject: for a certain grammar is plainly among those things which are indeed in a subject, but clearly are said of no subject'). The Chinese has not only relocated the sentence: it has also modified the Latin to reverse the original emphasis. *In Universam Dialecticam* says that non-substantial individuals unproblematically inhere 'in' subjects. The 名理探 takes inherence for granted, and cautions us not to make the mistake of supposing that *individual* accidents are 'said of' anything; that is, we are warned not to conflate particular accidents with general ones, which constitute the next division. It is not obvious that this deviation from the original hurts the train of thought. The real Aristotle has merely a throw-away comment, an afterthought contrasting particular accidents with individual substances, which can neither inhere in nor be predicated of anything. The Chinese Aristotle is alert to the chance that we might confuse particular and general in the case of the accidental categories, surely a very real possibility for new readers approaching the 十倫 (*shih lun*).[211]

The passage on the third division, general accidents, contains two additions: the Latin says neither that knowledge 'constitutes a genus' nor that 'it can also be divided' so as to be 'said of' some particular science. It is perfectly true, however, that general accidents can be predicated of relatively specific or absolutely particular non-substantial items (for example colour of whiteness and whiteness of this white respectively) because they are the accidental genera under which their instances fall; and so once more the 古 (*ku*) has been (helpfully) altered. But I am not so sure that the second addition is innocuous. This talk of 'division' must be introduced because what Li and Furtado have in mind is a taxonomy of being, developed by Porphyry, in which category theory becomes a classificatory model dividing and subdividing general kinds until a dendritic structure supposedly matching the articulation of reality is achieved.[212] On this conception genera do indeed seem to 'split' into subordinate species. But in the *Categories* any such notion hinders rather than helps. Because knowledge is 'said of' some particular science, the science *is* knowledge: all of the definition of knowledge applies to the

---

[210] *In Universam Dialecticam*, p. 332.

[211] Owen's 'Inherence' (in Owen 1986) contentiously argues that a non-substantial individual is not, say, Socrates' pallor or Plato's pallor, but rather the individual pale hue inhering in both of them, as opposed to some darker shade. But this view, valid or not, is irrelevant to our interests, since both *In Universam Dialecticam* and the 名理探 adopt the traditional interpretation, on which accidental individuals are real tokens, not lowest determinate kinds falling under general determinables.

[212] Both *In Universam Dialecticam* and the 名理探 only come to the *Categories* after commenting on Porphyry's *Isagoge* (see p. 76 above), but I have detected no evidence in the Latin that its reading of the Aristotelian text is ever biased by its preliminary treatment of Porphyry.

instance, contrary to what the image of 'dividing' the genus before predicating it of the individual science would most naturally be taken to imply.

The fourth and final division is of course the most important, since it yields the particular substances, the beings on which the being of everything else depends. The Latin reads: 'others are neither in a subject nor are said of any subject, like a certain horse: for nothing of this sort is either in a subject, or is said of a subject'.[213] The Chinese, which has been considerably expanded, both anticipates by immediately identifying these things as substances, and also distorts the teaching of the *Categories* by asserting that '*all* substances' are of this type. For not all substances are 'indivisible individuals':[214] the man 'said of' someone exemplifying the first division of being is a general substance. The Chinese for 'cannot depend on a subject', 不得賴底 (*pu te lai ti*), is probably elliptical for 'cannot depend accidentally on a subject', since 賴 (*lai*) usually has this sense in the 名理探, and so would not of itself exclude general substances; but of course these are by definition 'said of' their instances, which is just what the translation here denies of *any* substance. Damage has been done, but it will be made good in ch. 5, where it is made abundantly clear that there are general as well as particular substances.[215]

Substances 'do not depend on other beings outside their original category to get the designation "being"',[216] while accidents 'must rely on other beings, and only then should one designate them "beings"'.[217] This claim for the independence of substance does not, admittedly, mean that everything substantial is *ipso facto* an altogether unqualified entity, for there are many 'imperfect' substances requiring some manner of combination or completion; but, unlike accidents, they need only be combined with or completed by something else from within the category of substance. For example, matter and form are real categorial substances,[218] but are apparent only to the analytical intelligence: all

---

213 *In Universam Dialecticam*, p. 332: the 名理探 does later supply a reference to 'a particular horse' (p. 316); and the Latin itself is short of a second example to be found in the original Greek, which reads 'a certain man or a certain horse'.

214 'Individual' of course originally means 'indivisible' or 'atomic': the 'individuals' are what the *infima species*, the 'lowest species', 'divides' into. 不分一者 (*pu fen i che*), 'what is single and not cut up', is thus a perfect calque.

215 And in the commentary on ch. 4 we read that not being 'in' a subject 'is often used to signify substances' (常用以指自立之體, 名理探, p. 328): this criterion would cover both particular and general.

216 非有藉於本倫以外之他有以得謂有 (名理探, p. 328, corresponding to *In Universam Dialecticam*, p. 339).

217 須托他有然後謂之有者 (*ibid.*).

218 The vast majority of contemporary Aristotelian scholars are of the opinion that the *Categories* knows nothing of hylomorphic theory, which analyses all substances other than the prime mover into form and matter, but *In Universam Dialecticam* and the 名理探, subscribing to the unitarian reading already noted, freely integrate all Aristotelian theorising about substance, not to mention subsequent scholastic elaboration of his metaphysical and logical doctrines.

that exists autonomously in the created world is natural substances compounded of matter and form. The 名理探 expresses this by asserting that matter and form depend on each other for 'actual subsistence', 有 在 (*yu tsai*); furthermore, subsistence itself ununited with nature (在也者之不結於性, *tsai yeh che chih pu chieh yü hsing*) is similarly not yet actualised.

Here again we encounter an ontological thesis which, for the relativist, should count as perverted Indo-European reification. Scholastic philosophy distinguishes between *per se* existence (本在之有, *pen tsai chih yu*),[219] the condition of not being 'in' anything else, and *per se* subsistence (全自在者, *ch'üan tzû tsai che*), the stronger condition of actual, independent *per se* existence. All substances, particular or general, complete or 'imperfect', satisfy the weaker condition,[220] but only individual substantial compounds *per se* subsist. Once more the 名理探 betrays no linguistic 'hesitation' in its rendering of this complex thesis. Some or all (unaided) readers might fail to take in the difficult idea of the purely analytical separation of actual existence from the general nature which makes the subsisting particular what it is. But that failure would be the consequence of the translation's unremitting use of the technical vocabulary of the schools. We have no reason to suppose that Furtado would be unable to explain these logical distinctions to Li; or that so long as the Jesuit was sufficiently fluent, the lesson could not be conducted in 'proper' Chinese.

Much of the remainder of the commentary on ch. 2 is given over to the formulation and refutation of objections to the definition of accidents as things inseparable from the subject they are 'in'. A selection of these objections is worth passing in brief review: although the translation is faultless and unconnected to 'guidance and constraint' issues, it does provide those interested in cross-cultural communication with much food for thought.

First, 'the intellect and will of an existing man use him as a *per se* subject; but after he dies they cannot be said to be in him, although they can be said to be in the soul: therefore

---

[219] 名理探, p. 334.

[220] 'Saying that what is designated as substance *per se* exists is tantamount to asserting that it is not in another being, and does not undergo accidental union to exist in a subject. All substances do not undergo accidental union to exist in some subject: if general is in particular nature, that is called "being in a subject of predication"': 謂自立者為本在。即云非在於他有者。顧非就依結而在底之在也。凡自立者。皆無就依結而在何底者。公性在特性。則謂在於所稱之底 (名理探, p. 334, corresponding to *In Universam Dialecticam*, p. 346). The subsequent claim that 'the ways in which general is in particular nature, form is in matter, and matter is attached to the definition of form, are all distinctive modes of substantial inherence' goes some distance to allay our earlier worries (p. 123) about the description of the inherence of the general nature man in some particular man as 妙 (*miao*) in the sense of 'miraculous' rather than 'subtle': 'modes of substantial inherence' unambiguously refer us to relations within the category of substance, rather than to anything akin to the supernatural being of God.

the later and earlier subjects are not the same. Furthermore, the whiteness of the live man, when he later dies, is in his corpse: but again, how could one say that the man and his corpse are one subject?'[221] The answer is that one must distinguish between immediate (無隔之中底, *wu ke chih chung ti*) and mediate (有隔之終底, *yu ke chih chung ti*) subjects of inherence. The soul is the immediate subject in which the intellect and will inhere, while 'the man compounded of body and soul'[222] is only the mediate subject. 'Furthermore, if some quantity be applied to prime matter, then this is the immediate subject of the accidental white colour, and the man compounded of the quantified matter and the soul is the mediate subject of the accidental attributes.'[223] Although in both cases the mediate subjects are destroyed, the immediate ones are not; and the rule that accidents are inseparable from what they are 'in' applies only to immediate subjects.

Aristotle famously declares in *De Anima* that the soul is *not* an independent entity lodged within the body, and thus that we should say that the entire man, not his soul alone, is angry (408b11–15). This psychological hylomorphism, now regarded as one of the chief glories of his thought, was the occasion for much contorted exegesis on the part of Aristotle's mediaeval commentators, who sought to reconcile his philosophy of mind with the Christian doctrine of the afterlife. The enterprise is doomed to failure: identifying the soul as the immediate subject in which the intellect and will inhere is just to say, against Aristotle, that the soul, not the man, is angry. All converts, including the uneducated, must have been introduced to the conception of man as a soul–body compound, 靈魂與身所相合而成之人 (*ling hun yü shen so hsiang ho erh ch'eng chih jen*): without it even the most elementary Christian doctrine cannot be imparted, and only with it could the Jesuits combat what they would have seen as the flourishing evil of popular Chinese conceptions of the spirit. But what the highly educated Chinese convert is offered here is the technical solution to a problem which only arises from the forced marriage of Aristotelian ontology and psychology to Christian thanatology. A converted *literatus* would be new to Christianity, and the 名理探 would be his initial foray into Aristotle: but Li Chih-tsao and Furtado nevertheless expect him ultimately to deal with scholastic compromises between the true religion and the Philosopher.[224]

---

[221] 明悟與受德之在人也。以人為本底。人死後。不可謂在人。但可謂在靈魂。則後底與前底不同。又在活人之白者。其人死後。白在其屍。活人與屍。亦豈可謂一底哉 (名理探, pp. 335–6, corresponding to *In Universam Dialecticam*, p. 348). Note that the binome used here to translate 'the will', 受德 (*shou te*), is not the same as 愛欲 (*ai yü*), the one employed earlier in the introduction (p. 101 above). Such inconsistency is rare, but it does occur.

[222] 靈魂與身所相合而成之人 (名理探, p. 340, corresponding to *In Universam Dialecticam*, p. 352).

[223] 又元質。舉其著於某幾何者。則為白色諸依賴者無隔之中底。而其幾何之質。與靈性合成之人。乃其依賴者之終底也 (ibid.).

[224] Perhaps the Chinese were not entirely unprepared: 1623 saw the appearance in Hangchou of Fr. Giulio Aleni's 性學觕述 (*Hsing hsüeh ts'u shu, An Outline of Human Nature*), which according

The solution to the problem of the persistence of certain physical qualities after death also involves an innovative approach to a notorious difficulty in the interpretation of Aristotle. He insists that organisms are *essentially* alive, so that their corpses are no more real animals than are ones made of stone or wood (*De Generatione Animalium* 734b24–7): hence the puzzle of what to say about inanimate properties which seem not to alter on death. The scholastic answer is to conduct an exhaustive analysis of hylomorphic composites. These ultimately consist of 'prime matter' (元質, *yüan chih*), an absolutely featureless subject[225] in which, at the first stage of composition, bare quantity inheres. At the second stage quantified matter serves as the immediate subject 'in' which qualities such as colour inhere. Again the demands placed on the reader of the 名理探 are extreme. As usual, the meaning of 元質 (*yüan chih*) must be teased out of the context (or supplied by a tutor); and nothing is said to help the Chinese understand the scholastic habit of using a vocabulary of 'uniting', 'mixing' and 'combining' when what is in question is always a thought-experiment designed to illustrate metaphysical composition, rather than any sort of physical process.

The second sample objection observes that smelly things are known to leave their odours behind when handled: so if smell is an accidental attribute, why can it be separated from its subject?[226] A first response concedes that an odour can indeed pass from fruit to the air or one's hand, but suggests that Aristotle's inseparability principle means only that the smell must inhere in one subject or another, not that it must stick in one and the same subject. This answer is rejected. The second response claims that the original odour, which remains inseparably united to the fruit, generates a distinct but similar smell which itself properly inheres in either the air or the smelly hand. This answer is deemed preferable to the first, but still incorrect. The third, which is fully endorsed, is that fine particles of the fruit actually penetrate the air or settle on the hand, so that the accident is never separated from its original subject; the observation that old stored fruit is dry and wrinkled is said to attest to the fact that some bulk has disappeared.[227]

The translation of this passage from the Latin is exemplary; the only difference between them is that *In Universam Dialecticam* informs us that the first opinion is that of Boetius and Ammonius, that Alexander (*De Sensu et Sensibili*) and Thomas de

---

to Luk is 'an Aristotelian-Thomistic psychology' (Luk 1988, p. 178), and he subsequently expounded hylomorphism in the 三山論學記 (*San shan lun hsüeh chi, Learned Conversations at San-shan* [= Foochow]), again published in Hangchou (1627). In the 天主實義 (*t'ien chu shih i*) Ricci had already referred to the Aristotelian distinction between the vegetative soul, 生魂 (*sheng hun*), the sensitive soul, 覽魂 (*lan hun*), and the intellectual soul, 靈魂 (*ling hun*) (Melis 1994, p. 81).

[225] Most contemporary Aristotelian scholars either deny that Aristotle himself was committed to prime matter or at least heavily qualify his commitment.

[226] 名理探, p. 336, corresponding to *In Universam Dialecticam*, p. 348.

[227] *Ibid.*, pp. 340–1, corresponding to *In Universam Dialecticam*, p. 352.

Garbo (*summa quaestiones*) propose the second, and that Simplicius (and others) are responsible for the third. There are simple but strong grounds for dwelling on what some modern readers might impatiently prefer to skim as a serviceable example of the worst sort of dusty scholastic excess: namely, that from the vantage-point of Aristotelian scholarship the excess is splendid. This Coimbran book is the admirable thesaurus of a tradition culled from centuries, in some cases millennia, of meticulous, endlessly inventive effort all expended to one end, the better understanding of the Philosopher through whom we understand reality. The case of the smelly apple, even without any names, gives the reader of the 名理探 some sense of an exotic, but highly learned, civilisation. The Chinese rank among the world's great commentators; despite all the barriers to comprehension, perhaps the commentarial involutions of this translation would strike them as characteristic of true, recognisable culture.[228]

Third, since the sense of the 'in' figuring in the inseparability principle is specialised, various irrelevant senses in which separation is possible are enumerated and discarded.

> To discuss being in place and being in time, suppose that our God were to take the things of the world altogether to put them outside the motionless heaven (靜天 之外, *ching t'ien chih wai*),[229] then although there is there neither what can be designated place to occupy or time in which to be,[230] nevertheless they would be able to persist without destruction for a short time, like fish put outside water. Therefore there is a difference from 'not being able to exist separated from things'.[231]

The only divergence from the original is that in Latin one reads '. . . although all things in the universe were moved by God into *the vacuum*, where there is neither real place nor real time . . .'. Many readers, seventeenth-century Chinese or not, might be unsure of how to react to such a thought-experiment; and perhaps divergence of generic expectations across cultures creates a special problem. Philosophical commentaries in the Western tradition – indeed, Aristotle himself in many of his 'dialectical' discussions –

---

[228] Henderson 1991 is an exemplary comparative study of the Confucian, Homeric, Vedantic, Rabbinic, Christian and Islamic commentarial traditions. He cites the representation of Confucius himself as the editor and expurgator of what were to become canonical texts, the *Songs* in particular, as evidence for a specifically Chinese exaltation of commentary: '. . . expurgation and excision, to say nothing of editing and compiling, are essential commentarial activities in almost any tradition or civilisation. Thus, Confucius as portrayed by Confucian classicists resembles the Alexandrian scholars of Hellenistic antiquity more than he does the founders of other great religious or scriptural traditions . . . But while the Alexandrian scholars, in contrast to Homer, cut obscure figures in Western intellectual history, Confucius, the great commentator, was exalted in China as the "Great Sage and Teacher of Ten Thousand Generations"' (Henderson 1991, p. 30).

[229] An unexplained reference to traditional Western cosmology's outermost sphere of fixed stars – perhaps not inexplicable, if Li's and Furtado's previous translation of *De Caelo* was in circulation.

[230] 所居之處。所存之時。

[231] 名理探, p. 338, corresponding to *In Universam Dialecticam*, p. 349.

often contain *outré* material not at all necessarily accepted *in propria persona* by the author or compiler. However, it is for the reader to realise that not all objections, counter-objections and explanations are on an equal footing. The Latin reader knows perfectly well that only an idiot would confuse the manner in which accidents inhere in a substance with things' being located 'in' cosmic space and time, and so would not press the implications of this astounding counterfactual too hard. The Latin reader knows this without being told: what of his Chinese counterpart?

8 How many questions?

In ch. 4 the categories themselves are finally introduced on the basis of correlation with simple predicates:[232]

> Of the things which are said without combination, some signify substance; others signify quantity/how much; others signify quality/like what; others signify relation/what is mutually regarded; others signify place of contact; others signify what time; others signify situation; others signify having/being clothed; others signify action/making and acting; others signify passion/opposing and receiving.
>
> (*Categories* 1b25–7)[233]

In Greek the first category is οὐσία, an abstract noun derived from εἶναι, 'to be', conventionally rendered 'substance' in English, an anglicisation of the Latin *substantia*. 自立體 (*tzû li t'i*)[234] literally means 'self-supporting structure', and thus perfectly captures the idea that this category collects independent beings.[235] In the case of the second and third categories I have provided alternative English translations so that their now

---

[232] 取不合稱者。分立十倫 (名理探, p. 326).

[233] 不合而謂者。或指自立體。或指幾何者。或指何似者。或指互視者。或指切所者。或指何時者。或指體勢者。或指受飾者。或指作為者。或指抵受者 (*ibid.*, pp. 325–6). Ricci's 天主實義 (*t'ien chu shih i*) has its own list of categories, in some instances identical with what we find in the 名理探, in others, divergent. The differences are as follows: quality is 何如 (*ho ju*), rather than 何似 (*ho ssu*); relation is 相視 (*hsiang shih*), rather than 互視 (*hu shih*); place is 何所 (*ho so*), rather than 切所 (*ch'ieh so*); situation is 體勢 (*t'i shih*), rather than 體勢 (*t'i i*); having/being clothed is 穿得 (*ch'uan te*), rather than 受飾 (*shou shih*) (Melis 1994, p. 75, n. 22).

[234] Already in Ricci: see Melis 1994, p. 71.

[235] '. . . the word "substance" was imposed on this category on the basis of its double affection, obviously subsisting in itself and supporting other things . . .' (*In Universam Dialecticam*, p. 394). Graham, working on the assumptions that substance is read off as the answer to a Greek question of the form 'what is it?' and that substance is essence, proposes that a parallel Chinese exercise yields a very different category: '何 (*ho*) solicits an answer in terms of 類 (*lei*), kind (rather than essence)' (Graham 1989, p. 417). But *In Universam Dialecticam* and the 名理探 suppose that things fall into *natural* 類 (*lei*) because their essences make them members of their kinds; what Graham regards as linguistically predisposed exclusive alternatives are easily combined in the 十倫 (*shih lun*).

standard names can be recognised. The intriguing feature of 幾何者 (*chi ho che*) and
何似者 (*ho ssu che*) is that they bypass the Latin abstract nouns *quantitas* and *qualitas*
to approach the original Greek more closely. The Latin names are technical formations
from the indefinite adjective *quantus* and from *qualis*, which functions as either adjective or pronoun, interrogative or relative. *Quantus* and *qualis* approximate better to the
Greek than do their abstract derivatives, since ποσόν/πόσον and ποιόν/ποῖον are
normally either indefinite adjectives or interrogatives.[236] (In the case of 何時者 (*ho shih
che*), 'what time', both the Greek πότε/ποτέ and the Latin *quando* could be either
interrogatives or indefinite adverbs, 'when?' or 'when'.) 'Relation'/'what is mutually
regarded', 互視者 (*hu shih che*), translates *ad aliquid*, 'to something' or 'to what?',
itself a translation of πρός τι, 'towards something' or πρὸς τί;, 'towards what?'; thus in
this instance the Chinese avoids an interrogative rendering. 'Place of contact', 切所
(*ch'ieh so*), translates *ubi*/ποῦ/πού, 'where?' or 'where': again the question-form is
lost. I suspect that 'contact' has been added because the 名理探 wishes immediately to
select the sense of 'place' as 'immediate spatial container' from among all the meanings discusssed by *In Universam Dialecticam*. 'Having'/'being ornamented', 受飾者
(*shou shih che*), translates *habere*. The category is usually understood as 'possession'
in a wide sense, but the narrow Chinese rendering might be prompted by the following
illustration of 'having', 服 (*fu*), 'being dressed',[237] adapted from the Latin *calceatum
esse, armatum esse*, 'having shoes or armour on'. The final two categories are subsequently exemplified by 施感 (*shih kan*), 'affecting and influencing', and 承應 (*ch'eng
ying*), 'accepting and responding', respectively:[238] these are common phrases for action
and passion in native Chinese philosophy.[239]

The Chinese versions of some of the categories invoke the idea of interrogation; but
is their incorporation of question-forms meant to make the reader actually think of the
categories in terms of questions; and, if so, are they 'natural' ones? Ackrill speculates
that the presence of interrogatives in Aristotle's original list is no coincidence:

> How did Aristotle arrive at his list of categories? Though the items in categor-
> ies are not expressions but 'things', the identification and clarification of these
> things could, of course, be achieved only by attention to what we say. One way of

[236] Aristotle does elsewhere use the abstract noun ποιότης to designate a 'quality', but the word at 1b26
is ποιόν.

[237] 名理探, p. 326.   [238] *Ibid.*

[239] 'Aristotle is guided by grammatical voice to the categories of action and passion. In Chinese philosophy the great categorial distinction among processes is between *kan* 感 "arousal" and *ying* 應
"response", the activating and activated processes distinguished by the syntax of the ergative verb'
(Graham 1989, p. 422). 'Guidance and constraint' with a vengeance indeed. Since Chinese lacks
grammatical voice, Greek, 'ergative syntax', it should follow that the last two of the 十倫 (*shih lun*)
are miscegenated categories, misexpressing together what can only be said, or at least said well, in one
language or the other, but not both.

classifying things is to distinguish different questions which may be asked about something and to notice that only a limited range of answers can be appropriately given to any particular question . . . One must not, of course, suppose that in so far as Aristotle is concerned to distinguish groups of possible answers to different questions he is after all engaged in a study of expressions and not things.[240]

Graham's version of this hypothesis maintains that philosophers thinking in sufficiently different languages who pay 'attention to what we say' will end up with disparate, if not incommensurable, categorial schemes. His imaginary Chinese Aristotle's supposed preference for 'which?' over 'what?' questions leads to relativistic conclusions:

> It seems remarkable that one asks for the subject with 孰 *shu* 'which?', reserving 何 *ho* 'what?' for the object. *It is a further confirmation* that Chinese thinking proceeds not from the thing referred to but from a whole or aggregate from which one divides it . . . Aristotle starts with the isolated thing, asks 'what is it?', proceeds to describe it in isolation . . . 'Which?' on the other hand is a dichotomising question, starting from two or more things.[241]

Does this rampant relativism really find any support in the *Categories*? Pushed perhaps a little further than he himself takes it, Graham's argument would condemn the Aristotelian categories as nothing more than a bogus reification of Indo-European linguistic forms. The peculiarities of Greek grammar have encouraged the construction and success (in the West) of a scheme which, viewed from a larger linguistic perspective, is nothing more than the wrong-headed inflation of particular and limited linguistic phenomena into 'reality' itself, when the 'realities' (easily) accessible in some languages are (relatively) inaccessible in others. A quite specific difficulty for Graham's linguistic determinism is that, as explained,[242] the first category of *Topics* I.9, 'what it is', groups non-substantial items together with substances, so that the contention that Greek grammar somehow delivered 'substance' in response to τί ἐστι, 'what is it?', loses all plausibility. And more generally the fact that Aristotle is impressively alert to linguistic pitfalls[243] should temper any relativistic enthusiasm.

---

[240] Ackrill 1979, pp. 78–9. 'Alternatively, one may address oneself not to the various answers appropriate to various questions about a substance, but to the various answers to one particular question which can be asked about any thing whatsoever – the question "what is it?" . . . This approach may be said to classify subject-expressions (capable of filling the gap in "what is . . . ?") whereas the previous one classified predicate expressions (capable of filling the gap in "Callias is . . ."), though, as before, the point for Aristotle is the classification of the things signified by these expressions' (p. 79). The further suggestion that in *Topics* I.9 Aristotle 'starts by using "what is it" as a label for the category of substance' is incorrect: see pp. 73–4 above.

[241] Graham 1989, p. 419 (my italics), reaching a climax in the Whorfian pronouncement that 'a cosmology which starts from the question "which?" might be expected then to build on parallel classes with paired subjects and verbs. This is indeed what we find in China, with Yin and Yang as the unifying principles running down each side of the dichotomy' (p. 420).

[242] See p. 73 above.   [243] See n. 6 above.

So much for the *Categories*: but what of the larger significance of the questions of the 十倫 (*shih lun*)?[244] The 名理探 contains a section devoted to the issue of why the categories are ten in number. One possibility canvassed anticipates Ackrill's hypothesis:

> Ockham (峨加摩) asked what prime substance (初之自立者, *ch'u chih tzû li che*) is like to determine that the categories of things are ten. His explanation asserts that if one refers to a prime substance, some ask: 'what thing?' (何物, *ho wu*), and the response is to say 'substance'. Some ask about 'how much' (若干, *jo kan*), and the response is in terms of size and quantity. Some ask: 'what is it like?' (何似, *ho ssu*), and the response is in terms of colour. Some ask about direction (所向, *so hsiang*): then one establishes the category of relation. Some ask about what is done: then one establishes the category of action. Some ask about what is undergone: the response is to establish the category of passion. Some ask: 'what is it in?' (何在, *ho tsai*): this determines place. Some ask about physical situation, which introduces the category. Some ask: 'how much time?' (幾時, *chi shih*): this determines the category of time. Some ask: 'how clothed?' On which basis one establishes the category of having.[245]

The passage is neatly composed, and of course the reconstruction has remained perennially attractive. Nevertheless the 名理探 will have none of it: 'this reasoning, although plausible, has not yet obtained what is to be proved'.[246] Instead the commentary recommends the rationale suggested by Thomas Aquinas (篤瑪), which divides the ten categories into three groups, the essential properties of prime substance, its internal accidents, and its extrinsic relations. That 'why ten?' never receives an adequate answer is of no consequence; what does matter is that the Chinese explicitly considers the proposal that the categories were discovered by exhausting question-types, only to reject it.

9 Relatively speaking

In ch. 7 the definition of related things is terse: 'things which designate directed to another are called relatives' (*Categories* 6a36–7).[247] The original Latin apparently says

---

244 One might also wonder about the implications of ch. 8's reliance on a linguistic criterion for the analysis of quality: 'none of the characteristics of quality raised up until now is its exclusive property. But if one makes an assertion of similarity (相似, *hsiang ssu*) or dissimilarity (不相似, *pu hsiang ssu*), that is exclusive: for with reference to all things compared, if one says whether they are similar or not, it is always on the basis of quality (何似, *ho ssu*)' (*Categories* 11a15–19: 名理探, p. 478, corresponding to *In Universam Dialecticam*, pp. 494–6).

245 名理探, p. 349, corresponding to *In Universam Dialecticam*, pp. 363–4.

246 此論似然。而未有所證 (*ibid.*).

247 向他而謂。云互物者 (*ibid.*, p. 431). Since 'things which *designate*' translates the Latin 'things said to be relative' (*In Universam Dialecticam*, p. 446), one might think that the Chinese exposition is overly linguistic, but subsequently we read that 'to explain relative things, one should say that their *being* resides in having a direction' (解互物。當云其有。在有所向 (*Categories* 8a31–2: 名理探, p. 436).

rather more: 'those things are said to be relative which are said to be what they are of other things, or are said to be related to something in another manner'.[248] 'Of other things' is in the genitive case, and the accompanying commentary – not translated into Chinese – shows how the omitted text was understood, and why it disappears from the 十倫 (*shih lun*):

> The Philosopher calls relation 'to something' (*ad aliquid*) because thus relation is more expressly separated from the other accidents, since its nature is placed in something as it were transitive:[249] which also was the reason why he defined relatives in the plural, doubtless so as to show that a relation obtains between two things. Which fact Ammonius on this passage and Albertus (*tractatu de quanti-tate* ch. 3) noted, unless with Boetius and other interpreters you take the plural as standing for the singular. Moreover, the sense of the definition adduced is that relatives are those things, that is, entities, which are what they are (or, agreeing more closely with the Greek text, those very things they are, that is, according to their natures and essences) of other things, or are said to be related to something in another manner, that is, are explained in relation to another (*ad aliud*), either in the accusative or in another case, for that is what the words 'or in some other manner' signify, as Simplicius explained.[250]

The Chinese cannot distinguish singular from plural relatives. It could have emulated the genitive 'of other things' with something like 互視者乃他物之互也 (*hu shih che nai t'a wu chih hu yeh*), but this placement of 他物, 'other things', in attributive position governed by 之 cannot be modified to provide analogues to 'the accusative or another case'. Has lack of morphology put the Chinese at a disadvantage in the expression and analysis of relations?

'All relative things reciprocate: the lord is called lord of a minister, and the minister is called minister of a lord. Double is called double half, and half is called half double' (*Categories* 6^{b}28–31).[251] In the Chinese there is a difference between the first and the second pair of examples difficult to convey in English. The passive construction of 'lord of a minister' and 'minister of a lord', 臣所君 (*ch'en so chün*) and 君所臣 (*chün so ch'en*), might be represented as 'what is lorded by a minister' and 'what is ministered by a lord'. In 'double half' and 'half double', 半之倍 (*pan chih pei*) and 倍之半 (*pei*

---

[248] 'Ea vero dicuntur ad aliquid, quae id quod sunt, aliorum esse, aut ad aliquid aliquo alio modo dicuntur' (*In Universam Dialecticam*, p. 446).

[249] Just this claim is translated: 'the definition of the accidental constitution of relatives is that they all reside in coming from this and approaching that' (互也者之為依賴。其義。切在乎自此而逯彼者) (名理探, p. 431).

[250] *In Universam Dialecticam*, pp. 445–6.

[251] 夫凡互物者。彼此相轉應。君謂臣所君。臣謂君所臣。倍謂半之倍。半謂倍之半 (名理探 p. 433).

chih pan), the construction is simply modifier + 之 (*chih*) + noun. I am at a loss to account for the variation, since in both Latin and Greek the expression is uniform, '*x* (nominative) of *y* (genitive)': perhaps the Chinese is striving to introduce some (unwanted) constructional variation of its own, *in lieu* of impossible case-endings. The original Latin passage has a continuation the 名理探 leaves out:

> and relatives universally are spoken of in relation to those things with which they convert: for a slave is called slave of a master, and a master is called master of a slave: and double is called double half, and half is called half double, and so forth: although sometimes the expression differs in case (*quamquam interdum dictio casu differt*). For knowledge is knowledge of the knowable (*scibilis scientia*), and the knowable is knowable by knowledge (*scibile scientia scibile*), and the sense is the sense of what is sensible (*sensus sensibilis sensus*), and what is sensible is said to be sensible by the sense (*sensibile sensu sensibile*) (*Categories* 6b28–36).[252]

Perhaps here we really have at last encountered something inexpressible in Chinese. Not that (recognisable) morphological variation in the Latin is unproblematically uniform. The two occurrences of *scientia* may appear the same, but the first is nominative, the second, ablative. Although at some periods they were pronounced differently, they would in all probability have been phonetically identical to seventeenth-century Europeans. Thus the tokens of *scientia* are distinguishable on functional grounds alone – as if they were occurrences of 智 (*chih*), 'knowledge'. Granted, there is a difference in case-ending between the nominative *sensus* and the ablative *sensu*. But then we should reflect that the ablative Latin constructions translate Greek instrumental datives, τὸ ἐπιστητὸν ἐπιστήμῃ ἐπιστητόν and τὸ αἰσθητὸν αἰσθήσει αἰσθητόν: highly inflected languages have different numbers of cases, and the expressive 'work' is often distributed differently between shared cases. Are the Chinese at a grave disadvantage? Surely the immediate conclusion is that in this particular instance their lack of morphology is, if anything, a boon: Aristotle's point is that properly correlated relative pairs exceptionlessly 'reciprocate' *despite* case-difference, so that an isolating language spares one the need to disregard irrelevant, distracting variation. But it should also be conceded that heterogeneous patterns of inflection did make Western students of the *Categories* sensitive to *logical* differences in how *relata* are related; this example should be set beside chapter 1's suggestion that Greek's rich variety of moods *mildly* improved the chances that modal logic would develop.[253]

The commentary on ch. 7 demonstrates that lack of inflection does not debar the 名理探 from translating the most technical scholastic classifications. A question is

---

[252] *In Universam Dialecticam*, p. 448.   [253] See pp. 38–9 above.

raised concerning membership in the category of relation: are *relata* restricted to real entities, or are mental constructs, for example, also included? And, since relations themselves divide into 'real relations according to being' and 'relations of reason', do they all belong to the category? The eventual answer will be that membership should be restricted; but in the course of its formulation a distinction is made between 'things related according to being' (*relata secundum esse*) and 'things related according to what is said' (*relata secundum dici*):

> The first member of the analysis is things related according to being (就有而為互物, *chiu yu erh wei hu wu*); its second member is things related according to what is said (就謂而為互物, *chiu wei erh wei hu wu*). Everything which has a tendency towards another essentially and naturally (本性而有所向乎他物, *pen hsing erh yu so hsiang hu t'uo wu*) is a thing related according to being, such as matter and form, each of which tends towards the other essentially and naturally. A pair of similar things also tend towards each other essentially and naturally. Things related according to what is said divide on the basis of a pair of definitions. First, if things are all apprehended by the intellect (明悟所攝, *ming wu so shê*) according as they are directed to others, then all things related according to real being (實有, *shih yu*) are also referred to: they are all included on this definition, because they are all taken as what the intellect represents as directed to others. If the other definition is in question, then only absolute (超, *ch'ao*) things lacking relation are referred to: they are merely relative according to mental representation.[254]

The latter and proper definition of *relata secundum dici* applies to things which are intrinsically non-relational, but are conceived or explained in relation to something else (for example a head is thought of in terms of its torso). Thus the 十倫 (*shih lun*) manages to incorporate an extensive and sophisticated logical analysis of relations and *relata*, even if the translation is to some degree handicapped by the absence of morphology and case-differentiation.

10 Particular and general

Ch. 5, devoted to substance, brings us to the core of category theory. 'Everything which cannot be said of a subject and cannot be in a subject is designated as primary substance, and is substance to the highest degree' (*Categories* 2a11–13).[255] Although primary substances such as individual people are the beings *par excellence*, all substance,

---

[254] 名理探, p. 441, corresponding to *In Universam Dialecticam*, pp. 458–9.
[255] 凡不能稱底。又不能在底。是之謂初體。最切為自立 (名理探, p. 353). The Latin examples, 'a certain man and a certain horse', have been omitted – not an inconsequential omission, as we shall see (pp. 144–6 below).

particular and general, has precedence over the occupants of the accidental categories: 'substance is nobler than accident. Moreover, substances are directly designated as being, while accidents depend on substances for designation as being.'[256] 'Substance' has four significations: essence (本元, *pen yuan*); everything non-accidental, complete or incomplete; complete substance (全成之自立體, *ch'üan ch'eng chih tzû li t'i*); and primary substance (初之自立體, *ch'u chih tzû li t'i*).[257] The fourth signification is least qualified, because primary substances alone *per se* subsist.[258] 'Accordingly, one should designate secondary substances (次之自立, *tz'û chih tzû li*) as subsistent in reliance on primary substances, but the primary ones actually subsist on their own without relying on secondary substances.'[259]

Ch. 2's explication of the relations 'in' and 'said of' provided the means for determining that primary substances are ontologically basic; now that the categories themselves have been introduced, Aristotle takes the opportunity to state explicitly that nothing else could be without a foundation[260] in particular, individual substances: 'all beings are either said of or accidentally depend on[261] primary substances . . . Therefore were primary substances not actually subsistent, all other beings would also necessarily not exist'[262] (*Categories* 2a34–5, 2b5–6).[263] The commentary explains that whenever a genus in the category of substance can be 'said of' a species, it can also be 'said of' some primary substance: for example, if animal is predicated of man, it must also be predicable of a particular individual. Similarly, whenever an accidental genus inheres in a general subject, it must also be 'in' some primary substance: for example, if colour is 'in' physical body, it must also inhere in some particular body.[264] The transmission of Aristotelian ontology to the Chinese has been completed.

---

256 自立貴於依賴。況自立者。直謂為有。而依賴者。惟視自立者以謂為有耳 (名理探, p. 353).
257 *Ibid.*, corresponding to *In Universam Dialecticam*, p. 369.
258 See the explanation on p. 127 above.
259 緣次之自立。就初者而謂之在。而初者自為現在。不就次者而以為在也 (名理探, p. 353, corresponding to *In Universam Dialecticam*, p. 371).
260 Primary substance is 'the foundation of myriad being', 萬有之基, *wan yu chih chi* (名理探, p. 355).
261 The Latin says that 'all other things are either said of or *in* primary substances as subjects' (*In Universam Dialecticam*, p. 370); the 名理探 is taking the equivalence of 'in' and 'accidentally depend on' for granted in another alteration of the Aristotelian text.
262 The Latin runs 'therefore if primary substances do not *exist*, it is impossible for any of the other things to be' ('non existentibus igitur primis substantiis aliquid aliorum esse est impossibile', *In Universam Dialecticam*, p. 372). The Coimbran version has translated the Greek μὴ οὐσῶν τῶν πρώτων οὐσιῶν, 'were primary substances not to be', with the specification that the not-being in question is non-existence (as does Ackrill); the 名理探 goes a stage further by importing the scholastic equation of fully unqualified 'existence' with 'actual subsistence' into the text.
263 一切諸有。或稱初體。或依初體…故設初體若無現在。一切諸有俱亦必無 (名理探, p. 355).
264 *Ibid.*, pp. 355–6, corresponding to *In Universam Dialecticam*, p. 373.

The commentary entertains an objection (駁, *po*) to this argument for the primacy of particular substances:

> Making an affirmation on the basis of an inference from superior to inferior (由上推下而是, *yu shang t'ui hsia erh shih*), and again making a negation on the basis of an inference from inferior to superior (由下推上而非, *yu hsia t'ui shang erh fei*), are not valid (確, *ch'üeh*) according to the laws of inference (推之法, *t'ui chih fa*). Hence Aristotle's assertions that because animal can be said of man, it can also be said of a particular man, and again that were it incapable of being said of a particular man, it would also be incapable of being said of the species man, are both faulty inferences (其推論皆非也, *ch'i t'ui lun chieh fei yeh*).[265]

These scholastic principles ultimately derive from the *Prior Analytics*, which never took its place in the 名理探 curriculum. Without exposure to Western syllogistic, thinking in a language which the relativistic Sinologists of chapter 1 deem intrinsically unsuited to regimentation, could the Chinese manage at least this much formal logic? We are instructed to dispute (辯, *pien*) the objection by replying that such inferences are defective only when they rely on 'some given determinate inferior' (定為某一下, *ting wei mou i hsia*): because man is white, it does not follow that a particular individual is white as well; and if some particular individual is not black, it does not follow that man also is not. But if instead one means only one or another randomly selected man, 'an indeterminately signified particular individual' (無定指之不分一者, *wu ting chih chih pu fen i che*), then the inferences are necessarily valid. If the general nature of the human species (人類之公性, *ren lei chih kung hsing*) is white, then all particular individuals falling within the species must also be white, just as if each and every individual man is not black, then the species too will not be black.[266] (Note that these inferences are valid, but not sound.) The translation does not falter in the slightest. In the original one is informed that the valid positive argument is based on 'the first antepraedicamental rule', the negative, on 'a complete enumeration of parts'. The student reading in Latin can consult his elementary logic textbook. The student reading in Chinese cannot, but is equally well placed to comprehend a sort of informal demonstration by example expressed in his own language.

How surely does the 名理探 make its way through the complications in Aristotle's thesis that although particular individuals are primary, general substances also deserve a place in the category? 'Except for primary substance, all other beings are either said of or are accidents of genera and species. Therefore primary substances are also designated as substances in the strict sense. If you say of a particular individual that he is cultivated, then it is also permissible to make the predication of man and animal'

---

[265] *Ibid.*, p. 356, corresponding to *In Universam Dialecticam*, p. 373.
[266] *Ibid.*, pp. 356–7, corresponding to *In Universam Dialecticam*, p. 373.

(*Categories* 3a1–5).[267] In Latin we read: 'just as the primary substances are related to everything else, so the genera and species of the primary substances are related to all the rest: for all the rest are predicated of these. For you will say that a certain man is grammatical; you will therefore say that both man and animal are grammatical.'[268] Three changes have been introduced in the Chinese. First, we are told in so many words that beings are related to secondary substances in both respects, either 'in' them (as culture is 'in' animal) or 'said of' them (unexemplified: but as, for example, animal is 'said of' man). Second, this expansion permits the 名理探 to add a little argument to the effect that secondary substances are indeed substantial, since they too serve as subjects. Third, the Chinese avoids rendering 'for all the rest are predicated of these'. The claim might cause trouble, because it could sound as if all the rest are 'said of' genera and species. In fact the Latin has general 'praedicantur' rather than specific 'de subiecto dicuntur', but nevertheless the 名理探 completely eliminates a source of potential confusion. Li and Furtado do a scrupulous job of mending the crabbed writing of the *Categories* to produce a 十倫 (*shih lun*) which if still most exacting, in their view is a smoother text.

In the following passage Aristotle's attempt to make room for general substances is submitted to maximum pressure:

> What is signified as substance seems to be actual, essential subsistence *per se*. If one is discussing primary substances, they certainly signify actual *per se* subsistents. If one is discussing secondary substances, then one inspects them in accordance with the name used. If one says 'man' or 'animal', they also seem to signify essentially actual subsistence *per se*. But in the final analysis, this is not so: their signification seems rather as if one is talking about substance of a certain quality. Accordingly neither man nor animal is a single *per se* subsistent: they are predicated of many *per se* subsistents. The principles of the quality of genera and species and the quality of white are not the same. Whiteness is an extrinsic accident and does not explain the natures of things; genera and species control the essence and can define the nature (*Categories* 3b10–21).[269]

Aristotle finds himself pulled in two directions. On the one hand, although we have been repeatedly assured that all substances, primary and secondary, are substances inasmuch as none of them inheres 'in' anything, particular individuals remain

---

[267] 若除初體。其他諸有。所稱所依。惟宗惟類。故謂自立。於義亦切。如稱某甲。稱某文藝。亦可稱人。可稱生覺 (名理探, p. 359).

[268] *In Universam Dialecticam*, p. 374.

[269] 自立者所指。似實本自在。夫論初之體。固指實自在。若次之體者。就所用名相。云人云生覺。亦似指本然。而實自在者。究理則不爾。其指更若云。何似之自立。緣人與生覺。各非一自在。用稱多自在。宗類何似。與白何似。其理不同。白者依外。不釋物性。宗類統內。能解性義 (名理探, pp. 361–2).

substances 'to the highest degree' because they also are 'said of' nothing. To be a species is to exist predicated of a member of the species; but to be an individual substance is just to exist. But on the other hand, perhaps the idea that primary substances 'just' exist cannot withstand inspection. As we have stated,[270] 'Socrates is a man' does not merely tell us something *about* him; it identifies what Socrates *is*, and we might seriously doubt whether the simple contrast between 'in' and 'said of' suffices to capture the insight that natural substantial individuals are actually defined by certain of their properties. Hence the uneasy compromise attempted in the passage. It begins by casting doubt on the right of genera and species to the title 'substance' because of their very generality; but at the end it maintains that the qualities which they signify define substantial being.

This is a thoroughly modern reading of the *Categories* which sees the Aristotle of 3b10–21 as hovering between a simplistic ontology privileging the particular over the general and the profound, and unresolved, meditations on being to be found in *Metaphysics* Z and H. Of course the Philosopher of *In Universam Dialecticam* and the 名理探 is never in trouble, and the commentary in its exposition of this chapter marshals the complete supply of powerful metaphysical theorising available to the entire scholastic tradition. But even so, the quoted passage is tricky: how does the Chinese negotiate its difficult transitions? We find what we have already discovered time and again: that Li and Furtado, in turning the *Categories* into the 十倫 (*shih lun*), have made the original text over into a new version divergent not because of sheer ineptitude, but rather as a consequence of subtle interaction between *literatus*, Jesuit and potential native reader.

Our first point of significant contrast comes in the very first sentence. The Latin begins 'every substance seems to signify a certain this' ('omnis autem substantia hoc aliquid significare videtur').[271] 'A certain this', 'hoc aliquid', translates the original Greek's τόδε τι. 'Thisness' is particularity: Aristotle is saying that not being general is an *apparent* criterion for substantiality (and a real criterion for being substance 'to the highest degree'). But in Chinese unadorned 'this' has become 'actual, essential subsistence *per se*', 實本自在 (*shih pen tzû tsai*). That is, Li and Furtado have seen fit to replace Aristotle's own words with a scholastic formulation distinguishing between the merely existent and the actually subsistent. Given that primary substances alone subsist *per se*, this means that the sentence reads very oddly: surely the Philosopher himself would know that only 'substance' on its narrowest signification satisfies his description? This glossing goes well beyond our previous examples: for although the conception of primary substances as actually and independently subsistent combines a number of central Aristotelian ideas, the *Categories* simply refers to 'thisness', not to actuality. The Chinese procedure in this instance is, to say the least, what even the most liberal of

---

[270] See p. 123 above.   [271] *In Universam Dialecticam*, p. 378.

moderns would call violent over-translation. Li and Furtado could surely have stuck to the original by writing 自立者所指。似此 (*tzû li che so chih ssu tz'û*), but instead elected to inscribe their favoured interpretation within the text itself. While it is true that every translation, 'literal' or loose, good or bad, necessarily involves interpretation, by our standards the Jesuit and *literatus* show too little respect for what we regard as the real distinction between translating and explaining.

The second sentence of the Chinese inevitably develops its 'clarified' account. The Latin states that 'thisness' is indisputable in the case of primary substances because 'what is signified is individual and one in number'. Hence the Western reader is left in no doubt that particular reference is the immediate issue. The Latin continues: 'but in secondary substances while it seems that they similarly signify a certain this on account of the form of the appellation, when one says "man", or "animal": nevertheless, this is not true, but rather they signify a certain quality (*quale quid*)'. Here the contrast is telling, and brings us back to 'guidance and constraint' questions. The linguistic observation in Latin (and Greek) is that one could be misled by grammatical number into supposing that the general is particular: since 'man' and 'animal' are singular nouns like '(this) man' and '(this) animal', one might mistakenly suppose that their referents, the species man and the genus animal, are likewise particular beings. As we have seen, the 十倫 (*shih lun*) does of course discriminate between particular and general, some individual man, 不分一人 (*pu fen i jen*), as distinct from the species man, 人之類 (*jen chih lei*). If in Chinese one 'says man', 云人 (*yün jen*), 人 is not marked as either singular or plural; however, Chinese is without the morphological resources to suggest that general 'man' is actually a predicate of the many particular men, because without formally marked distinctions of number it cannot correlate '(a) man' with some man, 'man' through 'men' with men. But once more one could attempt to reverse the implication: if 人 cannot be morphologically altered for plurality, by the same token it has singular and plural signification indifferently, so that there is no 'form of appellation' *speciously* seeming 'to signify a certain this'; and the Chinese text does finally assert that secondary substances are 'predicated of many *per se* subsistents', 用稱多自在 (*yung ch'eng to tzû tsai*).

The 名理探 says that the signification of 'man' and 'animal' 'seems rather as if one is talking about substance of a certain quality', 何似之自立 (*ho ssu chih tzû li*), where the Latin does not mention substance ('they signify a certain quality'). The Western reader is left to doubt, at least momentarily, whether in that case so-called 'secondary substances' do not after all belong in the category of quality; the student of the 十倫 (*shih lun*) knows right off that qualified substance is substance, and thus is blinded to the threat which the admission that general predicates, substantial or not, do not signify a 'this' poses to the entire scheme of categories. In the end *In Universam Dialecticam* also carefully insists that generic quality is not on an equal footing with 'ordinary' qualities ('quale quid absolute'): 'the species and the genus define the quality with regard to substance: for they certainly signify substance of a certain quality (qualem quandam substantiam)'. The concept of definition is present; but there is no explicit mention of essential predication, as in the Chinese 'genera and species control the essence and can define the nature'. 'Control', 統 (*t'ung*), guarantees the status of 次之體者 (*tz'û chih t'i che*) as substance in the most emphatic manner possible.

In its commentary, however, the 名理探 considers an objection to the acceptance of 次之體者(*tz'û chih t'i che*) as substances which is phrased in terms of both particularity and subsistence. 'Subsistence *per se* is a condition uniquely possessed by all things which establish singular reference.'[272] But secondary substances neither establish singular reference nor subsist *per se*; hence the being of general natures depends on that of particular individuals.[273] The response is that subsistence characterises *all* items in the category of substance. True, particular individuals alone 'are designated as a mode of actual being' (現有其即, *hsien yu ch'i chi*),[274] but general natures, although they do not *completely* subsist (不盡然, *pu chin jan*),[275] nevertheless 'accept the mode of actualised subsistence by achieving actual union with the nature's mode of actualised subsistence *per se*'.[276] The nature which here enjoys a 'mode of actualised subsistence' is not one of the 'general natures', but rather a nature already – somehow – particularised to the extent that, and inasmuch as, it *is* the essence of some primary substance.[277] So completely general substance may be said to subsist indirectly by clinging to the shirt-tails, as it were, of an essential nature both particular and general – or neither. In the final analysis, all that Aristotle wishes to deny is that general natures are capable of 'actual subsistence in abstraction from what belongs to the category'.[278] This is the sort of thing which earns scholastic metaphysics (and some contemporary Aristotelians) a bad name: would a Chinese reader believe that the 十倫 (*shih lun*) so interpreted could truly serve as the blueprint for reality?

---

[272] 本自在者。乃諸畸一之物所獨有之情也(名理探, p. 365, corresponding to *In Universam Dialecticam*, p. 383); 畸一 (*chi i*) renders *suppositio*.

[273] 至于公性之在。則必係於不分一者之在 (*ibid.*).   [274] *Ibid.*, p. 366.   [275] *Ibid.*, p. 367.

[276] 公性就所現在之即以得現合於性所現本自在之即 (*ibid.*, p. 366, corresponding to *In Universam Dialecticam*, p. 384: I *believe* that my translation is accurate; the sentence, although fiendishly difficult, is logically constructed, and makes good sense (to a scholastic)).

[277] Cf. 'the subsistence by means of which some particular subsists and the subsistence by means of which the particular's human nature subsists are actually only one. Hence how could one say that the subsistence predicated of each substance is not univocal?' (就某甲所以在之在。與在某甲之人性所以在之在。實惟一在耳。則夫稱各體之在。豈可謂不同義者之在歟) (*ibid.*, p. 377, corresponding to *In Universam Dialecticam*, pp. 396–7).

[278] 不能脫乎屬倫而現在 (*ibid.*, pp. 368–9, corresponding to *In Universam Dialecticam*, p. 386).

A further objection suggests that the subsistence criterion creates problems for our view of the soul.[279] Since the soul is an incomplete entity, it cannot rank as a first-class occupant of the category of substance; but it does subsist *per se*, both attached to and separated from the body. Hence subsistence *per se* is not a distinguishing characteristic (獨情, *tu ch'ing*) of primary substances. The answer is that the soul does *not* subsist *per se*: 'in the man it is one part of a whole, acting as the formal cause'.[280] Previously the commentary had identified the soul as the immediate subject in which the intellect and will inhere,[281] thereby jeopardising Aristotle's anti-dualist psychology. Now it swings in the opposite direction: a 'formal cause', 模故 (*mo ku*), should be the *inseparable* organising principle of what is informed. How then can the soul sometimes exist apart from the body? The tortuous solution – not developed in the 名理探 – is to concede that the rational soul, unique among causes, is a separable entity, but also to insist that it cannot permanently remain in the incorporeal state, and must eventually be reunited with its body. Thus the doctrine of the resurrection of the flesh helps to accommodate religion with philosophy. Perhaps resurrection joined the Eucharist on the (partially) proscribed list, so that the Chinese reader remained uncertain of quite how to reconcile these various psychological passages, let alone of how this philosophy of mind relates to the Christian doctrine he had been taught.

Finally, we come to a problem which originates in a few words not translated into Chinese, the solution of which, however, is carried over into the 名理探. *Categories* 2a11–13, which were rendered as 'everything which cannot be said of a subject and cannot be in a subject is designated as primary substance, and is substance to the highest

---

[279] In Chinese, 人之靈魂 (*jen chih ling hun*), 'the human soul' (名理探, p. 366); in Latin, 'anima rationalis', 'the rational soul' (*In Universam Dialecticam*, p. 384). Nevertheless, perhaps the use of 靈魂 (*ling hun*) rather than 靈 (*ling*) on its own is significant. Traditional Chinese psychology views the soul as consisting of ten components, three of which, the 魂 (*hun*), are associated with 陽 (*yang*), the positive, solar, male principle, the other seven, the 魄 (*p'o*), with 陰 (*yin*), the negative, lunar, female principle. 'The *p'o* were sometimes believed to stay in the corpse until decomposition was complete, when they would return to the earth, which was *yin*. The *hun* were supposed to go out of the body at the last breath; some of the *hun* might stay in the commemorative tablets of the dead person and receive sacrifices, but no part was expected to survive outside the body for more than a few generations of the descendants of the deceased' (Luk 1988, p. 194). Obviously, nearly all of this would be anathema to Christians; but the collaborating converts and Jesuits might well feel that 魂 (*hun*) is a far less corrupt psychic conception than 魄 (*p'o*), and so decide to employ 靈魂 (*ling hun*) to translate *anima*. (One might be tempted to speculate that 靈魂 (*ling hun*) is specifically 'the rational soul', especially in the light of Ricci's usage in the 天主實義 (*t'ien chu shih i*: see n. 224 above). However, since the 名理探 goes on to identify the 靈魂 (*ling hun*) as the living man's formal cause, the entire soul must be meant, since both the sensitive and vegetative souls also serve as contributory formal principles.)

[280] 為其在人。乃全者之一分。且為其模故也 (名理探, p. 369, corresponding to *In Universam Dialecticam*, p. 386).

[281] See p. 128 above.

degree', continues 'like a certain man and a certain horse' (2a14: 'ut quidam homo, et quidam equus').[282] The commentary suggests that ' "a certain man and a certain horse" are cited as place-holders for those things on behalf of which they are offered as proof, *scil.* Socrates and Plato, for under that form they are not primary categorial substances, but rather vague individuals, as we shall say later'.[283] What is responsible for this interpretation is one of the true abominations of pre-Fregean quantification theory. For the scholastics, 'all men' and 'a man' must be referring terms no less than 'Socrates'. 'Socrates' refers to Socrates; 'all men' refers to all men; and 'a man' refers to a man who is not Socrates or Plato or . . . , but rather just *a* man, a betwixt-and-between 'vague' entity. Having introduced these unholy things, the commentary raises an objection which is translated: all vague individuals (游移特一 (*yu i t'e i*), literally 'varying individuals') like 'a man' (一人, *i jen*) or 'a horse' (一馬, *i ma*) are primary substances, but are not covered by their definition, which states that primary substances cannot be predicated of subjects. But 'a man' is predicable of all the individual men (可用一人以稱某某, *k'o yung i jen i ch'eng mou mou*), given that 'a man's' definitional formula (故, *ku*) applies to each and every one of them. The definition of primary substance is thus defective.[284]

Two answers. The first maintains that vague individuals are primary substances because they are *not* predicated of a plurality. A vague individual is not predicated of the individuals as of subjects to whose essence it attaches: rather, it is just the same as them (惟一而已, *wei i erh i*). If one asserts that an individual is 'a man', *all* one is saying is that he is this or that individual (指其為此一人彼一人云爾, *chih ch'i wei tz'û i jen pi i jen yün erh*).[285] Most unfortunately, the Chinese are steered away from this solution, which tries to account for quantification without postulating 'vague' referents, and towards an alternative answer which denies that vague individuals are primary substances because they are compounds of 'general nature and indeterminate particular *differentia*' (公性與未定之特殊所成者, *kung hsing yü wei ting chih t'e shu so ch'eng che*).[286] The discussion concludes with a majestic but obscure declaration:

> In the chapter Aristotle does not refer to determinate particular individuals, but rather to vague individuals, because determinate particular individuals do not suffice for the determinate domain of intellectual constancy. But if one is dealing with vague individuals, then abstracted from determinate and limited *differentiae*

[282] *In Universam Dialecticam*, p. 370.

[283] 'Haec afferuntur loco exempli pro iis, pro quibus verificantur, scilicet pro Socrate et Platone, nam sub ea forma non sunt primae substantiae praedicamentales, sed vaga individua ut postea dicemus' (*ibid.*, p. 372).

[284] 名理探, p. 380, corresponding to *In Universam Dialecticam*, p. 398.

[285] *Ibid.*, p. 381, corresponding to *In Universam Dialecticam*, p. 400.　　[286] *Ibid.*

they preserve the shared nature in order. Therefore the intellect employs them to constitute the domain of constancy.[287]

The idea is that real primary substances are ephemeral, while vague individuals partake of the constant invariance of the species; and the objects of philosophical knowledge ought to be general and unchanging. That is all very well, but desperately implausible as a rationale for the substitution of particular by vague individuals in *Categories*, ch. 5. In fact the unembroidered original on which the Chinese is based is not enthusiastic: 'Aristotle preferred to use this example rather than some determinate individual, if we believe Scotus, so as to sustain the majesty of philosophy, which does not descend to particular individuals.'[288] On the whole the Coimbran authors tend not to believe Scotus.

Comparison with the Latin version of the objection brings out vividly the embarrassing plight in which the 名理探 finds itself: 'it is objected that a certain man and other vague individuals are primary substances, but the definition does not accommodate them; hence it is not adequate. *The major premiss comes from Aristotle, who brought it forward as an example*: the minor is proved, since a certain man is said of many men, as of subjects.'[289] With 2a14 untranslated in the Chinese, one is left wondering why anyone would think – rightly or wrongly – that vague individuals *should* fall under the definition of primary substance. To compound the difficulty, in the response it is certainly implied that Aristotle himself *does* refer to them (he 'does not refer to determinate particular individuals, but rather to vague individuals'): where? The situation can be at least partially retrieved, because a subsequent bit of the *Categories*, also interpreted as referring to vague individuals, is translated: 'a certain man' ('quidam homo') is in the species man (2a16–17): but instead of 一人 (*i jen*), the Chinese has only 人.[290] If in the end the reader of the 十倫 (*shih lun*) might hesitate in drawing the line between particular and general, the reason is to be found in the tangle of late scholastic logic, not in any supposed inadequacies in the referential or quantificational resources of the Chinese language.

11 Translating the untranslatable

'Aristotelian Whispers' ends without a summarising conclusion: our purpose has been to grope towards reading the 名理探 as it might have been understood (or misunderstood),

---

[287] 亞利[Aristotle] 篇中。不舉有定之某特一。而舉游移之特一。緣定特一者不足為明悟恆然之定界。而游移之特一。則脫乎定限之殊。第存所共之性。故明悟用之以為恆然之界焉 (*ibid.*).

[288] *In Universam Dialecticam*, p. 400.   [289] *Ibid.*, p. 398, my italics.

[290] *In Universam Dialecticam*, p. 370, 名理探, p. 354.

not to produce some definitive catalogue of successes and failures according to rigid translational criteria. But in the end we return to the beginning of the *Categories* to consider one of the most astonishing passages in the 十倫 (*shih lun*).

The first chapter introduces certain semantic distinctions for subsequent use.[291] In Latin: 'those things are called denominatives which have their nominal appellation from something, different only in case; as grammarian has (its/his) appellation from grammar, and the brave man from bravery' (*Categories* 1a12–15);[292] and then the commentary explains that 'denominatives are things which, really derived from some prior form, take their name from it, at the beginning the same as the name of the form, different, however, at the end'.[293] This, if anything, one would judge to be simply untranslatable. In defining denominatives Aristotle does not merely take advantage of some grammatical feature the more easily to express the doctrine; the doctrine itself is phrased in terms of morphological change. In Chinese: 'things which complete their names from some other thing do so in accordance with a subject and a form. The designation is compound: for example, virtue and man. They are both called courageous, but the man's designation as courageous comes from the virtue.'[294] Only in the commentary do these things receive a label: 'in the West they are called "denominatives"; the translation is "names of combined appellation" '.[295]

If one read only so far, the translation of 1a12–15 would have to be judged a failure. The 十倫 (*shih lun*) may say that these names 'are completed from some other thing', but the example hardly demonstrates this: if in English the virtue is 'courage', the man, 'courageous', in Chinese the 德 (*te*) is 勇 (*yung*) just as the 人 (*jen*) is 勇: 勇 is invariant. Furthermore, on coming to 'have their nominal appellation from something, different only in case', the translation veers off completely: what do 'a subject and a form' have to do with morphological root and case-ending?

Appearances alter dramatically when we inspect the commentary,[296] where the references to 'subject and form' become clear. First, an accidental form and one of its particular instances which characterises an individual substance bear names which match at the

---

[291] Wardy 1992 contains a discussion of some aspects of the translation of ch. 1 not replicated here.

[292] 'Denominativa ea dicuntur, quae ab aliquo nominis appellationem habent, solo differentia casu: ut a Grammatica Grammaticus appellationem habet, et a fortitudine fortis' (*In Universam Dialecticam*, p. 306). Nothing corresponds to 'its/his' in the English, and a choice between them would, of course, compel a choice between the object, the grammarian, and the word 'grammarian'; but in the Latin there is no possessive here, and so no choice to be made.

[293] *Ibid.*, pp. 305–6.

[294] 由彼他物。以成厥名。是緣底模。合成而謂。如德與人。皆稱謂勇。人之謂勇。由德而謂 (名理探, p. 292).

[295] 西言得諾靡納第勿 [*denominativa*]。譯云合稱之名 (*ibid.*, p. 293).

[296] 名理探, pp. 313–14, corresponding to *In Universam Dialecticam*, pp. 327–30.

beginning but differ at the end,[297] just as the Latin commentary said. Second, their essential principles match in being, but differ in mode; since the form on its own is an abstract entity, while inhering in the concrete subject it actually characterises the particular.

> For instance, if knowledge constitutes the form, knowing, the source for making the predication of a man, then in talking on opening one's mouth what is uttered is 'know', and that is all. But if one interprets the ending, then there is a difference between reference to the virtue and reference to the man.[298]

Li and Furtado's wonderful solution to this daunting translation problem is to take advantage of 者 (*che*), a multi-purpose functional particle. 智 (*chih*) is the abstract noun, 'knowledge', and 智者 (*chih che*) is the state of knowing. Thus, just as if I say 'courageous', the first two syllables of the denominative expression are identical to the noun 'courage' naming the virtue, but the suffix indicates derivation, so if I say 智者 (*chih che*), the first graph is the abstract noun 智 (*chih*) naming the virtue, but the following functional particle indicates that the graph is now being employed differently.

We might applaud this feat of translational ingenuity – but does it matter? Is the doctrine of denominatives anything more than a trivial fragment of Indo-European linguistics? A section of the Latin commentary – untranslated for obvious reasons – shows that what is translated is far more than a piece of grammatical lore useless to the reader of the 名理探. 'Those things which according to a certain case of their name do not differ from the nominal form are not to be excluded from the number of the denominatives. For example Grammaticus, Grammatica, Grammaticum in the feminine gender, in which it plainly coincides with its form, which is Grammatica, although St Augustine teaches the opposite.'[299] Bearing a name differing in case from the nominative naming the abstract accidental form is the norm for the *things* which are 'denominatives'; but the norm is not a necessary condition, since 'if we attend rightly, difference in mode of signification is prior, for since the form is in a different state taken by itself and taken compounded with the subject, we use a word differently composed for the signification of the mode added to the form'.[300] The strategy developed to deal with (occasional) invariants such as *grammatica* ('grammar')/*grammatica* ('female grammarian') could have been easily adapted to deal with invariance in Chinese as the rule rather than the exception.

How do the semantic distinctions of ch. 1 prepare for category theory? Let us remember that the great purpose of the *Categories* is to convince us that although there are

---

[297] 兩者之名。在始則相合。在末則相異 (名理探, p. 313).
[298] 比如智為模。智者為其所由以稱人者。論啟口所稱之智。惟一而已。譯其末。則有指德指人之異焉 (ibid.).
[299] *In Universam Dialecticam*, p. 329.   [300] *Ibid.*, p. 330.

irreducibly many ways to be, substance and the particular take precedence over accidents and the general. Universals such as human being and wisdom are real, but particular individuals like Confucius and Confucius' wisdom take pride of place; and Confucius' wisdom depends on Confucius for being. That is why it is metaphysically important that 'we say', not that wisdom is Confucius; or that Confucius is wisdom; but that Confucius is wise: to the philosophical grammarian, correct identification of subject and predicate and the fact that 'wise' is 'only' an adjective reveal that this individual instance of the quality wisdom is Confucius'.

And is it also metaphysically important that the Chinese cannot quite say that? 'As Cajetan rightly explains, as white is the effect of whiteness, and is thereby posterior by nature to whiteness, so the name of this effect presupposes the name of its cause, *scil.* of whiteness – not that the compound name in accordance with the rule of grammar is always derived from the abstract.'[301] The Coimbran authors hardly imagine that *albus* ('white') comes from *albedo* ('whiteness') in any merely etymological sense: the reverse is evidently the case. What 'we' should be concerned with is the structure of reality, not of one or another language, familiar or exotic. Sometimes, as here, relations of linguistic dependence run opposite to ontological dependence. When that happens, we should do philosophical rather than linguistic 'grammar'. The heroic attempt to use the 者 (*che*) construction as an analogue for denominative morphology is phonetically plausible; and the contrast between abstract noun referring to the accidental form and noun +者 (*che*) referring to the particular accident of the individual substance is just what is wanted. But the fact remains that 智 (*chih*) without the 者 (*che*) is not at all the same as an Indo-European morpheme stripped of its accidence: 智 (*chih*) is not internally affected, as it were, by the presence of 者 (*che*), and can always be perceived as semantically complete, unlike many Greek, Latin or English roots (an Indo-European modification of the Chinese example might be printed 'for instance, if know-ledge constitutes the form, know-ing, the source for making the predication of a man, then in talking on opening one's mouth what is uttered is "know-", and that is all'). But as the Western philosopher knows that white comes from whiteness, never mind about 'white' and 'whiteness', so the Chinese philosopher can know that 智者 (*chih che*) indicates a particular accident falling under the accidental universal 智 (*chih*), never mind that the simple collocation of the two graphs just hints at the metaphysical 'derivation'. 'What we say' can, in the right context, mean 'what we philosophers have learnt to say'; and whether or not he taught him any Latin, Furtado gave Li Chih-tsao difficult but real access to one of his native culture's crowning achievements, the language of the philosophical schools.

---

[301] *Ibid.*, pp. 328–9.

Epilogue

In chapter 2 we watched Aristotle's *Categories* being transmitted to the Chinese as the focus of a monumental, centuries-old commentarial tradition. Even without the elaborate referencing system and syllogistic format of the original, much of the richness and power of this extraordinary exegetical machinery, with its forceful combination of authority and close reasoning, has come across in the Chinese version of the commentary – at times, it must be admitted, in the Chinese version of the *Categories* itself. For we have detected occasional blurrings between authorial text and explanatory armature which would be unacceptable today. It is tempting, of course, to ask whether that division was deliberately neglected; but perhaps this question would have been meaningless to the Jesuit, if he took his goal as conveying to a new readership 'what Aristotle was really saying'. And that task could simply not have been accomplished (it was plainly assumed), whatever the audience, without the resources of a vast and sophisticated technical vocabulary and all its associated distinctions and definitions.

The reader's dominant impression must surely be one of enormous, and enormously ingenious, inventiveness: of language being put to new and difficult work with great skill and precision. (The list of Aristotelian Chinese jargon will reinforce that impression, if reinforcement is needed.) But the sheer scale of the achievement should not be allowed to dwarf or conceal signs of stress or mismatch, of forced or improper renderings, even, perhaps, of failures of translation, if they exist. For the *Categories* project to help us get to grips with the challenge of linguistic relativism, we have had to engage at close quarters with particular cases, in all their subtlety and detail. The question has been whether what might be called the single most influential text in the history of Western metaphysics could be seen, embarrassingly, as little more than a local outgrowth of one language (or language family) and its idiosyncrasies.

Time and again expectations that 'Chinese simply could not cope' with the *Categories* have been dashed. Abstruse but crucial distinctions – such as those between *per se* existence and *per se* subsistence, between primary and secondary substances, and between these and accidents both general and particular – are perfectly conveyed.

Instances of apparent native 'nominalism' disappear in the light of the translation's fidelity to the dominant, and highly persuasive, reading of the *Categories* as moving effortlessly from words to the world. Even the two sections of the text where the relativist case threatened to take the upper hand, those concerning *relativa* and *denominativa*, were immediately and successfully explicated by what the Chinese philosophical tradition would call 'translation of the meaning'. It turned out, too, that here the relevant features of the Chinese language could be construed, not as distorting, still less missing, Aristotle's intent, but as actually better suited to reproduce certain logical properties of the items in question. Thus absence of morphology helpfully avoids the specious appearance of variation amongst (names for) genuine correlates which inflection for case imposes on Greek or Latin: and if, on the other hand, it is urged that such grammatical variation encourages recognition of the range of types of correlate, well, who is to choose between inflected Indo-European and uninflected Chinese on this score? Again, while the original example of *denominativa* found unexpected expression in a striking use of the functional graph 者 (*che*), the cardinal point is that that distinction was not merely successfully conveyed, but conveyed in such a way that the underlying ontology was just as sharply delineated as in the Latin. And this was not the only passage in which the concerns of the commentarial tradition were well served by the 名理探: the distinction between 'simple' and 'compound' names deserves mention in this connection.

If 'the Chinese reader' (whoever he was) found the *Categories* and the commentary in which it was nested strange, comparison with native traditions of philosophical teaching and learning has strongly suggested that that strangeness would lie at least as much in the Western emphasis on the canons of correct reasoning as sure roads to truth and harmony as it would in the (of course unfamiliar) metaphysics which the text was taken to articulate. (Western readers, in their turn, have found themselves drawn into the alien world of neo-Confucian, anti-Buddhist polemic.) The commentary seems to have taken some pains to isolate the *Categories* from its less palatable associations, both historical (thus Aristotle appears chiefly as sage and respected adviser to a great king) and theological (we noted the absence of allusions to the difficult doctrines of transsubstantiation and the Trinity), even if the quarantine was decidedly imperfect. The reader was spared little, however, when it came to what strikes us as the fantastically ramified exegesis of the *Categories*, and nothing at all in the matter of jargon. *In Universam Dialecticam* is very much a book of its time and (cultural) place: a *school* book from a scholastic tradition. But the very fact that its strangeness can be appreciated, even savoured, by us moderns in the West reveals that it is not locked in the seventeenth century, and we have found no evidence that Aristotle, too, could not make the transition from fourth-century BCE Greek, to seventeenth-century Latin, to seventeenth-century Chinese.

'Because the language was so rarefied, thorns have come into my throat, and several times on account of difficulties I have set aside my pen.' What Li Chih-tsao said of Aristotle, I can say of Li Chih-tsao; but learning to perceive my Aristotle in his 亞利 has taught me much about both Aristotelian language and language itself. Whether or not there was a 'Chinese reader', I hope that the readers of this book will share my conviction that Li and Furtado did not labour in vain.

Glossary of technical terms

This glossary is not at all comprehensive: it includes only an illustrative sample of terms of art (not all of which are discussed in the main text), to permit the reader to gain an impression of how the 名理探 (*ming li t'an*) creates *en passant* a scholastic vocabulary for itself. Graphs employed to render distinct Latin terms receive more than one entry. Where necessary I have provided the Latin original as well as an English translation. The first listing is for Sinologists, and is organised by radical and stroke-number. The second is for readers without Chinese, and is in alphabetical order.

不分一者 (*pu fen i che*: 名理探, p. 316)	particular individual
互視 (*hu shih*: p. 325)	relation
作所以然 (*tso so i jan*: pp. 34, 336)	efficient cause
作為 (*tso wei*: p. 326)	action
依 (*i*: p. 27)	accidental attribute
依合 (*i ho*: p. 316)	accidental combination
依模 (*i mo*: p. 336)	accidental form
依結乎底 (*i chieh hu ti*: p. 336)	inherence
依賴 (*i lai*: p. 327)	accident
倫 (*lun*: p. 289)	category
元質 (*yüan chih*: p. 340)	prime matter
內 (*nei*: p. 362)	essence
內有 (*nei yu*: pp. 333, 345)	essence
次質 (*tz'û chih*: p. 336)	secondary matter
次體 (*tz'û t'i*: p. 353)	secondary substance
函內性 (*han nei hsing*: p. 345)	essential
切所 (*ch'ieh so*: p. 325)	place
初情 (*ch'u ch'ing*: p. 481)	primary quality
初自立 (*ch'u tzû li*: p. 349)	primary substance
剖析 (*p'ou hsi*: p. 27)	to analyse
動感 (*tung kan*: p. 470)	affection

153

動成 (*tung ch'eng*: p. 470)   affective quality

動者 (*tung che*: p. 336)   motion

反 (*fan*: p. 329)   contradictory

受德 (*shou te*: p. 335)   the will

受飾 (*shou shih*: p. 326)   having

即 (*chi*: pp. 336, 366)   mode

可不然 (*k'o pu jan*: p. 313)   accidental

合一之結 (*ho i chih chieh*: p. 336)   real identity

合底 (*ho ti*: p. 342)   concrete subject

合成者 (*ho ch'eng che*: p. 334)   compound

合稱之名 (*ho ch'eng chih ming*: p. 293)   *denominativa*

合限 (*ho hsien*: p. 27)   term

名理探 (*ming li t'an*: p. 289)   dialectic

何似 (*ho ssu*: p. 325)   quality

何時 (*ho shih*: p. 325)   time

固然之稱 (*ku ran chih ch'eng*: p. 342)   necessary predicate

天主 (*t'ien chu*: pp. 333, 335)   God

天文 (*t'ien wen*: p. 10)   astronomy

宗 (*tsung*: pp. 291, 314, 326)   genus or class

實互 (*shih hu*: pp. 439, 440)   real relation

實別 (*shih pieh*: p. 341)   actually distinct

專而無合 (*chuan erh wu ho*: p. 333)   simple

就有而為互物 (*chiu yu erh wei hu wu*: p. 441)   *relata secundum esse*

就謂而為互物 (*chiu wei erh wei hu wu*: p. 441)   *relata secundum dici*

幾何 (*chi ho*: p. 325)   quantity

底 (*ti*: pp. 293, 313)   subject

形 (*hsing*: pp. 349, 350)   physical, corporeal

形性學 (*hsing hsing hsüeh*: p. 315)   physics

彼此相轉應 (*pi tz'û hsiang chuan ying*: p. 433) to reciprocate

往作為 (*wang tso wei*: p. 350)   transitive action

德 (*te*: pp. 349, 441)   potential

思互 (*ssu hu*: pp. 439, 440)   relation of thought

性 (*hsing*: p. 289)   nature

情 (*ch'ing*: pp. 27, 291, 333)   affection, condition

情 (*ch'ing*: p. 339)   proper character

意想 (*i hsiang*: p. 315)   concepts

愛欲 (*ai yü*: pp. 12, 16)   the will

愛知學 (*ai chih hsüeh*: pp. 1, 16)   philosophy

懷理 (*huai li*: p. 364)   mental definition

抵受 (*ti shou*: p. 326)   passion

指 (*chih*: p. 315)   designate, signify

推論 (*t'ui lun*: pp. 2, 13)	inference
掌展拓廣狹 (*chang chan t'o kuang hsia*: pp. 328–9)	extension
據 (*chü*: p. 333)	proof
收論 (*shou lun*: p. 356)	inference
效 (*hsiao*: p. 336)	effect
文藝 (*wen i*: pp. 6, 27)	rhetoric
所以然 (*so i jan*: p. 439)	cause
所向之為 (*so hsiang chih wei*: p. 336)	goal
斷通 (*tuan t'ung*: p. 28)	analysis
施 (*shih*: p. 441)	action
施動者 (*shih tung che*: p. 336)	mover
既然之須 (*chi ran chih hsü*: p. 34)	hypothetical necessity
旨 (*chih*: p. 315)	signification
明學 (*ming hsüeh*: p. 12)	speculative science
明悟 (*ming wu*: pp. 12, 335)	intellect
明辨 (*ming pien*: p. 10)	inference
有 (*yu*: p. 313)	being
有也者 (*yu yeh che*: p. 289)	existent
有在者 (*yu tsai che*: pp. 328, 339)	subsisting being
有隔之終底 (*yu ke chih chung ti*: p. 340)	mediate subject
本元 (*pen yüan*: pp. 315, 328, 333)	essence
本在之有 (*pen tsai chih yu*: p. 334)	*per se* existence
本然 (*pen jan*: pp. 313, 314)	essential
本理 (*pen li*: p. 356)	definition
本自 (*pen tzû*: p. 368)	*per se*
本自在之有 (*pen tzû tsai chih yu*: p. 353)	*per se* subsistent being
模 (*mo*: pp. 292, 328)	form
模別 (*mo pieh*: p. 341)	formally distinct
模效 (*mo hsiao*: p. 439)	formal effect
殊 (*shu*: pp. 291, 326)	*differentia*
游移特一 (*yu i t'e i*: p. 380)	vague individual
為 (*wei*: p. 326)	actual
為所以然 (*wei so i jan*: p. 34)	final cause
無屬 (*wu shu*: p. 314)	*simpliciter*
無隔之中底 (*wu ke chih chung ti*: p. 340)	immediate subject
率基 (*shuai chi*: p. 439)	virtual basis
率基之別 (*shuai chi chih pieh*: p. 379)	virtual distinction
現在 (*hsien tsai*: pp. 332, 342)	actually subsistent
現在之稱 (*hsien tsai chih ch'eng*: p. 342)	existential predicate
理 (*li*: p. 290)	principle
理 (*li*: p. 328)	mode

理學士 (*li hsüeh shih*: p. 439) — philosophers
生覺 (*sheng chüeh*: p. 336) — animal
界理 (*chieh li*: p. 364) — objective definition
留作為 (*liu tso wei*: p. 350) — immanent action
直然之須 (*chih jan chih hsü*: p. 34) — absolute necessity
直通 (*chih t'ung*: p. 28) — simple apprehension
相對 (*hsiang tui*: pp. 537, 541) — opposite
確 (*ch'üeh*: p. 356) — valid
稱 (*ch'eng*: p. 289) — appellation, predicate
積 (*chi*: p. 346) — intensity
缺 (*ch'üeh*: p. 345) — privation
義 (*i*: p. 290) — definition
能 (*neng*: p. 326) — potential
能推 (*neng t'ui*: p. 342) — extension
能覺之模 (*neng chüeh chih mo*: p. 373) — sensitive form/soul
脫底 (*t'uo ti*: p. 342) — abstract subject
自在 (*tzû tsai*: pp. 328, 335) — subsistence *per se*
自立 (*tzû li*: pp. 290, 314, 316) — substance
自立體 (*tzû li t'i*: pp. 316, 325, 327) — substance
號 (*hao*: pp. 315, 325) — signified
解 (*chieh*: p. 337) — definition
解釋 (*chieh shih*: p. 27) — to define
證 (*cheng*: pp. 329, 347) — proof
譚藝 (*t'an i*: pp. 10, 11, 27) — grammar
質 (*chih*: pp. 326, 328) — matter
賴 (*lai*: pp. 316, 328) — attribute
超形性學 (*ch'ao hsing hsing hsüeh*: p. 289) — *Metaphysics*, metaphysics
超有 (*ch'ao yu*: p. 290) — transcendent being
超模 (*ch'ao mo*: pp. 437, 438) — absolute form
遊互視者 (*yu hu shih che*: p. 441) — transcendental relation
辨藝 (*pien i*: p. 6) — logic
辯 (*pien*: p. 326) — disputation
限解 (*hsien chieh*: pp. 333, 339) — strict definition
開展 (*k'ai chan*: p. 481) — extension
靈 (*ling*: p. 314) — soul
靈魂 (*ling hun*: p. 335) — soul
靜天 (*ching t'ien*: p. 338) — the fixed stars
題論 (*t'i lun*: p. 27) — proposition
類 (*lei*: p. 291) — species
體執 (*t'i i*: p. 326) — situation
體模 (*t'i mo*: pp. 335, 336) — substantial form

absolute form	超模 (*ch'ao mo*: 名理探, pp. 437, 438)
absolute necessity	直然之須 (*chih jan chih hsü*: p. 34)
abstract subject	脫底 (*t'uo ti*: p. 342)
accident	依賴 (*i lai*: p. 327)
accidental	可不然 (*k'o pu jan*: p. 313)
accidental attribute	依 (*i*: p. 27)
accidental combination	依合 (*i ho*: p. 316)
accidental form	依模 (*i mo*: p. 336)
action	作為 (*tso wei*: p. 326)
action	施 (*shih*: p. 441)
actual	為 (*wei*: p. 326)
actually distinct	實別 (*shih pieh*: p. 341)
actually subsistent	現在 (*hsien tsai*: pp. 332, 342)
affection	動感 (*tung kan*: p. 470)
affection, condition	情 (*ch'ing*: pp. 27, 291, 333)
affective quality	動成 (*tung ch'eng*: p. 470)
to analyse	剖析 (*p'ou hsi*: p. 27)
analysis	斷通 (*tuan t'ung*: p. 28)
animal	生覺 (*sheng chüeh*: p. 336)
appellation, predicate	稱 (*ch'eng*: p. 289)
astronomy	天文 (*t'ien wen*: p. 10)
attribute	賴 (*lai*: pp. 316, 328)
being	有 (*yu*: p. 313)
category	倫 (*lun*: p. 289)
cause	所以然 (*so i jan*: p. 439)
compound	合成者 (*ho ch'eng che*: p. 334)
concepts	意想 (*i hsiang*: p. 315)
concrete subject	合底 (*ho ti*: p. 342)
contradictory	反 (*fan*: p. 329)
to define	解釋 (*chieh shih*: p. 27)
definition	本理 (*pen li*: p. 356)
definition	義 (*i*: p. 290)
definition	解 (*chieh*: p. 337)
denominativa	合稱之名 (*ho ch'eng chih ming*: p. 293)
designate, signify	指 (*chih*: p. 315)
dialectic	名理探 (*ming li t'an*: p. 289)
differentia	殊 (*shu*: pp. 291, 326)
disputation	辯 (*pien*: p. 326)

effect	效 (*hsiao*: p. 336)
efficient cause	作所以然 (*tso so i jan*: pp. 34, 336)
essence	內 (*nei*: p. 362)
essence	內有 (*nei yu*: pp. 333, 345)
essence	本元 (*pen yüan*: pp. 315, 328, 333)
essential	函內性 (*han nei hsing*: p. 345)
essential	本然 (*pen jan*: pp. 313, 314)
existent	有也者 (*yu yeh che*: p. 289)
existential predicate	現在之稱 (*hsien tsai chih ch'eng*: p. 342)
extension	掌展拓廣狹 (*chang chan t'o kuang hsia*: pp. 328–9)
extension	能推 (*neng t'ui*: p. 342)
extension	開展 (*k'ai chan*: p. 481)
final cause	為所以然 (*wei so i jan*: p. 34)
the fixed stars	靜天 (*ching t'ien*: p. 338)
form	模 (*mo*: pp. 292, 328)
formal effect	模效 (*mo hsiao*: p. 439)
formally distinct	模別 (*mo pieh*: p. 341)
genus or class	宗 (*tzung*: pp. 291, 314, 326)
goal	所向之為 (*so hsiang chih wei*: p. 336)
God	天主 (*t'ien chu*: pp. 333, 335)
grammar	譚藝 (*t'an i*: pp. 10, 11, 27)
having	受飾 (*shou shih*: p. 326)
hypothetical necessity	既然之須 (*chi ran chih hsü*: p. 34)
immanent action	留作為 (*liu tso wei*: p. 350)
immediate subject	無隔之中底 (*wu ke chih chung ti*: p. 340)
inference	推論 (*t'ui lun*: pp. 2, 13)
inference	收論 (*shou lun*: p. 356)
inference	明辨 (*ming pien*: p. 10)
inherence	依結乎底 (*i chieh hu ti*: p. 336)
intellect	明悟 (*ming wu*: pp. 12, 335)
intensity	積 (*chi*: p. 346)
logic	辨藝 (*pien i*: p. 6)
matter	質 (*chih*: pp. 326, 328)
mediate subject	有隔之終底 (*yu ke chih chung ti*: p. 340)
mental definition	懷理 (*huai li*: p. 364)
Metaphysics, metaphysics	超形性學 (*ch'ao hsing hsing hsüeh*: p. 289)
mode	即 (*chi*: pp. 336, 366)

mode	理 (*li*: p. 328)
motion	動者 (*tung che*: p. 336)
mover	施動者 (*shih tung che*: p. 336)
nature	性 (*hsing*: p. 289)
necessary predicate	固然之稱 (*ku ran chih ch'eng*: p. 342)
objective definition	界理 (*chieh li*: p. 364)
opposite	相對 (*hsiang tui*: pp. 537, 541)
particular individual	不分一者 (*pu fen i che*: p. 316)
passion	抵受 (*ti shou*: p. 326)
per se	本自 (*pen tzû*: p. 368)
per se existence	本在之有 (*pen tsai chih yu*: p. 334)
per se subsistent being	本自在之有 (*pen tzû tsai chih yu*: p. 353)
philosophers	理學士 (*li hsüeh shih*: p. 439)
philosophy	愛知學 (*ai chih hsüeh*: pp. 1, 16)
physical, corporeal	形 (hsing: pp. 349, 350)
physics	形性學 (*hsing hsing hsüeh*: p. 315)
place	切所 (*ch'ieh so*: p. 325)
potential	德 (*te*: pp. 349, 441)
potential	能 (*neng*: p. 326)
primary quality	初情 (*ch'u ch'ing*: p. 481)
primary substance	初自立 (*ch'u tzû li*: p. 349)
prime matter	元質 (*yüan chih*: p. 340)
principle	理 (*li*: p. 290)
privation	缺 (*ch'üeh*: p. 345)
proof	據 (*chü*: p. 333)
proof	證 (*cheng*: pp. 329, 347)
proper character	情 (*ch'ing*: p. 339)
proposition	題論 (*t'i lun*: p. 27)
quality	何似 (*ho ssu*: p. 325)
quantity	幾何 (*chi ho*: p. 325)
real identity	合一之結 (*ho i chih chieh*: p. 336)
real relation	實互 (*shih hu*: pp. 439, 440)
to reciprocate	彼此相轉應 (*pi tz'û hsiang chuan ying*: p. 433)
relata secundum dici	就謂而為互物 (*chiu wei erh wei hu wu*: p. 441)
relata secundum esse	就有而為互物 (*chiu yu erh wei hu wu*: p. 441)
relation	互視 (*hu shih*: p. 325)
relation of thought	思互 (*ssu hu*: pp. 439, 440)
rhetoric	文藝 (*wen i*: pp. 6, 27)

secondary matter	次質 (*tz'û chih*: p. 336)
secondary substance	次體 (*tz'û t'i*: p. 353)
sensitive form/soul	能覺之模 (*neng chüeh chih mo*: p. 373)
signification	旨 (*chih*: p. 315)
signified	號 (*hao*: pp. 315, 325)
simple	專而無合 (*chuan erh wu ho*: p. 333)
simple apprehension	直通 (*chih t'ung*: p. 28)
simpliciter	無屬 (*wu shu*: p. 314)
situation	體執 (*t'i i*: p. 326)
soul	靈 (*ling*: p. 314)
soul	靈魂 (*ling hun*: p. 335)
species	類 (*lei*: p. 291)
speculative science	明學 (*ming hsüeh*: p. 12)
strict definition	限解 (*hsien chieh*: pp. 333, 339)
subject	底 (*ti*: pp. 293, 313)
subsistence *per se*	自在 (*tzû tsai*: pp. 328, 335)
subsisting being	有在者 (*yu tsai che*: pp. 328, 339)
substance	自立 (*tzû li*: pp. 290, 314, 316)
substance	自立體 (*tzû li t'i*: pp. 316, 325, 327)
substantial form	體模 (*t'i mo*: pp. 335, 336)
term	合限 (*ho hsien*: p. 27)
time	何時 (*ho shih*: p. 325)
transcendent being	超有 (*ch'ao yu*: p. 290)
transcendental relation	遊互視者 (*yu hu shih che*: p. 441)
transitive action	往作為 (*wang tso wei*: p. 350)
vague individual	游移特一 (*yu i t'e i*: p. 380)
valid	確 (*ch'üeh*: p. 356)
virtual basis	率基 (*shuai chi*: p. 439)
virtual distinction	率基之別 (*shuai chi chih pieh*: p. 379)
the will	受德 (*shou te*: p. 335)
the will	愛欲 (*ai yü*: pp. 12, 16)

References

Ackrill, J. L.1979. *Aristotle's* Categories and De Interpretatione *Translated with Notes and Glossary*, Oxford.

Allinson, R. E. (ed.) 1989. *Understanding the Chinese Mind: The Philosophical Roots*, Hong Kong.

Anscombe, G. E. M. 1959. *An Introduction to Wittgenstein's* Tractatus, London.

Aristotle, 1978. *Categories and De Interpretatione*, ed. L. Minio-Paluello, Oxford.

  1979. *Topics and Sophistici Elenchi*, ed. W. D. Ross, Oxford.

  1995. *Aristotle's Posterior Analytics, Translated with Notes*, ed. J. Barnes, 2nd edition, Oxford.

Bloom, A. 1981. *The Linguistic Shaping of Thought: A Study in the Impact of Language on Thinking in China and the West*, Hillsdale, N.J.

Chao, Y.-R. 1955. 'Notes on Chinese Grammar and Logic', *Philosophy East and West* 5: 31–41.

Chomsky, N. 1967. *Aspects of the Theory of Syntax*, Cambridge, Mass.

  1969. *Current Issues in Linguistic Theory, Janua Linguarum*, Series Minor 38, The Hague.

Chroust, A.-H. 1973. *Aristotle: New Light on his Life and on Some of his Lost Works*, vol. I, *Some Novel Interpretations of the Man and his Life*, London.

Cicero, 1971. *Tusculan Disputations*, trans. J. E. King, London.

Collegium Conimbricense, 1976. *In Universam Dialecticam Aristotelis*, Hildesheim.

Davidson, D. 1980. *Essays on Actions and Events*, Oxford.

  1984. *Inquiries into Truth and Interpretation*, Oxford.

Denyer, N. C. 1981. 'Time and Modality in Diodorus Cronus', *Theoria* 47: 31–53.

Diderot, D. 1875. *Œuvres complètes de Diderot*, ed. J. Assézat, Paris, vol. I.

Diogenes Laertius, 1972. *Lives of Eminent Philosophers*, trans. R. D. Hicks (2 vols.), Cambridge, Mass.

Dudink, A. and Standaert, N. n.d. 'Ferdinand Verbiest's 窮理學 (1683)', unpublished.

Düring, I. 1957. *Aristotle in the Ancient Biographical Tradition*, Göteborg.

Engelfriet, P. 1993. 'The Chinese Euclid and its European Context', in Jami and Delahaye 1993.

  1998. *Euclid in China: The Genesis of the First Chinese Translation of Euclid's* Elements *Books I–VI* (Jihe yuanben; Beijing, 1607) *and its Reception up to 1723*, Leiden.

Etiemble, 1988. *L'Europe chinoise I: de l'Empire romain à Leibniz*, Paris.

方豪(Father Fang Hao), 1967–73. 中國大主教史人物傳, Hong Kong.

Fang, W.-C. 1984. 'Chinese Language and Theoretical Thinking: A Review Article', *Journal of Oriental Studies* 22: 25–32.

Flew, A. G. N. (ed.) 1968. *Logic and Language* (First Series), Oxford.

Frankenhauser, U. 1996. *Die Einführung der buddhistischen Logik in China*, Wiesbaden.

Frede, M. 1987. *Essays in Ancient Philosophy*, Oxford.

Furth, M. 1988. *Substance, Form and Psyche: An Aristotelian Metaphysics*, Cambridge.

Gallagher, L. (ed.) 1953. *China in the Sixteenth Century: The Journals of Matthew Ricci: 1583–1610*, New York.

Geach, P. T. 1981. *Logic Matters*, London.

Gernet, J. 1985. *China and the Christian Impact: A Conflict of Cultures*, trans. J. Lloyd, Cambridge.

Girdansky, M. 1963. *The Adventure of Language*, New York.

Givón, T. 1978. 'Universal Grammar, Lexical Structure and Translatability', in Guenthner and Guenthner-Reutter 1978.

Graham, A. C. 1978. *Later Mohist Logic, Ethics and Science*, London.

  1989. *Disputers of the Tao: Philosophical Argument in Ancient China*, La Salle, Ill.

Granet, M. 1934. *La Pensée chinoise*, Paris.

Guenthner, F. and Guenthner-Reutter, M. (eds.), 1978. *Meaning and Translation: Philosophical and Linguistic Approaches*, London.

Guttenplan, S. 1986. *The Languages of Logic*, Oxford.

Haack, S. 1978. *Philosophy of Logics*, Cambridge.

Hacking, I. 1968. 'A Language without Particulars', *Mind* 77: 168–85.

Hall, D. and Ames, R. 1987. *Thinking Through Confucius*, Albany.

Hall, E. 1959. *The Silent Language*, New York.

Hansen, C. 1983. *Language and Logic in Ancient China*, Ann Arbor.

  1985. 'Chinese Language, Chinese Philosophy, and "Truth" ', *Journal of Asian Studies* 44: 491–519.

  1987. 'Classical Chinese Philosophy as Linguistic Analysis', *Journal of Chinese Philosophy* 14: 309–30.

  1989. 'Language in the Heart-mind', in Allinson 1989.

  1991. 'Should the Ancient Masters Value Reason?', in Rosemont 1991.

Harbsmeier, C. 1979. *Zur philosophischen Grammatik des Altchinesischen im Anschluß an Humboldts Brief an Abel-Rémusat*, published with his German translation of Humboldt, *Brief an M. Abel-Rémusat über die Natur grammatischer Formen im allgemeinen und über den Geist der chinesischen Sprache im besondern*, Stuttgart–Bad Cannstatt.

  1981. *Aspects of Classical Chinese Syntax*, London and Malmö.

  1989. 'Marginalia Sino-Logica', in Allinson 1989.

  1991. 'The Mass Noun Hypothesis and the Part–Whole Analysis of the White Horse Dialogue', in Rosemont 1991.

  1998. *Science and Civilisation in China* (vol. 7), *Part I: Language and Logic*, Cambridge.

Harris, R. 1980. *The Language Makers*, London.

  1981. *The Language Myth*, London.

Hawkins, E. L. 1893. *The Oxford Handbook of Logic Deductive and Inductive, Specially Adopted for the Use of Candidates for Moderations at Oxford with Questions that have been Set in the Schools, together with Answers to the Same*, 5th edition, Oxford.

Henderson, J. B. 1991. *Scripture, Canon, and Commentary: A Comparison of Confucian and Western Exegesis*, Princeton.

Hirsch, E. 1993. *Dividing Reality*, Oxford.

Hobbes, T. 1973. *Leviathan*, London.

Hoijer, H. (ed.) 1954. *Language in Culture, Conference on the Interrelations of Language and Other Aspects of Culture*, Chicago.

Holzman, D. 1956. 'Conversational Tradition in Chinese Philosophy', *Philosophy East and West* 6: 223–30.

Humboldt, W. von 1827. *Lettre à M. Abel-Rémusat sur la nature des formes grammaticales en général, et sur le génie de la langue chinoise en particulier*, Paris.

Hummel, A. 1943. *Eminent Chinese of the Ch'ing Period*, vol. I, Washington.

Jami, C. and Delahaye, H. (eds.) 1993. *L'Europe en Chine: Interactions scientifiques, religieuses et culturelles aux XVIIE et XVIIIE siècles*, Paris.

Katz, J. 1978. 'Effability and Translation', in Guenthner and Guenthner-Reutter 1978.

    1988. 'The Refutation of Indeterminacy', *Journal of Philosophy* 85: 227–52.

Kirwan, C. 1978. *Logic and Argument*, London.

Lakoff, G. 1973. 'Fuzzy Grammar and the Performance/Competence Terminology Game', in *Papers from the Ninth Regional Meeting, Chicago Linguistic Society*, Chicago.

Lemmon, E. J. 1984. *Beginning Logic*, Wokingham.

Li Chih-tsao (李之藻), 1965. 名理探 (*ming li t'an*), Taipei.

Lippiello, T. and Malek, R. (eds.) 1997. *Scholar from the West: Giulio Aleni S. J. (1582–1649) and the Dialogue between Christianity and China*, Monumenta Serica Monograph Series XLII, Nettetal.

Lloyd, G. E. R. 1990. *Demystifying Mentalities*, Cambridge.

Luk, B. H.-K. 1988. 'A Serious Matter of Life and Death: Learned Conversations at Foochow in 1627', in Ronan and Oh 1988.

    1997. 'Aleni Introduces the Western Academic Tradition to Seventeenth-Century China: A Study of the *Xixue fan*', in Lippiello and Malek 1997.

Malotki, E. 1983. *Hopi Time: A Linguistic Analysis of the Temporal Concepts in the Hopi Language*, Berlin.

Melis, G. 1994. 'Temi e tesi della filosofia europea nel "Tianzhu Shiyi" di Matteo Ricci', in *Atti del convegno internazionale di studi Ricciani*, Macerata.

Monumenta Paedagogica Societatis Jesu, 1965– . Rome.

Müller, W. n.d. 'Raum und Zeit in Sprachen und Kalendern Nordamerikas und Alteuropas', *Anthropos* 57: 568–90.

Mungello, D. E. 1989. *Curious Land: Jesuit Accommodation and the Origins of Sinology*, Honolulu.

    1994. *The Forgotten Christians of Hangzhou*, Honolulu.

Nietzsche, F. 1973. *Beyond Good and Evil*, trans. R. J. Hollingdale, London.

    1987. *Jenseits von Gut und Böse: Vorspiel einer Philosophie der Zukunft*, Augsburg.

Owen, G. E. L. 1986. *Logic, Science and Dialectic: Collected Papers in Greek Philosophy*, ed. M. Nussbaum, London.

Passmore, J. 1961. *Philosophical Reasoning*, London.

Peterson, W. J. 1988. 'Why Did They Become Christians? Yang T'ing-yün, Li Chih-tsao, and Hsü Kuang-ch'i', in Ronan and Oh 1988.

Pinxton, R. (ed.) 1976. *Universalism versus Relativism in Language and Thought*, The Hague.

Prior, A. N. 1955. *Formal Logic*, Oxford.

Quine, W. V. 1960. *Word and Object*, Cambridge, Mass.

    1969. *Ontological Relativity and Other Essays*, New York.

    1974. *Methods of Logic*, 3rd edition, London.

    1980. *Elementary Logic*, 2nd edition, London.

    1981. *Theories and Things*, London.

1986. *Philosophy of Logic*, 2nd edition, London.

1987. 'Indeterminacy of Translation Again', *Journal of Philosophy* 84: 5–10.

Ramsey, F. P. 1990. *Philosophical Papers*, ed. D. H. Mellor Cambridge.

Reding, J.-P. 1986. 'Greek and Chinese Categories: A Reexamination of the Problem of Linguistic Relativism', *Philosophy East and West* 36: 349–74.

Resnik, M. 1988. 'Second-order Logic Still Wild', *Journal of Philosophy* 85: 75–87.

Robins, R. 1976. 'The Current Relevance of the Sapir–Whorf Hypothesis', in Pinxton 1976.

Ronan, C. E. and Oh, B. B. C. (eds.) 1988. *East Meets West:The Jesuits in China, 1582–1773*, Chicago.

Rosemont, H. Jr. 1974. 'On Representing Abstractions in Archaic Chinese', *Philosophy East and West* 24: 71–88.

1991 (ed.) *Chinese Texts and Philosophical Contexts: Essays Dedicated to Angus C. Graham*, La Salle, Ill.

Ross, J. R. 1972. 'The Category Squish; Endstation Hauptwort', in *Papers from the Eighth Regional Meeting, Chicago Linguistic Society*, Chicago.

Russell, B. 1956. *Logic and Knowledge, Essays 1901–1950*, ed. R. C. Marsh, New York.

Ryle, G. 1968. 'Systematically Misleading Expressions', in Flew 1968.

Sainsbury, M. 1991. *Logical Forms: An Introduction to Philosophical Logic*, Oxford.

Schenkeveld, D. M. 1992. 'Prose Usages of AKOYEIN "to Read"', *Classical Quarterly* n.s. 42: 129–41.

Schmitt, C. B. and Skinner, Q. (eds.) 1988. *The Cambridge History of Renaissance Philosophy*, Cambridge.

Sedley, D. 1977. 'Diodorus Cronus and Hellenistic Philosophy', *Proceedings of the Cambridge Philological Society* n.s. 23: 74–120.

Semedo, A. 1655. *The History of the Great and Renowned Monarchy of China*, trans. E. Tyler, London.

Spence, J. D. 1985. *The Memory Palace of Matteo Ricci*, London.

Standaert, N. 1994. 'The Investigations of Things and the Fathoming of Principles (*Gewu Qiongli*) in the Seventeenth-Century Contact between Jesuits and Chinese Scholars', in Witek 1994.

Steiner, G. 1992. *After Babel: Aspects of Language and Translation*, 2nd edition, Oxford.

Strawson, P. F. 1952. *Introduction to Logical Theory*, London.

1971. *Logico-Linguistic Papers*, London.

Usener, H. 1887. *Epicurea*, Leipzig.

Verhaar, J. W. M. (ed.) 1967–. *The Verb 'Be' and its Synonyms*, in *Foundations of Language*, supplementary series, Dordrecht.

Verhaeren, H. 1935. 'Aristote en Chine', *Bulletin catholique de Pékin* 22 (1935).

Wardy, R. 1992. 'Chinese Whispers', *Proceedings of the Cambridge Philological Society* n.s. 38: 149–70.

Webb, J. 1669. *An Historical Essay Endeavouring a Probability That the Language of the Empire of China is the Primitive Language*, London.

1678. *The Antiquity of China, or an Historical Essay, Endeavouring a Probability That the Language of the Empire of China is the Primitive Language Spoken Through the Whole World Before the Confusion of Babel*, London.

Whorf, B. 1967. *Language Thought and Reality*, ed. J. Carroll, Cambridge, Mass.

Wiggins, D. 1980. *Sameness and Substance*, Oxford.

Williams, C. J. F. 1981. *What is Existence?*, Oxford.

Wilson, M. 1994. 'Can We Trust Logical Form?', *Journal of Philosophy* 91: 519–44.

Witek, J. W. (ed.) 1994. *Ferdinand Verbiest (1623–1688): Jesuit Missionary, Scientist, Engineer and Diplomat*, Monumenta Serica Monograph Series XXX, Nettetal.

Wittgenstein, L. 1978. *Tractatus Logico-Philosophicus*, trans. D. F. Pears and B. F. McGuinness, London.

    1981. *Tractatus Logico-Philosophicus*, London.

Wright, A. (ed.) 1953. *Studies in Chinese Thought*, Cambridge.

Wu, K.-M. 1987. 'Counterfactuals, Universals, and Chinese Thinking', *Philosophy East and West* 37: 84–94.

Index

accident, 85, 105, 116, 121–6, 129–31, 138; *see also i*
    'accident'; substance
Ackrill, John, 72 n. 4, 120 n. 197, 132–4, 138 n. 262
actual, 114; *see also wei*
Adam, 89–90, 106
affection, 105, 113 n. 168; *see also ch'ing*
ai chih hsüeh 愛知學 'philosophy', 90–1
ai yü 愛欲 'the will', 101, 128 n. 221; *see also shou te*
Albertus Magnus, 109, 135
Aleni, Guilio, 90 n. 76, 99 n. 108, 128 n. 224
Alexander of Aphrodisias, 129
Alexander the Great, 93–4, 96 n. 94
Ames, Roger, 26, 30–3, 55, 56
Ammonius, 64 n. 219, 84, 117, 129, 135
angels, 106–7
Anscombe, Elizabeth, 42 n. 143
Anselm, 4–5, 38
Aquinas, St Thomas, 39 n. 135, 76 n. 16, 83 n. 49,
    128–9 n. 224, 134
Archytas, 83 n. 49
argument, 48–50, 75, 81–2; see also dialectic
Argyropulos, Johannes, 76
Aristotle, 51, 54 n. 185, 69–79, 89, 93–7, 117–18,
    130, 151
    Analytics, 76, 83, 103, 106, 109 n. 148, 112, 139
    categories, 22, 71–5, 86 n. 62, 112–113, 116–17,
      119–20, 122 123, 131–4, 148–9; *see also lun*
    Categories, 69–70, 72, 73–6, 80 n. 39, 82–6, 99,
      100, 103, 105, 106 n. 140, 116, 120, 121, 123 n.
      205; *see also In Universam Dialecticam*
      Aristotelis; ming li t'an; shih lun
    causes, 86 n. 62, 107, 144; *see also tso so i jan; wei*
      so i jan
    De Anima, 115, 128
    De Caelo et Mundo, 79, 80 n. 38; *see also hüan yü*
      ch'üan
    De Generatione Animalium, 129
    De Interpretatione, 76, 112–13
    Nicomachean Ethics, 102 n. 121
    Politics, 95

Prime Mover, 96; *see also* God
psychology, 101–2, 128, 144; *see also* soul
Sophistici Elenchi, 72, 76, 100
syllogistic, 33–4, 35, 103, 139, 150
    Topics, 72, 73–4, 76, 100, 103, 106 n. 140, 113, 133
art, 98–101
attribute, 46
Augustine, St, 100, 108, 148

Barnes, Jonathan, 103 n. 126
being, 51–5, 72, 73, 87, 114–16, 120–31, 141; *see*
    also existence
Benveniste, Emile, 69–70 n. 1, 72 n. 6
Bloom, Alfred, 25–9
Boethius, 76
Boetius, 129, 135
Bonaventure, St, 39 n. 135
Bororo, 39
Buddhism, 71, 80–1, 82, 85–6, 151

Cajetan, 149
categories: *see* Aristotle, categories; Kant
    Humboldtian, 22–3
Chao, Yuen Ren, 1, 33 n. 117, 39 n. 136, 55
ch'ao hsing che 超性者 'metaphysics', 110–11; *see*
    also ch'ao hsing hsing hsüeh; metaphysics/
    Metaphysics
ch'ao hsing hsing hsüeh 超形性學 'metaphysics/
    Metaphysics', 83 n. 47, 116; *see also ch'ao hsing*
    che; metaphysics/*Metaphysics*
che 者, 148–9, 151
cheng 證 'proof', 109
cheng ming 正名 'name rectification', 31, 57–8, 104
ch'eng 稱 'appellation', 'predicate', 112, 117 n. 184,
    118 n. 191, 119 n. 195, 122, 123 n. 204, 131 n.
    232, 137 n. 255, 138 n. 262, 140 nn. 267, 269,
    142, 143 n. 277, 145, 148 n. 298; *see also* logic,
    predication
chi jan chih hsü 既然之須, 'hypothetical necessity',
    107; *see also* necessity

166

ch'i 氣, 61, 67, 81
chieh 解 'commentary', 123
chih 智 'knowledge', 66
chih 質 'matter', 114 n. 172; *see also* matter
chih jan chih hsü 直然之須 'absolute necessity', 107;
    see also necessity
chih shih 治世 'government', 101
chih t'ung 直通 'simple apprehension', 105
Chinese
    ambiguity, 6–10
    conditionals, 8, 25–30
    disjunction, 39
    'genius' of, 23, 37
    interrogatives, 132
    logic, 22–5, 67, 81–2; *see also* logic
    mood, 8
    morphology, lack of, 6–8, 22, 117, 135–7, 142,
      151
    negation, 37, 39
    nouns, 32, 60–2, 67
    quantifiers, 37, 146
    quotation, 117 n. 184, 119 n. 195; *see also yeh*
    semantics, 55
    syntax, 23
    tense, 8
    word-classes, 21, 24, 32
ch'ing 情 'affection', 105, 113 n. 168; *see also*
    affection
Chomsky, Noam, 13 n. 33, 20 n. 56
Christianity, 77–81, 98, 102, 115–16, 128
    Crucifixion, 115 n. 175
    resurrection, 144
    transubstantiation, 85–6, 115 n. 175, 122, 124
    Trinity, 115
Chroust, Herman, 95 n. 91, 96 nn. 92, 94
Chuang Tzu, 64 n. 220, 91
ch'üeh 確 'valid', 139; *see also* logic, validity
Cicero, 92, 109
Clavius, 78
Clement of Alexandria, 88 n. 69, 108, 111
complexio 'combination', 118
conceptual schemes, 16–19; *see also* translation,
    radical
Confucius, 29 n. 102, 30–1, 81, 94, 102, 108 n. 146,
    130 n. 228
Couto, Sebastian, 76

Damascene, St, 83 n. 49
Davidson, Donald, 17–19, 25, 48, 67
definition, 105, 113, 143; *see also t'ui lun, chieh shih*
Denyer, Nicholas, 39 n. 133
Derrida, Jacques, 58, 63
dialectic, 58–9, 63, 66, 74, 76 n. 15, 77, 78 n. 22, 81,
    88–90, 93, 97–111, 112–13; *see also* argument
Diderot, Denis, 41 n. 140

differentia 113, 114; *see also shu*
Diodorus Cronus, 38–9, 41
Diogenes Laertius, 69, 88 n. 69, 92
Diogenes the Cynic, 93
Dionysius, 115
Dudink, Adrian, 83 n. 44
Duns Scotus, 146

εἶναι 'to be', 51–2, 54, 87, 131
Engelfriet, Peter, 83 n. 46
English, 8, 25–8, 38, 54, 59, 67, 117, 117 n. 184, 147,
    149
Epicurus, 88
essence, 53, 105, 114, 121–3, 129, 131 n. 235, 143;
    see also nei chi i li; pen yuan
ethics, 97, 101–2
Etiemble, 77 n. 18
Euclid, 78, 83 n. 46
Evans, Gareth, 40 n. 138
existence, 4–5, 25 n. 77, 42, 51–5, 114, 127, 141; *see*
    also being

fa 法 'law', 'rule', 'regulation', 81, 100 n. 113, 108 n.
    145, 109 n. 147, 139
fei 非 'wrong/false', 97–8, 100 n. 114, 118–19, 139;
    see also shih
form, 53, 114, 126–7; *see also mo*
Frankenheimer, Uwe, 71 n. 3
Frede, Michael, 72 nn. 4, 6, 73 nn. 7, 8, 74 nn. 9, 10,
    75 n. 11
Frege, Gottlob, 46, 66 n. 226
Furtado, Francisco 傅汎濟 (Fu Fan-chi), 70, 71, 75,
    76, 78 n. 22, 79 n. 32, 80, 83, 86 n. 62, 91, 92 n.
    80, 93, 95, 96 n. 94, 98, 102, 103, 111, 114, 120,
    124, 125, 127, 128, 140, 141–2, 148, 149, 152
Furth, Montgomery, 73 n. 7

Garbo, Thomas de, 129–30
Geach, Peter, 47
genus, 113, 114, 116 n. 177; *see also tzung*
Gernet, Jacques, 24–5, 77 n. 18
Givòn, Talmy, 39 n. 137
God, 96, 113–16, 130; *see also* Aristotle, Prime
    Mover; *t'ien chu*
Graham, Angus, 4–6, 10, 32 n. 112, 33–4, 35, 37, 38,
    42 n. 142, 51–8, 61 62, 62–6, 69–70 n. 1, 72, 87,
    113 n. 165, 118, 131 n. 235, 132 n. 239, 133
Granet, Marcel, 24
Greek, 4, 8, 21, 24, 37, 38, 42 n. 142, 51, 54, 67, 69,
    70, 73, 117–18, 117 n. 184, 131–3, 142, 149
Grunebaum, Gustave von, 39 n. 135
Guttenplan, Samuel, 35–6, 49 n. 165

Haack, Susan, 49, 50
Hacking, Ian, 59–60

Hall, David, 26, 30–3, 55, 56

Han Fei Tzu, 64 n. 220

Hangchou, 70, 78, 79, 80, 85 n. 61, 86 n. 62, 87 n. 64, 128–9 n. 224

Hansen, Chad, 34, 55–7, 60–2, 65, 67–8, 118

Harbsmeier, Christoph, 8–9, 26, 32 n. 114, 37–8, 39, 55 n. 186, 56, 57 n. 196, 59 n. 201, 60 nn. 204, 206, 61, 63

Harris, Roy, 9 n. 19, 57–8, 63 n. 213

Hawkins, E. L., 66 n. 226

Henderson, John, 130 n. 228

Heraclides Ponticus, 92

Hieronymus, 110

Hippocrates, 97

Hirsch, Eli, 67 n. 227

ho hsien 合限 'term', 105, 113 n. 164; *see also* logic, terms

Hobbes, Thomas, 52–3

Hoijer, Harry, 15 n. 39

hsing 性 'nature', 139, 140 n. 269, 145, 146 n. 287

hsing chih shih 性之識 'physics', 110

hsiu shen 修身 'self-cultivation', 101–2

Hsün Tzu, 57

hüan yü ch'üan 寰宇詮, 79; *see also* Aristotle, *De Caelo et Mundo*

Humboldt, Wilhelm von, 19–25, 37

huo 或 'or', 39

i 依 'accident', 105, 123 n. 204, 138 n. 256, 140 n. 267; *see also* accident

i 義 'definition', 31

i 意 'idea', 65–6

i hsiang 意想 'concept', 119

In Universam Dialecticam Aristotelis, 75–7, 79 n. 32, 83–7, 120, 121–2, 123–4, 142–3; *see also* Aristotle, *Categories*; *ming li t'an*

Indo-European, 10, 20–1, 26 n. 91, 27, 32, 33 n. 117, 37, 41, 42 n. 142, 51, 53, 54, 61, 64, 69, 87, 114–15, 127, 133, 148–9, 151

infinity, 113–16

Isagoge, 76, 83, 100, 103, 105, 125 n. 212; *see also* Porphyry

Jesuits, 75–9, 82–3, 86–7, 87–90, 95, 99, 106, 111, 115 n. 175, 128, 144 n. 279

Kahn, Charles, 51

Kant, Immanuel, 22, 38

Katz, Jerrold, 13, 17–18

Kirwan, Christopher, 36–7, 40 n. 138, 49 n. 167

ku 古 'ancient (text)', 123, 125

kuei 規 'criteria', 101, 104, 108 n. 145, 109, 110 n. 152, 112 n. 163

Kwakiutl, 59–60

language
artificial, 35–9, 42–4, 52
context, 7–10
feature-placing, 59–60
inflection, 38–9, 41, 64–5, 117, 135–7
interrogatives, 70 n. 1
natural, 35–9, 40–4, 48–51, 52
pragmatics, 7–8, 29, 41
reference, 16–17, 59–60
semantics, 8–9, 17–19, 30–4, 56–9
structure, 2, 6, 11–13
syntax, 41, 50

Latin, 21, 24, 38 n. 132, 39 n. 135, 70–1, 82, 114, 117, 117 n. 184, 132, 142, 149

Legalism, 94

lei 類 'species', 86 n. 62, 94, 113, 131 n. 235, 139, 140 nn. 267, 269; *see also* species

Lemmon, Edward, 49 n. 167

li 理 'pattern', 'principle', 'mode', 66, 90, 96 n. 95, 99 n. 108, 104 n. 130, 105, 106, 110 n. 152, 113 n. 168, 140 n. 269

Li Chih-tsao 李之藻, 70, 71, 75, 76, 78–83, 86 n. 62, 87 n. 64, 91, 93, 95, 96 n. 94, 98, 102, 103, 111, 114, 120, 124, 125, 127, 128, 140, 141–2, 148, 149, 152

Li T'ien-ching 李天經, 80–2

Li Tsu-pin 李次霦, 83

ling 靈 'soul', 100 n. 112, 110 n. 152, 114 n. 173, 128, 144 n. 279; *see also* soul

Lloyd, Geoffrey, 2, 11, 19 n. 55

logic, 22–5, 71, 75, 77, 81–2, 97–107, 107–11, 112; *see also* Chinese, logic
Aristotelian, 86
inference, 81–2, 97–8, 101–10, 113 n. 168, 139; *see also t'ui lun*
logical atomism, 44, 45–7
logical form, 32–4, 35–50, 66–7
logical 'translation', 35–9, 40–1, 48–51
modal, 38–9
predicate calculus, 33–4, 36, 49, 59
predication, 73–4, 117, 122–3, 139, 145; *see also ch'eng*
proposition, 64–6, 103, 104, 105, 113, 117–20; *see also* λόγος; *t'i lun*
quantification, 145–6
reference, 119–20
second-order, 45–6
sentential calculus, 48–9
subject–predicate form, 33–4, 44–7, 54
syllogism, 84, 103
terms, 104, 105, 113, 117–19; *see also ho hsien*
validity, 36, 39–41, 48–51, 66–7, 106–7, 110, 113
Western, 90 n. 76

λόγος, 118; *see also* logic, proposition

Lounsbury, Floyd, 39

lun 倫 'category', 86 n. 62, 112–13; *see also*
    categories

Malotki, Ekkehart, 14–15
Marius Victorinus, 39 n. 135
matter, 114, 126–7, 129; *see also chih* 'matter'; *yüan chih*
Mencius, 93
mentalities, 2
metaphysics/*Metaphysics*, 83 n. 47, 100, 103–4,
    110–11, 112, 114, 116, 117, 122, 143, 149, 150;
    see also ch'ao hsing che; *ch'ao hsing hsing hsüeh*
miao 妙 'miraculous', 'subtle', 115 n. 174, 123, 127 n. 220
ming 命 'destiny', 103
ming li t'an 名理探, 70–1, 83–7, 101; *see also*
    Aristotle, *Categories*; *In Universam Dialecticam Aristotelis*
ming wu 明悟 'the intellect', 101
mo 模 'form', 114n. 172, 148 n. 298; *see also* form
mo ku 模故 'formal cause', 144
Mohists, 10, 63–6, 82, 113 n. 165, 118
Mungello, David, 77 n. 18, 78 n. 27, 87 n. 64, 115 n. 175

Needham, Joseph, 1
necessity, 107; *see also chi jan chih hsü*
nei chi i li 內之義理 'essence', 105; *see also* essence
neng 能 'potential', 114; *see also* potential
Nietzsche, Friedrich, 20–1, 44 n. 149

Ockham, William of, 134
ὅρος 'term', 105 n. 132; *see also* logic, terms
οὐσία 'substance', 25 n. 77, 131
Owen, Gwilym, 125 n. 211

Parmenides, 54
particulars, 45–7, 61–2, 121, 137–46
Passmore, John, 72 n. 6
pen yuan 本元 'essence', 138; *see also* essence
Peterson, Willard, 78 n. 24
Philoponus, 84 n. 53
φιλοσοφία 'philosophy', 90–2
philosophy
    analytical, 35, 44, 46, 51, 52, 72
    Chinese, 10, 30–4, 40, 52, 56–9, 61–2, 63–6, 88,
        90–8, 132
    Greek, 40, 51, 54, 56–8, 63–5, 74, 87, 88, 90–8,
        114, 121
    Hellenistic, 38–9
    Western, 5, 51, 53, 61–6, 69, 93, 104–5
pien 辨 'to discriminate', 99–100, 113 n. 166
pien 辯 'to dispute', 57–8, 64, 99–100, 113 n. 166,
    139

Plato, 4–5, 38, 54 n. 185, 62, 64–6, 75, 83 n. 49, 92 n.
    78, 100, 114, 118, 121, 122 n. 200
Pliny the Elder, 94 n. 85
Plotinus, 39 n. 135
Plutarch, 54 n. 185, 93 n. 82
po 駁 'to refute', 99 n. 108
politics, 101–2
Porphyry, 76, 125; *see also Isagoge*
potential, 114; *see also neng*
Prior, Arthur, 40 n. 139
Pythagoras, 90, 91–2

quantification, 10
Quine, Willard van Orman, 11, 13, 16–19, 25, 47, 67

Ramsey, Frank, 45–7
Reding, Jean-Paul, 2 n. 3, 5 n. 9
relatives, 72, 76 n. 14, 134–7
Resnik, Michael, 50–1
Ricci, Matteo, 6, 77, 78, 86 nn. 62, 63, 106, 108 n.
    146, 128–9 n. 224, 131 nn. 233, 234, 144 n. 279
Rosemont, Henry Jr., 6 n. 11, 7, 21, 30
Russell, Bertrand, 43–4, 45, 52
Ryle, Gilbert, 43–4 n. 147

Sainsbury, Mark, 40 n. 138
Sanskrit, 21
Schenkeveld, Dirk, 64 n. 219
scholasticism, 53, 85, 102, 105, 114, 127, 128,
    129–30, 136, 138 n. 262, 139, 141, 143, 145–6
Sedley, David, 38–9
shih 是 'right/true', 97–8, 100 n. 114, 118–19, 139;
    see also fei
shih lun 十倫 '*Ten Categories*', 105, 111, 112, 116,
    140, 141–2, 143; *see also* Aristotle, *Categories*
shou te 受德 'the will', 128 n. 221; *see also ai yü*
shu 殊 'differentia', 113, 114 n. 172, 145, 146 n. 287;
    see also differentia
Simplicius, 130, 135
Sivin, Nathan, 67 n. 228
so i jan 所以然 'causes and reasons', 104
Socrates, 94, 121
soul, 101–2, 115, 127–9, 144; *see also ling*
σοφία 'wisdom', 90–2
species, 86 n. 62, 113, 141; *see also lei*
Standaert, Nicholas, 77 n. 18, 83 n. 44, 99 n. 108, 108
    n. 146
Steiner, George, 87 n. 66
Strawson, Peter, 49, 59
substance, 46, 72, 74–5, 84, 85, 115, 121–2, 125–7,
    131, 133, 137 146; *see also* accident; *tzû li t'i*
συμπλοκή 'combination', 118

tao 道, 62, 111
Tarski, Alfred, 56

teleology, 75
theology, 78, 115–16, 122, 151
t'i lun 題論 'proposition', 105, 113; *see also* logic, proposition
t'ien chu 天主 '(the Christian) God', 115, 116 n. 176; *see also* God
t'ien hsüeh 天學 'theology', 116 n. 177; *see also* theology
time, 47–8
τόδε τι 'a certain this', 141
translation, 70–1, 82–7, 111, 119, 146–9; *see also* logic, logical 'translation'
   dissonance/strain, 4–10, 18–19, 115
   radical, 16–19; *see also* conceptual schemes
truth, 32–3, 36, 55–9, 118–19; *see also* logic, validity
tso so i jan 作所以然 'efficient causation', 107; *see also* Aristotle, causes
ts'û 辭 'phrase', 'proposition', 65–6, 113 n. 165, 118
tuan t'ung 斷通 'analysis', 105
t'ui lun 推論 'inference', 81–2, 97–8, 100 n. 113, 108 n. 143, 110 n. 152, 113 n. 168, 139; *see also* logic, inference
   chieh shih 解釋 'definitional', 105
   p'ou hsi 剖析 'analytical', 105
tzû li t'i 自立體 'substance', 115 n. 174, 116 n. 176, 123 n. 204, 131, 138; *see also* substance
tzung 宗 'genus', 113, 114 n. 172; *see also* genus

universals, 45–7, 121, 137–46

Valla, 84
Verbiest, Ferdinand, 83

Wardy, Robert, 77 n. 19, 147 n. 291
Webb, John, 7
wei 為 'actual', 114; *see also* actual
wei so i jan 為所以然 'final causation', 107; *see also* Aristotle, causes
wen 文 'language', 'literature', 'text', 112 n. 163, 113, 119
Whitehead, Alfred North, 46
Whorf, Benjamin, 10, 11–15, 16–18, 19, 25, 26, 28, 30, 40–1, 54–5, 56, 59, 70, 133 n. 241
   on Hopi time, 14–15
Wiggins, David, 122 n. 201
Williams, Christoper, 53
Wilson, Mark, 40 n. 138, 48 n. 164
Wittgenstein, Ludwig, 1, 42–3, 56
Wright, Arthur, 63 n. 213
wu 無 'there are not', 10, 53; *see also yu*
wu ch'eng 五稱 'five predicates', 105

Xenocrates, 83 n. 49

yang 陽, 86 n. 62, 144 n. 279
Yang Chu 楊朱, 102
yeh 也 (quotational device), 119 n. 195; *see also* Chinese, quotation
yin 陰, 86 n. 62, 144 n. 279
yu 有 'there are', 10, 52, 53–6, 114–15, 116 nn. 176, 178, 134 n. 247, 137, 138 nn. 256, 263; *see also wu*
yüan chih 元質 'prime matter', 129; *see also* matter

Zeno, 89

CPSIA information can be obtained at www.ICGtesting.com
Printed in the USA
BVOW040424061112

304791BV00003B/23/A

9 780521 028479